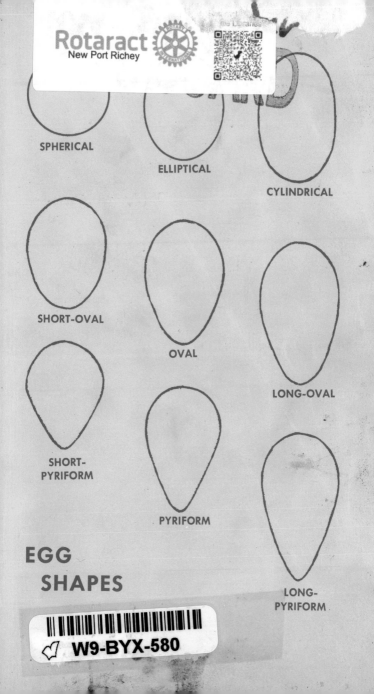

SPHERICAL

ELLIPTICAL

CYLINDRICAL

SHORT-OVAL

OVAL

LONG-OVAL

SHORT-
PYRIFORM

PYRIFORM

LONG-
PYRIFORM

EGG
SHAPES

A Field Guide
to Birds' Nests

THE PETERSON FIELD GUIDE SERIES

Edited by Roger Tory Peterson

1. Birds (eastern) — *R.T. Peterson*
1A. Bird Songs (eastern) — *Cornell Laboratory of Ornithology*
2. Western Birds — *R.T. Peterson*
2A. Western Bird Songs — *Cornell Laboratory of Ornithology*
3. Shells of the Atlantic and Gulf Coasts, W. Indies — *Morris*
4. Butterflies (eastern) — *Klots*
5. Mammals — *Burt and Grossenheider*
6. Pacific Coast Shells (including Hawaii and Gulf of California) — *Morris*
7. Rocks and Minerals — *Pough*
8. Birds of Britain and Europe — *Peterson, Mountfort, Hollom*
9. Animal Tracks — *Murie*
10. Ferns (ne. and cen. N. America) — *Cobb*
11. Eastern Trees — *Petrides*
11A. Trees and Shrubs — *Petrides*
12. Reptiles and Amphibians (e. and cen. N. America) — *Conant*
13. Birds of Texas and Adjacent States — *R.T. Peterson*
14. Rocky Mt. Wildflowers — *Craighead, Craighead, and Davis*
15. Stars and Planets — *Menzel and Pasachoff*
16. Western Reptiles and Amphibians — *Stebbins*
17. Wildflowers (ne. and n.-cen. N. America) — *R.T. Peterson and McKenny*
18. Mammals of Britain and Europe — *van den Brink*
19. Insects (America north of Mexico) — *Borror and White*
20. Mexican Birds — *R.T. Peterson and Chalif*
21. Birds' Nests (east of Mississippi River) — *Harrison*
22. Pacific States Wildflowers — *Niehaus and Ripper*
23. Edible Wild Plants (e. and cen. N. America) — *L. Peterson*
24. Atlantic Seashore — *Gosner*
25. Western Birds' Nests — *Harrison*
26. Atmosphere — *Schaefer and Day*
27. Coral Reefs (Caribbean and Florida) — *Kaplan*
28. Pacific Coast Fishes — *Eschmeyer, Herald, and Hammann*
29. Beetles — *White*
30. Moths — *Covell*
31. Southwestern and Texas Wildflowers — *Niehaus, Ripper, and Savage*
32. Atlantic Coast Fishes — *Robins, Ray, and Douglass*
33. Western Butterflies — *Tilden and Smith*
34. Mushrooms — *McKnight and McKnight*
35. Hawks — *Clark and Wheeler*
36. Southeastern and Caribbean Seashores — *Kaplan*
37. Eastern Forests — *Kricher and Morrison*
38. Birding by Ear — *Walton and Lawson*

THE PETERSON FIELD GUIDE SERIES

A Field Guide to the
Birds' Nests

United States east of the Mississippi River

Hal H. Harrison

Color photographs by
Hal H. Harrison
Bird sketches by
Ned Smith
Map and endpapers by
Mada Harrison

*Sponsored by the National Audubon Society,
the National Wildlife Federation,
and the Roger Tory Peterson Institute*

HOUGHTON MIFFLIN COMPANY · BOSTON

For information about permission to reproduce selections
from this book, write to Permissions, Houghton Mifflin
Company, 2 Park Street, Boston, Massachusetts 02108.

Library of Congress Cataloging in Publication Data

Harrison, Hal H.
A field guide to birds' nests of 285 species found
breeding in the United States east of the Mississippi River.

(The Peterson field guide series; 21)
Includes bibliographical references and index.
1. Birds—Eggs and nests—Identification. 2. Birds—United
States—Identification. I. National Audubon Society.
II. National Wildlife Federation. III. Title: A field guide to
birds' nests of 285 species...
QL675.H37   598.2′5   74-23804
ISBN 0-395-20434-8

Printed in the United States of America

K 13 12 11 10 9 8 7 6 5 4

For
MADA
from Doolin's Run
to Eternity

Editor's Note

A Field Guide to the Birds, the first book in the Peterson Field Guide Series, was published in 1934, and the visual principle on which it was founded proved a sound one. Although this book has since been extensively modified and revised, one important feature was lacking, a description of the nest and eggs of each species, an omission dictated by the limitations of space. Hence this new book by Hal Harrison, the foremost photographer of birds' nests. It is intended as a companion to *A Field Guide to the Birds,* and seeks to fill the gap and to furnish information that had to be omitted if the bird guide was to remain a size to fit in the pocket. Actually, nesting is seasonal; information on nidification is helpful to the field observer only during the spring and summer months.

The area covered by this book is somewhat smaller than that of its companion volume; it is restricted in scope to the United States east of the Mississippi River. Its usefulness diminishes on the Plains and in the more boreal parts of Canada.

I think I may take some indirect credit for Mr. Harrison's career, because I recall a letter received from him more than thirty years ago, when he was a newspaperman in Tarentum, Pennsylvania. He stated that my own work, and particularly my *Field Guide to the Birds,* had induced him to abandon the world of the press and to seek fulfillment as an interpreter of nature — by lecturing, writing, and photographing birds. In turn he inspired his son, George, who is now the distinguished editor of *National Wildlife* and *International Wildlife* Magazines and also a fine nature photographer in his own right. Although Hal Harrison has filmed a variety of nature subjects and lectured throughout the country with these films, he has always had a special interest in finding and photographing nests.

At the turn of the century, ornithology went through a phase of collection; birds were collected (shot) and then classified. Eggs were also collected, by professionals and amateurs alike; however, much of the collecting by amateurs contributed little to the science of ornithology. Today the collecting of eggs — or, rather, their shells — would be meaningless. It no longer fits the climate of the times. In the modern context, only research concerned with embryology or with protein analysis (as a taxonomic tool) would justify the taking of eggs.

Not so long ago it was feared that drawing attention to nests by means of a guide such as this might lead to a resurgence of nest-robbing. Now this fear is no longer valid; egg collecting is a thing of the past, prohibited by law, and replaced by the game of bird-listing — collecting sight records — and by birdbanding.

Bird nesting has now come of age with the discovery that hard pesticides of the hydrocarbon complex may affect the calcification of eggs and result in thin-shelled eggs that break or fail to hatch. Monitoring nests has become a highly organized procedure, yielding data important to the concerned environmentalist. These data are filed and analyzed at the Laboratory of Ornithology, Cornell University, Ithaca, New York.

There are dangers, of course, in careless or too frequent visits to nests. But whether you are a bander, a photographer, a systematic nest observer, or simply an armchair type, this book with its beautiful photographs and informative text will enhance and enlarge your ornithological horizons.

ROGER TORY PETERSON

Preface

PROBABLY no facet of bird watching will replace the sport of "listing" as the most popular activity of avian devotees throughout the world. It is invigorating, competitive, and affords an outdoor activity that demands no more from the participant than he cares to give. In some, however, this initial involvement has sparked a desire to know more about the bird than its correct name. One development, inspired to a great extent by the North American Nest Record Card Program, sponsored by the Laboratory of Ornithology at Cornell University, might simply be called "nesting."

Begun in 1965, the program caught on rapidly and appealed to so many bird watchers all over North America that in a few years the Laboratory of Ornithology was receiving over 20,000 records a year from more than 1000 contributors. Over 100 regional centers throughout the continent coordinate the distribution and collection of cards. These are sent to program headquarters at Cornell University. After they are edited, the information is stored on computer tapes and memory discs where it is available to qualified researchers. Over 1000 records each have been assembled for at least 24 different species.

Even the casual bird watcher is almost certain to find a few nests, some with eggs, as he tramps the woods and fields. Often the owner of a nest has quietly slipped away and is not immediately available for identification. So what nest is it? If one has the time and patience to wait, the owner may return. If the clutch of eggs is incomplete and incubation has not started, the observer may watch for a day or longer without an answer to his question. A field guide to birds' nests illustrated with color photographs and containing a descriptive text to explain the birds' nesting biology seemed the obvious answer.

The present book had its inception 15 years ago when I undertook the task of photographing in color all the wood-warblers of the United States. That project included photographing nests and eggs as well as living birds. The original plan was never completed but a spin-off idea evolved. With more than 30 color photographs of wood-warblers' nests and eggs as a nucleus, the idea of photographing nests and eggs of other species in the eastern United States seemed interesting and challenging. This *Field Guide* is the culmination of the second project.

It would have been an awesome accomplishment to have found without help the 222 nests with eggs that I photographed. To find these same nests with young when the parents were making trips to the nest to feed them would have been difficult enough, but to find them with eggs when the adults offered little help required the assistance of many kind and interested friends. My debt to them is so great that the very existence of this book is testament to my obligation. Space does not permit naming them all. There were occasions when I was indebted to an entire bird club, as when the Brooks Bird Club of West Virginia turned out to help me locate the nest and eggs of the Swainson's Warbler that appear on page 177. There were, in addition, faithful friends who helped throughout the years I worked on the photography, studied the biology of thousands of nests, and prepared the final text. These I must not neglect.

Foremost is my wife, Mada, to whom this book is rightfully dedicated. With few exceptions, she was beside me when every picture was taken, and in many cases it was she who found the nest. It was also Mada who did the initial editing of the text, typed the manuscript, sketched the drawings for the endpapers, prepared the area map, and made the index. Her dedication to the production of the book has equaled my own.

For help in finding nests in western Pennsylvania, my debt to Joseph A. Grom can never be repaid adequately. I owe a debt of thanks to Earl Schriver. To Ralph H. Long, Jr., whose infinite patience and perseverance resulted in many of the photographs taken in Maine, I am forever grateful. Griffing Bancroft, Charles E. Carter, and W. Wilson Baker were especially helpful in Florida; Bart Snyder and Nelson Hoy in New Jersey; Carl and Laura Richter, Irma Chipman, and my son, George, in Wisconsin. It was George who took the only photograph in the book for which I cannot take credit — that of the Greater Prairie Chicken on page 50. I am also indebted to him for encouragement and for neverending faith in my ability to complete this work.

I am especially grateful to August and Wilda Bodisch, James Bond, Eugene Eisenmann, Marguerite Geibel, Cyrilla Mansmann, Vernon Norris, Russell T. Norris, Frank W. Preston, Russell L. Pyke, Raymond Sickles, Everett and Ruth Shoop, and Kenneth Vierling.

My thanks also to Jane Bancroft, Thomas J. Diez, Mary Donald, Erma J. Fisk, Peggy Fowler, Beulah Frey, Robert W. Fuller, Albert A. Ganier, Bruce Glick, Samuel A. Grimes, Frederick and Frances Hamerstrom, Vera H. Hebert, Grant Heilman, Robert Howe, George Hurley, Betty Ingalls, John Kaspar, Barney Kinzer, Edwin V. and Betty Komarek, Mary Leberman, Robert C. Leberman, Patricia Long, Janet Mathison, Erard Matthiessen, Eugene P. Nelson, Kenneth C. Parkes, Robert Personious, Dorothy and Fred Poole, Charles Platt, Jr., Ray Quigley, William B. Robertson, Jr., Ralph W. Schreiber, Charles G. Sibley, Fred Sibley, Elmer Simpson, Eleanor Sims, Robert N. Spear, Jr., Betty Starr, Clark Townsend,

Winston J. Wayne, Roberta White, Gladys Whitmore, Betty Winstead, and Robert E. Woodruff.

General information on the status of species in each of the 26 states included was compiled mainly from latest editions of books accepted as "official" for those states. Where such publications were not available, ornithological societies cooperated by furnishing checklists indicating breeding species and their present status within those states. Following are these sources: Thomas O. Imhof, *Alabama Birds;* Noble Proctor and Fred Sibley, *Preliminary List of Connecticut Birds;* Delmarva Ornithological Society, *Breeding Birds of Delaware;* Alexander Sprunt, Jr., *Florida Bird Life;* Thomas D. Burleigh, *Georgia Birds;* Harry R. Smith and Paul W. Parmalee, *A Distributional Check List of the Birds of Illinois;* Earl Brooks, *Common Birds of Indiana;* Robert M. Mengel, *The Birds of Kentucky;* Ralph S. Palmer, *Maine Birds;* Robert E. Stewart and Chandler S. Robbins, *Birds of Maryland and the District of Columbia;* Robbins and Willet T. VanVelzen, *Field List of the Birds of Maryland;* Wallace Bailey, *Birds in Massachusetts;* Dale O. Zimmerman and Josselyn Van Tyne, *A Distributional Check-List of the Birds of Michigan;* Norman A. Wood, *Birds of Michigan;* Mississippi Ornithological Society, *Field Check-List;* Audubon Society of New Hampshire, *Yearly Check List;* New Jersey Audubon Society, *Check List for Birds of New Jersey;* Witmer Stone, *Bird Studies at Old Cape May;* E. M. Reilly and Kenneth C. Parkes, *Preliminary Annotated Checklist of New York State Birds;* Thomas Gilbert Pearson, Clement Samuel Brimley, and Herbert Hutchinson Brimley, *Birds of North Carolina;* Arthur R. Harper, *Ohio's Birds;* W. E. Clyde Todd, *Birds of Western Pennsylvania;* Earl L. Poole, *Pennsylvania Birds;* Merrill Wood, *Birds of Pennsylvania;* Rhode Island Ornithological Club and Audubon Society of Rhode Island, *Check-List of Rhode Island Birds;* Alexander Sprunt, Jr., and E. Burnham Chamberlain, *South Carolina Bird Life,* rev. ed., with supplement by E. Milby Burton; Tenessee Ornithological Society, *Field List of Tennessee Birds;* Green Mountain Audubon Society, *Breeding Birds of Vermont;* Joseph James Murray, *A Check-List of the Birds of Virginia;* Maurice G. Brooks, *A Check-List of West Virginia Birds;* George A. Hall, *The List of West Virginia Birds;* Owen W. Gromme, *Birds of Wisconsin;* L. Kumlien and N. Hollister, *The Birds of Wisconsin,* with revisions by A. W. Schorger.

In addition to books dealing entirely or in part with birds' nests and eggs, files of *The Auk* and *The Wilson Bulletin* were used. Many contributors to these publications have been quoted, and I regret that space limitations make it impossible to name them individually. My thanks are nonetheless sincere. I referred often to *The Condor, The Jack-Pine Warbler, The Cardinal, The Living Bird,* and *American Birds* (formerly *Audubon Field Notes*). I am most in debt to Arthur Cleveland Bent for his 23 volumes of *Life*

Habitats: *Above*, northern freshwater marsh; *center*, northern spruce forest; *below*, swamp.

Histories of North American Birds, published by the Smithsonian Institution. Although advanced research often disproves statements made in the Bent series, there is no doubt that this monumental work is the foundation for much of our knowledge of bird biology. Most researchers whose papers appear in contemporary literature used Bent's classic volumes as the jumping-off place for their studies. In addition to Bent I made reference to the following: American Ornithologists' Union, *Check-List of North American Birds,* 5th ed. (and Thirty-second Supplement); Glover M. Allen, *Birds and Their Attributes;* G. Ronald Austing, *The World of the Red-tailed Hawk;* G. Ronald Austing and John B. Holt, Jr., *The World of the Great Horned Owl;* John A. Burton (ed.), *Owls of the World;* David F. Costello, *The World of the Gull;* Herbert Friedmann, *The Cowbirds* and *Host Relations of the Parasitic Cowbird;* Ludlow Griscom and Alexander Sprunt, Jr. (eds.), *The Warblers of North America;* Mary Louise Grossman and John Hamlet, *Birds of Prey of the World;* Francis Hobart Herrick, *Wild Birds at Home;* Francis H. Kortright, *The Ducks, Geese and Swans of North America;* Louise de Kiriline Lawrence, *A Comparative Life-History Study of Four Species of Woodpeckers;* R. M. Lockley, *Puffins;* John Bichard May, *The Hawks of North America;* Harold Mayfield, *The Kirtland's Warbler;* Howard L. Mendall, *The Ring-necked Duck in the Northeast;* Margaret M. Nice, *The Watcher at the Nest;* Sigurd T. Olson and William H. Marshall, *The Common Loon in Minnesota;* Ralph S. Palmer (ed.), *Handbook of North American Birds,* Vol. 1; Roger Tory Peterson, *A Field Guide to the Birds;* Olin Sewall Pettingill, Jr., *Ornithology in Laboratory and Field,* 4th ed.; Richard Pough, *Audubon Land Birds* and *Audubon Water Bird Guide;* Edgar M. Reilly, Jr., *The Audubon Illustrated Handbook of American Birds;* Chandler S. Robbins, Bertel Bruun, and Herbert S. Zim, *Birds of North America;* William G. Sheldon, *The Book of the American Woodcock;* John Sparks and Tony Soper, *Owls;* Alexander Sprunt, Jr., *North American Birds of Prey;* Robert Carrington Stein, *The Behavioral, Ecological and Morphological Characteristics of Two Populations of the Alder Flycatcher, Empidonax traillii (Audubon);* Gardner D. Stout (ed. and sponsor), *The Shorebirds of North America.*

Ned Smith, old and valued friend from years in Pennsylvania, generously consented to put aside a backlog of work to contribute his talent. His sketches add greatly to the value of the book.

For their encouragement when the task of undertaking this book became a reality, I am indebted to Roger Tory Peterson, Richard B. McAdoo, and Paul Brooks. I am also grateful to Roger Peterson for his careful reading of the manuscript and for the many helpful suggestions that resulted. My thanks are here expressed to members of the Houghton Mifflin Company staff who helped with production of the Field Guide, but particularly to Helen

Phillips, whose fine editing and personal interest in the book were
so evident, and to Katharine Bernard, who was most patient and
understanding of my problems in selecting and fitting the illustrations.

HAL H. HARRISON

Contents

Habitats: *Above,* southern pine flats; *center,* slough; *below,* cypress swamp.

About This Book

INCLUDED IN THIS *Field Guide* are descriptions of range, habitat, nest, and eggs, with miscellaneous notes for 285 species of birds that breed regularly in all or some of the 26 states lying entirely east of the Mississippi River. Precedent for choosing this approach rather than one involving specific biomes such as mountains, forests, swamps, prairies, etc., was established in 1951 with the publication of *A Guide to Bird Finding East of the Mississippi* by Olin Sewall Pettingill, Jr. In considering the appropriate area to be included, I came to the same conclusion as Dr. Pettingill, who wrote: "The average bird finder, like most other Americans, pictures his country in terms of states." Since this *Field Guide* is directed primarily to the average nest finder, the format I have adopted seemed to be the most convenient and easiest for use of the book.

Species Included: There are more than 285 species nesting in the 26 states of our area. Almost yearly some new species nests here for the first time. As I write, Miami is being invaded by six or more species of nesting parrots and parakeets. In 1972, a Blue-gray Tanager nested in Broward County, Florida. A colony of Fulvous Tree-Ducks has bred successfully on Virginia Key, Dade Co., Fla. since 1968. Red-whiskered Bulbuls, Java Sparrows, and Spot-breasted Orioles have maintained a precarious breeding status in the Miami area for a few years; and the latter, at least, seem destined to stay. The first North American nesting of the Manx Shearwater was reported on Penikese Island, Massachusetts, in June, 1973. Should these species be included? Not yet, I believe; not until their status is well established like that of the Cattle Egret, Smooth-billed Ani, Common (Ring-necked) Pheasant, Common Starling, and House Sparrow.

When Pymatuning Swamp in northwestern Pennsylvania was dammed in 1932 to create Pymatuning Lake, the ecological picture of the region changed so drastically that for several years Pennsylvania recorded nesting American Wigeons, Northern Pintails and Shovelers, Redheads, Green-winged Teal, and Ring-necked Ducks. Today, none of these species nest in Pennsylvania, yet many bird books continue to include that state in the breeding range of these waterfowl.

Western Species: Some western species nest occasionally in eastern states bordering the Mississippi River, but only those species that nest regularly year after year are included.

Rarities: Finally, there are some rarities whose nests have been seen by few professional ornithologists and are not likely to puzzle amateurs. The last known nest of Bachman's Warbler was found in South Carolina 57 years ago, although the bird itself has been observed several times since then. The Ivory-billed Woodpecker may still nest somewhere in southern swamps, but no one is quite sure. White-tailed Tropicbirds may now be breeding on some remote island in Florida Bay or the Dry Tortugas. These and species of similar status do not appear.

Order of Species: Species are basically in the order designated in the American Ornithologists' Union *Check-List of North American Birds* (5th ed., 1957). However, this order — and some names—has been modified within certain groups essentially to conform to recent revisions by Amadon-Brown (hawks), Delacour (waterfowl), and Jehl (shorebirds). Names, both common and scientific, are basically in compliance with the 1957 A.O.U. list as modified by the Thirty-second Supplement to the list, published in *The Auk* for April 13 and October 1, 1973. Most guides for the identification of birds, as well as local, state, and regional checklists, are organized in A.O.U. order. The bird watcher has learned to locate species names quickly in these publications, where species are not arranged in alphabetical order. His familiarity with this system makes the use of the nest guide a simple and convenient extension of an everyday habit.

Subspecies: Subspecies are ignored here. Generally, the eggs of the races of species are indistinguishable; nests typically follow the same basic pattern, although materials used in construction may vary according to what is available. In some cases the materials used are virtually diagnostic of a subspecies. One is the Northern Parula warbler. The race breeding in Maine nests in *Usnea* lichen. The southern race invariably places its nest in Spanish moss. Birds in between nest on open tree limbs in trashy structures. Another example is the Yellow-throated Warbler. Along the southern Atlantic Coast the bird hides its nest in Spanish moss. Inland, where the airplant does not grow, a subspecies known as the Sycamore Warbler (*Dendroica dominica albilora*) builds an open nest saddled to the horizontal limb of a tree, often a sycamore.

Time of Nesting: Exact time of year when each species nests is not given, principally because it is impossible to be accurate. Not only does the nesting time vary from south to north in the range of the same species, but it varies greatly in the same species in the same geographic location. Red-shouldered Hawks in Florida typically start to nest in late February, but the same species in New England may not nest until April or May. In Florida, not all Red-shouldered Hawks nest in February. There are some whose breeding cycle may not reach the egg-laying period until late March or early April. On January 30, 1968, I found hundreds of Double-crested Cormorants incubating eggs on Hemp Key, Pine Island Sound, Florida. On March 11, 1969, when I visited Hemp Key, the cormorants were just beginning to build nests — a difference of two months. On May 17, 1969, I saw about 400 Double-crested Cormorant nests with eggs on Ship Island in Blue Hill Bay, Maine.

Young in the Nest: There are other subjects in bird biology outside the province of this book. One, which might seem closely related, is that of young birds in the nest. When the eggs have hatched, a new phase in the bird's breeding cycle has been reached. The subject of nestling birds and fledglings is a complete study in itself, one that might challenge a researcher-photographer to attempt a field guide to baby birds.

Courtship: Only when courtship is involved directly with nest building, as in grebes and in some species of herons, has it been mentioned.

Illustrations: Photographers may be interested to know that nearly all color photographs in this *Field Guide* were taken with a 3¼ x 4¼ Crown Graphic with a 135 mm Graflex Optar lens, using groundglass focusing and flash. In a few exceptions a Hasselblad camera was employed. Daylight-type Ektachrome sheet film was used in the Graphic; Kodak Ektachrome X in the Hasselblad for the 2¼ x 2¼ transparencies. Since the problem of movement, so vexing in the photography of live birds, is not encountered in taking pictures of nests with eggs, it was possible to expose at a small aperture (generally at f/32) to assure the sharp picture so essential in portraying accurately the markings on eggs.

Measurements: Because of the future changeover in the United States to the metric system, all statistics are given in duplicate: U.S. first, followed by the same measurement in metric terms, rounded to the first decimal except for egg measurements, which are exactly as given by the U.S. National Museum in Bent's *Life Histories.* Equivalents are: 25.4 millimeters (mm) or 2.54 centimeters (cm) per inch; 30.48 centimeters or .3048 meters (m) per foot; .9144 meters per yard; 1.609 kilometers (km) per mile; .4047 hectares (ha) per acre; 39.37 inches or 3.28 feet per meter; .3937 inches per centimeter.

CENTIMETERS (I CM. = 10 MM.)

Comparison of millimeter and inch scales.

Bibliography: Space limitations preclude a formal bibliography. Listed in the Preface are books and checklists pertaining to the 26 individual states, and other books and periodicals which I used in my work on this guide.

Breeding Range

Range here refers only to the *breeding* or *nesting* range of the species solely within the boundaries of the 26 states and the District of Columbia; many of the species of course also nest elsewhere — in Canada, west of the Mississippi, south of the United States, and even in other parts of the world. The range is adequate to inform the reader where the bird nests in eastern United States.

The range description in each species account will help in two basic ways. (1) If you find a nest and are trying to identify the owner, the range given will indicate whether the bird you are considering may be expected to nest in the area where your nest is found. For example, you have a nest on the ground under a pine tree in New York; it seems to fit the description of a Kirtland's Warbler nest. The range tells you that this species has never been found nesting anywhere but in Michigan. (2) You live in Virginia, and every spring and fall you have Yellow-rumped Warblers in your yard. You decide you would like to see the nest of this interesting bird. Where should you look? The range will tell you that you will waste time looking for it in your own state, which is far south of the normal breeding range, and that you will have to go to New England or some other region to the north.

The information included under **Breeding range** is general in scope. The fact that a species nests in South Carolina does not necessarily mean that it breeds in all parts of South Carolina. To narrow the possibilities, consult the **Habitat** section given in the account. For example, the Clapper Rail is a common nesting bird in South Carolina, but if you happen to be visiting in a mountainous part of that state you are a long way from the nearest Clapper Rail's nest, which should be looked for along the Atlantic Coast in the saltmarshes.

Also, you should bear in mind that where you find a bird in winter, or at any time of year other than the nesting season, is not necessarily an indication of where this species breeds. Possible exception would be "resident" birds — those that do not migrate but are generally found in the same area the year round, birds like Cardinals, chickadees, nuthatches, some woodpeckers, Common Starlings, some hawks and owls, and others. Even permanent resident birds can wander at times in the nonbreeding season, so a Northern Mockingbird might show up at a winter feeding station far north of its normal breeding range.

In some cases the stated breeding range may be unavoidably inaccurate by the time this book is published: many birds continue to extend their breeding range annually. A good example is the Cattle Egret. If this book had been published in 1953, I would have told you that it nested only in the Lake Okeechobee region of Florida. Now, 22 years later, I have stated its range as including much of eastern United States; and the bird continues to appear in new areas every year. To have the guide as up to date as possible at the time of publication, I have leaned heavily on *American Birds,* published by the National Audubon Society, which devotes its entire October issue each year to the nesting season. The information comes from bird watchers everywhere who annually report changes in breeding status of species in their states. This compilation of changes from scattered and often otherwise unattainable data makes available a review of the current status of nesting birds.

Habitat

The species accounts refer only to the *breeding* or *nesting* habitat of a species within its range in our area and are not concerned with the winter or other nonbreeding habitat of the bird. Even during the breeding season the place where an adult bird is discovered is not necessarily the place where the nest is located. A Mourning Dove may be found daily feeding in a cornfield, yet Mourning Doves do not nest normally in cornfields. A grove of pines would be a more likely place to look for the nest. A Belted Kingfisher may be seen regularly perched on a branch overhanging a pond, but the nest of the bird may be in the side of a sandbank a half mile away from where it is fishing. A flock of Herring Gulls perched on the top of a fish house in a Maine village may be nesting on a grassy island 4 miles (6.4 km) out to sea.

It is difficult to pinpoint the habitat of some species. It is easy to say that Piping Plovers nest on sandy beaches, that Common Loons nest at the edges of northern lakes, that Chimney Swifts nest in chimneys. But where do Common Starlings nest? The temptation is to write "everywhere." And how do you state exactly where one should look for the nest of a Northern House-Wren — in the pocket of a bathrobe, in an old shoe, in the radiator of an automobile, or in a birdbox? All are right, you know.

Nest

While knowledge of the breeding range and habitat of a species is basic to finding or identifying the nest, it is also necessary to pinpoint the typical site chosen and to have a detailed description of the nest itself. In the species accounts an order has been followed, depending at times on the amount of information available.

Colony Nesting: Where birds typically nest in colonies, the fact has been noted. The degree to which birds are colonial has been emphasized in such terms as "congested colonies," "loose colonies," "scattered colonies," or "singly." This information will be helpful, but it serves only to narrow the search. If a nest is found after the breeding season, the presence of similar nests in the same area would be the only indication of a colony.

Nest Site: The site in which the nest is located is often diagnostic. While some species will choose a variety of sites, many are highly specialized, and this is often important in identification. An Ovenbird invariably nests on the ground in an open woods; a Palm Warbler nests on or near the ground, rarely more than 2 or 3 ft. (.6–.9 m) above the ground; a Blackburnian Warbler places its nest high in a tree, seldom less than 10–15 ft. (3.0–4.6 m) above the ground. The nest of a Common Loon is always on the ground, generally along the shore of a northern lake; all woodpeckers nest in cavities; all Leach's Storm-Petrels, Bank Swallows, and Belted Kingfishers nest in burrows; Horned Larks nest in depressions in the ground; and Chuck-will's-widows build no nests at all.

As much as possible, I have tried to be specific about the site of the nest, giving such facts, when available, as the height above the ground, types of vegetation commonly chosen, precise location of a nest when placed in a tree (fork, distance out from trunk, surroundings, and even the appearance of the structure as seen from the ground). This, it is hoped, adds to information concerned with "What nest is this?" or "Where shall I look?"

Nest Description: The nest itself is described in detail. Materials used will vary with availability. For some species this has been noted, but the reader should bear in mind that Spanish moss would be no more available to a bird in Ohio than spruce needles would be to a bird in Mississippi. The basic structure of the nest of most species is so uniformly true to type that even though the materials used may vary, the format generally does not. An American Robin's nest in Maine with *Usnea* built into it still looks very much like a Robin's nest in Maryland with mud and grasses predominating.

Birds, like people, often display individual traits that defy the rules. There is much truth in the old saying "Birds never read the books." Consequently, we find a maverick Wood Thrush that has built its nest almost entirely of paper napkins and facial tissues, a Song Sparrow that built the whole structure with short pieces of wire, a Northern Oriole that wove the framework of its deep basket from pieces of monofilament fishline, a Robin that laid its eggs in a bale of straw inside a shed, and a Hermit Thrush that is "supposed" to build on the ground but decided to place its nest 8 ft. (2.4 m) above ground on a horizontal limb of a tree.

Nest-building Behavior: Most birds build a new nest each year. Some that have more than one brood each season will build a new nest for each brood. Other species, especially birds of prey, will often repair old nests and use them year after year.

In describing nest construction, I have generally noted the fact that the female builds the nest alone, or that both sexes build, or that the male accompanies the female as she builds. To find a singing male Cape May Warbler and follow him during the nest-building period will not help you locate the nest. The female alone is the builder. To follow either a male or a female Blue-gray Gnatcatcher while the nest is being built may be quite rewarding. Both actively engage in construction.

Usually a nest is made as inconspicuous as possible — not with you in mind, be assured, but by an instinct that guides the species in hiding the nest from any predator that might threaten survival. In some species this instinct dictates that no nest at all is best. The Common Nighthawk lays its eggs on a gravel roof, the Whip-poor-will places its two eggs on a bed of oak leaves on the ground, the Killdeer chooses a bed of gravel or cinders to conceal its eggs; all have evolved in this way and survived better.

The Brown-headed Cowbird is a different case. It too builds no nest, but its instinct to lay eggs in other birds' nests has evolved along an entirely different route from that of Killdeers and Whip-poor-wills.

Evolution of Nests: You might logically ask why birds must build nests at all. The necessity arose as birds evolved from exothermal (cold-blooded) creatures into animals that could no longer abandon their eggs to hatch in the heat of their environment. As warm-blooded organisms, they were compelled to supply warmth for their eggs through incubation — transmission of heat from the parent's body. This necessitated the development of protective measures, not only for the exposed eggs, but also for the incubating parent.

Thus nest building became a necessary part of the breeding cycle. It is likely that the first nests were nothing but depressions scraped in the ground. Some may have been in natural cavities among rocks or tree roots, or in hollow trees. As I have pointed out, such primitive nests are still used today by many species.

Additional protection may have resulted when the first birds elevated their nests by placing them in vegetation off the ground. They were the first birds to depend entirely upon accumulated materials for holding eggs. Their nests were probably loose platforms of sticks and twigs, the type still built by most herons and related birds.

The ultimate in nest-building evolution is the cupped nest characteristic of many birds, particularly passerines. These vary greatly in adaptation to environment. Although some species, like Robins, build solid cups of mud and grasses in the forks of trees or on horizontal branches, others, like orioles and vireos, may hang pensile nests on twigs at the ends of branches. Eastern Phoebes and Barn Swallows plaster their cupped nests to the sides of vertical structures. Eastern Bluebirds, wrens, chickadees, Brown Creepers, and Tree Swallows still use cavities as nesting sites and build cupped nests within these cavities. Some birds that still nest on the ground have the added protection of cupped or even domed nests like those built by the Ovenbird, Eastern and Western Meadowlarks, Bachman's Sparrow, and Hermit Thrush. Camouflage of the nest itself has been carried to a high degree by the Ruby-throated Hummingbird, Blue-gray Gnatcatcher, and Eastern Wood-Pewee, whose meticulously woven and decorated nests look like part of the structures upon which they are saddled.

Nest Measurements: Where average measurements of a nest are available, they are given in this order: outside diameter, height (distance from top of rim to outside bottom of nest), inside diameter of cup, depth (distance from top of rim to inside bottom of cup). If all these statistics were not found, those available are given. Where measurements vary from this order, they are self-explanatory.

Eggs

On each page of the species accounts, information concerning eggs is given in the order indicated below by the boldface headings.

Number of Eggs Laid: The total number laid by one female in one nesting is called a clutch or set. This number varies from 1 egg for species like the Common Puffin and the Leach's Storm-Petrel to as many as 20 for a Common Bobwhite. The females of a species do not always lay the same number of eggs per clutch. Where variations occur, normal possibilities are given first, followed by the number of eggs commonly laid. For example, a Common Crow may lay 3–8 eggs, commonly 4–6; a Swainson's Warbler typically lays 3 eggs, sometimes 4, rarely 5.

Some species normally have 2 broods each season. It is not unusual for the female of such a species to lay fewer eggs in the second clutch than in the first. The Robin commonly lays 4 eggs in its first set, 3 in the second. Species that normally raise only 1 brood each year will usually make two or more attempts to breed successfully if the first nest is destroyed. The Eastern Bluebird, for instance, is a persistent layer. In a Maine experiment, 5 nests with eggs were taken from one pair of birds in one season (May 1 and 27, June 13 and 24, July 6). In about 76 days the birds had built 5 bulky nests and laid 5 complete clutches of eggs.

The same or closely related species nesting in areas widely separated geographically or ecologically may show variations in clutch size. A Cardinal in Florida typically lays a complete clutch of 3 eggs; in Ohio the same species commonly lays 4. The normal set of eggs laid by a Common Screech-Owl in Florida is 2 or 3; the same species in New York will almost always lay at least 4 eggs. Further examples can be found in the Parulidae (wood-warblers). The clutch laid by most members of this large family is 4 eggs, sometimes 5. Three outstanding exceptions are in species that range far north of most Parulidae: the Tennessee Warbler commonly lays 6 eggs, sometimes 7; the Cape May Warbler normally lays 6 or 7 eggs, sometimes more; and the Bay-breasted Warbler rarely lays fewer than 5 eggs, sometimes 6 or 7.

One theory advanced to explain this difference is that the southern individual has a more constant or stable food supply for the young and does not "need" to lay larger sets of eggs to perpetuate the species. It is also suggested that the more uniform southern climate permits a smaller clutch because the young are subjected to fewer risks from unfavorable weather. Birds nesting on sea islands may have smaller egg clutches than those breeding on the mainland, a concomitant of predator-free conditions and more stable weather, which favor optimal survival of young.

It is not uncommon for ducks to lay in each other's nests. The result is sets of eggs which appear to be abnormally large. This happens occasionally in other families, so allowances should be made for this possibility when an inordinate number of eggs is found in one nest. A Wood Duck typically lays 10–15 eggs in a complete clutch, yet as many as 40 eggs have been found in one nest. Such a nest is referred to as a "dump nest."

In most species, one egg is laid daily until the clutch is complete. Some species lay every other day and occasionally a lapse of 3 days may occur. Even in species that normally lay daily, a day may be missed during the production of a full set.

Size of Eggs: Egg sizes are given in millimeters, the standard measurement in oology for many years. Length is given first; the greatest width next. All measurements are average for the species, which means that in the field you may discover eggs both larger and smaller than the sizes given here. The measurements are those published in Bent's *Life Histories* of North American Birds from data recorded in the United States National Museum, Smithsonian Institution, and data taken from other large collections of eggs in public and private repositories.

If you wish to measure eggs, dividers or calipers will be necessary. A millimeter ruler would be convenient, although the conversion rule given on page xix and on the back cover of the book offer assistance. Precision is imperative, especially in measuring small eggs where differences are slight.

Among species included, the Ruby-throated Hummingbird lays the smallest egg, av. 12.9 x 8.5 mm; the Mute Swan lays the largest, av. 112.8 x 73.5 mm.

Shape of Eggs: The endpapers have been designed to help you learn the terminology of egg shapes and markings which has been used throughout the *Field Guide*. Egg shapes not only vary from species to species, but they often vary from individual to individual within a species, and may even vary within the same clutch. When this situation may be expected the fact is noted, as for the eggs of a Northern Mockingbird, which are "typically oval, occasionally short- or long-oval."

Reasons for variations in egg shapes are not always clear, but probable deductions can be made in many cases. Seabirds that lay a single egg on a precipitous cliff generally lay pyriform eggs. This certainly helps to keep the egg from rolling off a narrow ledge. An owl that lays its eggs in the comparative security of a tree cavity has no need for such protection. Most owl eggs tend to be more or less spherical. To incubate successfully up to 20 eggs, a Common Bobwhite might have a problem covering 20 round eggs, but the clutch is made more manageable when the eggs are decidedly pointed and fit well into a compact area. Most shorebirds lay eggs that are large for the size of the female. They tend to be quite pointed and may be incubated with the pointed ends turned inward, thus taking up less space.

Eggshells: The texture of the surface varies greatly. Most are smooth to the touch but some are granulated and rough, such as eggs of many raptors. Whatever the texture, all eggshells are perforated with countless minute pores that permit air to reach the growing embryo. Eggshells may be glossy as in woodpeckers, lusterless as in many of the passerines, or they may be chalky as in grebes and cormorants. Some eggs that are dull when laid may acquire before hatching a slight gloss from constant contact with the incubating bird's body.

Egg Color and Markings: In describing the color and markings of eggs, I have first stated the ground color. The eggs of many widely different species are white, but most eggshells are pigmented, and the variation in both ground color and markings is wide. Oologists describe egg hues with a multitude of terms that would require a chart for interpretation: Brussels brown, sayal brown, Prout's brown, hazel, warm sepia, cartridge buff, bister, Saccardo's umber, court gray, greenish glaucous, aniline lilac, Rood's lavender, Quaker drab, Isabella, buckthorn brown, vinaceous drab, ecru drab, citrine drab, tawny olive, etc. I decided that the average user of this guide would prefer to have colors stated in more familiar terms even if they lack the nuances of the more elaborate terminology.

Shapes and sizes of markings on eggs are described in 10 general terms that cover well the possible varieties: blotched, spotted, dotted, splashed, scrawled, streaked, marbled, wreathed, capped, and overlaid. Drawings on the endpapers depict these terms, and reference should be made to these illustrations when descriptions are studied. An egg may have one or more of these markings on its shell: the eggs of a Herring Gull are described here as "marked with grayish spots and blotches of irregular size overlaid with brown spots and blotches"; Red-winged Blackbird eggs as "Pale bluish green; spotted, blotched, marbled, scrawled with browns, purples, black; mostly concentrated at large end." In many species the markings tend to be heaviest around the large end, sometimes forming a wreath or cap. During an egg's descent through the oviduct, the large end comes first and often picks up the greater supply of pigment from the cellular walls.

Heaviest pigmentation is generally found in open nests where cryptic colors help protect the eggs from predators and may also protect the embryos from intense radiation of the sun. White eggs or eggs with little pigment are characteristic of hole-nesting species. Not all cavity-nesting birds lay white eggs, however. Chickadees, nuthatches, and titmice are examples. Since these species also build cupped nests within a cavity, these birds may still be evolving from a time when they too built nests and laid eggs in the open.

Incubation: The act or process by which a bird applies its body heat to an egg is called incubation. In most species, just before the beginning of incubation the bird develops a brood spot on the ventral surface of its body, a featherless area with an abundant supply of blood vessels that help pass heat from the bird's body to the eggs upon which it sits. Most species develop a single brood patch in the center of the ventral surface, but some species may have 2 or 3 patches. Some alcids, like Common Puffins, Razorbills, and Dovekies, have 2 brood spots, one on each side of the body, despite the fact that they generally lay 1 egg.

In researching this phase of breeding behavior, I found more discrepancies and more lack of definite information than for any other subject. In some species there is a dearth of information concerning the part played by the male, female, or both sexes in the incubation process. It is generally true that the female assumes the dominant role; but how much the male participates, if at all, is too often a matter of guesswork. The subject is in need of further study in many species.

Length of the incubation period is another subject where information is often inaccurate or unavailable. To quote accurately the incubation period of any species, one should know first the researcher's definition of "incubation period." Does he mean the time required to hatch a full clutch of eggs, or does he refer to the time necessary to hatch a single egg within a clutch? It seems to me that the most accurate method of determining the incubation period is to mark the last egg laid and then check accurately in days or hours the time required for that egg to hatch. If, however, a bird starts to incubate before the last egg is laid (and in some species incubation starts with the laying of the first egg) the period may be calculated for the entire clutch — the total number of days the adult spends on the nest incubating. This does not give accurate incubation time for a single egg, and in some species would vary considerably from bird to bird, since all individuals do not start to incubate after laying the same number of eggs. The size of the clutch laid by individual females may also vary, so the time of hatching for a full clutch might be longer or shorter within a species.

Other factors are involved in lengthening or shortening the period of incubation. A very cold wet period may delay hatching for a day or more as compared to incubation during a normal or a favorably warm dry period. The degree of attentiveness (time spent on the nest) of the incubating bird will have some effect on the number of days or hours required to hatch a clutch.

In stating the incubation period for most species I have given a range of days denoting the shortest to the longest time required to hatch the eggs. Where the period is unknown, I have said so. Where the period is uncertain, I have occasionally given the time as "probable."

Notes

Perhaps the section in the species accounts labeled **Notes** should be more accurately defined as a catchall. There are so many interesting facts I want to tell about each species and so many that do not fit into any specific category that I have used **Notes** as a means of crowding in bits of information pertinent to the breeding biology of the species. Thus it is difficult to summarize here what is included in this section; a bit of everything, I suppose.

Sometimes the facts are amplifications of points referred to under **Breeding range, Habitat, Nest,** and **Eggs;** and again, they may be entirely different from any facts given in those categories. The best example, perhaps, is the Brown-headed Cowbird. For many years I have made a study of this species, and some of the unusual aspects of its biology never cease to amaze me. Trying to crowd into the notes all that I wanted to say was indeed frustrating.

The notes are mostly concerned with my own experiences, but a multitude of facts were also gleaned from field experiences of others. It is my hope that this conglomeration of tidbits helps to make the book more interesting and informative.

A Field Guide
to Birds' Nests

THE GEOGRAPHICAL AREA
COVERED BY THIS GUIDE

**Includes the 26 states entirely
east of the Mississippi River**

COMMON LOON *Gavia immer*

Breeding range: New England west through extreme n. U.S.
Habitat: Freshwater lakes, large and small, often in undisturbed wilderness. Nesting sites vary, but small wooded islands are favored; usually protected from prevailing winds and wave action.
Nest: As close to water as possible, often continuously wet. May be on bare ground, floating bog, muskrat house, or attached to shoreline vegetation. Little material used before laying; as incubation progresses adults add vegetation from nearby, producing a mass of reeds, rushes, grasses, and twigs. Diam. 2 ft. (61 cm) or more; center slightly hollow.
Eggs: 2, frequently 1, rarely 3; av. 88.9 x 56.2 mm. Oval to long-oval. Shell thick, somewhat granular; slight gloss. Shades of greenish or brownish olive, usually with scattered spots or blotches of brown or black. Incubation by both sexes, but mostly by female; commonly 29 days, starting with laying of 1st egg. 1 brood.
Notes: Incubating bird faces water, slips off nest and dives when disturbed, surfacing many yards (or meters) away. One bird attends eggs at all times unless frightened by intruder. Same site may be used in succeeding years. In an experiment in Minnesota 6 of 8 man-made islands of native vegetation were accepted as nesting sites by loons.

1

RED-NECKED GREBE *Podiceps grisegena*

Breeding range: Known to nest in at least 3 Wisconsin lakes.
Habitat: Sloughs, marshes, shallow lakes, and ponds of 10 acres (4 ha) or more containing emergent vegetation.
Nest: Usually solitary but sometimes in loose colonies. Anchored in or to the fringe of emergent plants (rushes, flags, cattails, sedges). A low, flat (slightly above water level), carelessly built floating mass of rotted vegetation. Male often dives for and carries plant material to female at nest. Diam. 2 ft. (61 cm), with 6 in. (15.2 cm) saucer-shaped depression for eggs.
Eggs: 3–6, usually 4–5; av. 53.7 x 34.5 mm. Intermediate between oval and long-oval. Shell smooth or slightly chalky. Pale blue or buff when fresh; later stained brownish by mud and debris; usually wet. Incubation by both sexes; 22–23 days, starting with 1st egg. 1 brood.
Notes: Red-necked Grebes are very shy, conceal nests well, and cover eggs with wet plant material when not in attendance. Often

abandon clutches before incubating or before all eggs hatch. Rarely nest less than 30–50 ft. (9.1–15.2 m) apart and defend their territories vigorously. Wisconsin population (about 50 pairs) appears stable but tenuous; is remnant of previously larger population, not a recent extension of range (Kaspar).

2

PIED-BILLED GREBE *Podilymbus podiceps*

Breeding range: All eastern states. Permanent resident in s. Atlantic and Gulf states.

Habitat: Freshwater ponds, marshes, sloughs, ricefield reservoirs, flooded areas. Requires open water, aquatic vegetation.

Nest: In water 1 ft. (30.5 cm) or more deep anchored to or built around or among dead or growing vegetation. A shallow depression slightly above water level in a sodden floating mass of decaying aquatic plant material. Typically anchored to an underwater foundation of rotted plants. Both sexes build. Diam. 1 ft.

Eggs: 3–10, usually 4–8, laid at irregular intervals; av. 43.4 x 30.0 mm. Elliptical to oval. Shell generally smooth, sometimes slightly chalky; surface dull or with light luster. Pale blue or green when laid, turning buff or brown during incubation. Incubation by both sexes, more often the female; 23 days, beginning with 1st egg. Probably 1 brood.

Notes: Nests early; in North starts building soon after ice disappears. Defends an area of 30 yds. (27.4 m) or more around the nest from other grebes. Associates and nests amicably with gallinules, coots, rails, and other marsh birds. Often approaches nest under water, surfacing at rim. Adults are wary and difficult to catch sight of on the nest. They cover eggs with debris when not incubating.

3

LEACH'S STORM-PETREL *Oceanodroma leucorhoa*

Breeding range: Atlantic Coast, Maine to Massachusetts.

Habitat: Offshore islands in areas of cold water with high plankton density.

Nest: Using both bill and feet, male alone digs a burrow in a bank or in an open field under a stump, rock, or brush. Av. entrance 2½ x 3¼ in. (6.4 x 8.3 cm); av. length 20 in. (50.8 cm); digging time 2–3 days. The egg chamber may or may not be lined with grass, rootlets, twigs, bark, dry leaves. Male calls female to burrow; mating occurs inside. Some burrows are reused many years.

Eggs: 1; av. 32.5 x 24.0 mm. Elliptical to nearly oval. Shell smooth, dull. White, unmarked. Incubation by both sexes; 41–42 days. One bird may incubate 1–5 days without relief. Change at nest made only at night. 1 brood.

Notes: Musky petrel odor strong in nest area. Birds never seen  on nesting islands during daylight. Changing at nest, at night, often involves hordes of fluttering birds. On ground, seeking or leaving burrow, birds are awkward, stumbling; flutter before becoming airborne. Unfinished burrows in late summer presumably are dug by pre-breeders. Birds at least 2 yrs. old at 1st breeding. Adults found in burrows without eggs in midsummer may be forming pair bonds. Pairs probably mate for life.

4

BROWN PELICAN *Pelecanus occidentalis*

Breeding range: Coasts of N. and S. Carolina; Atlantic and Gulf Coasts of Florida; formerly to Texas. (No records for Georgia.)
Habitat: Islands, mainly in shallow coastal waters, lagoons, tidal rivers, small inlets.
Nest: Strictly in colonies, often on islands with nests of herons, egrets, and cormorants (nests grouped by species). Only a few feet (1 m or more) apart on ground or in trees, generally mangroves. On ground, built of sticks, reeds, leaves, grass, available materials. Arboreal nests of same materials but more substantial; firmly anchored to mangrove branches 8–20 ft. (2.4–6.1 m) above water. Male gathers material; female builds. Much stealing of material from unguarded nests. Diam. 18–24 in. (45.7–61.0 cm); height 4–10 in. (10.2–25.4 cm) for ground nest.
Eggs: 3, sometimes 1–2; av. 73.0 x 46.5 mm. Oval to long-oval. Shell has lusterless rough granular surface. White; blood-stained (see illus.). Incubation by both sexes; 30 days. 1 brood. Eggshell-thinning noted in recent years.
Notes: Endangered species. S. Carolina and Florida nesting populations seem fairly stable; elsewhere alarmingly down. Time of egg-laying varies. Known to have nested every month; fall breeding now rare. Age at 1st breeding, 3–5 yrs.

5

DOUBLE-CRESTED CORMORANT *Phalacrocorax auritus*

Breeding range: Locally, Maine to Florida and Gulf of Mexico inland to Mississippi R. in suitable habitat. Present breeding status difficult to define because of abandonment of old colonies due to human disturbance.

Habitat: Undisturbed areas with nearby reliable food supply on coastal islands, reefs, large rocks, cliffsides, remote swamps.

Nest: In colonies. On Northeast Coast: generally close-grouped ground nests on cliffs and rocky islands with communal space between groups; often near nests of gulls and eiders. Inland and in the South: at any height in live or dead trees near water; often 30 or more nests per tree; frequently near colonies of pelicans and herons. Foundation of seaweed, sticks, and rubbish; finer material for lining. Male brings material; female builds, requiring about

4 days; material added throughout season. Old nests often rebuilt. Outside diam. 2 ft. (61 cm); inside diam. about 9 in. (22.9 cm), depth 4–6 in. (10.2–15.2 cm).

Eggs: 3–4 often 5, rarely 2 or 6; northern race (*P. a. auritus*) av. 61.6 x 38.8 mm; southern race (*P. a. floridanus*) av. 58.2 x 36.8 mm. Long-oval to cylindrical. Shell pale bluish with extensive white chalky surface; soon stained. Incubation by both sexes; 25–29 days. 1 brood.

Notes: Nests filthy with guano, dead fish, dead young. 3 yrs. old at 1st breeding.

6

ANHINGA *Anhinga anhinga* (Water-turkey, Snake-bird)

Breeding range: Coastal Plain, N. Carolina south to Florida and Gulf states; Mississippi Valley north to Kentucky.

Habitat: Sheltered quiet waters of ponds in cypress swamps, freshwater sloughs, marshy lakes, canals, mangrove-bordered bays, lagoons, tidal streams. Principally freshwater species.

Nest: Anhingas are mostly colonial, up to several hundred pairs separated into clusters of 8–12 pairs; often near herons, ibises, and cormorants. In willows, buttonbush, pond apples, mangroves 5–20 ft. (1.5–6.1 m) above water or ground. Base of twigs, coarse sticks, dead leaves; lining of leaves or twigs with foliage. Male establishes nest site and gathers material; female builds. May use same nest each year. Outside diam. 18–20 in. (45.7–50.8 cm), height 6 in. (15.2 cm).

Eggs: 4, sometimes 3 or 5; av. 52.5 x 35.0 mm. Oval to long-oval. Shell pale bluish white with chalky coating; becomes glossy and nest-stained during incubation. Incubation by both sexes; 25–28 days, beginning before clutch complete.

Notes: At least 2 yrs. old at 1st breeding. May pair before arrival or on breeding grounds. Young in nest often differ widely in size; suggests egg-laying irregularity.

MAGNIFICENT FRIGATEBIRD p. 12
Fregata magnificens

GREAT BLUE HERON *Ardea herodias*
(including Great White Heron)

Breeding range: All e. U.S. Permanent resident in South.
Habitat: Shallow saltwater or freshwater areas with trees suitable for nesting. Remote inaccessible situations favored.
Nest: Generally in colonies among nests of other herons, ibises, cormorants, pelicans; usually earlier than other species. In congested communities, often several nests in one tree; securely lodged in crotch or on limb of tree (many varieties) up to 130 ft. (39.6 m) from ground. Sometimes in bushes, low mangroves, rarely on ground. Flimsy to compact platform of large sticks; lined with fine twigs and green leaves. Male brings material to female, who places it in nest. Outside diam. 25–40 in. (63.5–101.6 cm).

Eggs: 3–6, usually 4; av. 64.5 x 45.2 mm. Oval to long-oval. Shell smooth or slightly rough. Pale bluish green, unmarked. Incubation by both sexes; 28 days.
Notes: Our largest heron. Great White Heron (*A. h. occidentalis*) is color morph of Great Blue Heron. In Florida, mated blue and white birds not uncommon. Wurdemann's Heron, now not recognized by A.O.U., has been supposed to be offspring of mating of Ward's (*A. h. wardi*) and Great White Herons.

GREAT (COMMON) EGRET *Casmerodius albus*

Breeding range: S. U.S. north to New England and Michigan. Species continues to extend range north and west.

Habitat: Cypress, mangrove, willow swamps, bushy lake borders, ponds, islands, deciduous woods with tall trees.

Nest: Solitary or in small to large colonies with other species of herons, cormorants, anhingas, pelicans. In trees or shrubs usually 10–30 ft. (3.0–9.1 m) above ground. Nests of Great Egrets and Great Blue Herons up to 80 ft. (24.4 m) from ground not uncommon in forests of tall trees. In North, beech trees and red maples often chosen; in South; colonies in cypress usual. Author found small colony on Florida island in bed of prickly pear cactus. Generally built of sticks and twigs; may or may not be lined with leaves, moss, finer materials. Larger and more substantial than nests of small herons but not so bulky as nest of Great Blue Heron. Male selects nest site, helps build. Diam. approximately 2 ft. (61 cm).

Eggs: 3–4, rarely more; av. 56.5 x 40.5 mm. Long-oval. Shell smooth, little or no gloss. Blue or greenish blue, unmarked. Incubation by both sexes; 23–24 days. 1 brood.

Notes: Species almost extirpated by plume hunters in early 20th century. Breeding status now excellent.

9

SNOWY EGRET *Egretta (Leucophoyx) thula*

Breeding range: S. U.S. north to New York (Long I.), Massachusetts, Maine. Steadily extending range northward.

Habitat: Fresh and saltwater marshes; cedar swamps, willow and buttonwood ponds, rice plantations, mangrove islands.

Nest: In colonies, thousands in some heronries; at periphery of range, single nestings, usually with other herons. In tree or shrub, averaging 5–10 ft. (1.5–3.0 m) from ground, some to 30 ft. (9.1 m). Flat, elliptical, loosely woven of slender twigs on foundation of heavy sticks; additional available material often used: reeds, rushes, dead cane, holly, etc. Building by both sexes, requiring 5–7 days. Male selects territory; both sexes vigorously defend. Outside diam. 1–2 ft. (30.5–61.0 cm).

Eggs: 4–5, sometimes 3, rarely 6; laid about every other day; av. 43.0 x 32.4 mm. Oval. Shell smooth, little or no gloss. Pale greenish blue, unmarked. *Indistinguishable from eggs of Little Blue Heron or Tricolored Heron.* Incubation by both sexes; 18 days, possibly longer. 1 brood.

Notes: Positive identification of nest and eggs not possible without seeing bird. Principal causes of nest failure: predation by Fish Crows, snakes, owls, raccoons, man. When alligators are present in water below nests, swimming predators are usually absent.

10

LITTLE BLUE HERON *Florida caerulea*

Breeding range: Coastal and inland in South; along Atlantic Coast to New Jersey; casual to New England. Range gradually extending northward. Permanent resident in Florida and Gulf Coast.

Habitat: Inland freshwater marshes, coastal mangrove bays, saltwater marshes, marine islands.

Nest: In colonies; in homogeneous groups, often near other herons. Placed 8–15 ft. (2.4–4.6 m) above water in mangrove, buttonbush, holly, swamp privet, other low shrubs. Loosely woven platform of twigs and sticks; egg cavity may or may not be lined with leaves and finer materials. Material gathered by male; female builds, requiring 3–5 days. Outside diam. 16–20 in. (40.6–50.8 cm); height 6–8 in. (15.2–20.3 cm).

Eggs: 3–5, generally 5, laid in from 5 to 8 days; av. 44.0 x 33.5 mm. Typically oval. Shell smooth, no gloss. Pale greenish blue, unmarked. *Indistinguishable from eggs of Tricolored Heron or Snowy Egret.* Incubation by both sexes; 22–23 days, starting after laying of 2nd egg. 1 brood.

Notes: Positive identification of nest and eggs not possible without seeing bird. Neither immature white nor intermediate blue-patched birds believed to breed, although they often roost and mingle with breeding adults. In a study of 50 nests, 34 had 4 eggs, 9 had 5 eggs, 7 had 3 eggs.

11

REDDISH EGRET *Dichromanassa rufescens*

Breeding range: Permanent resident western coast of Florida from Florida Bay north to Pine I. Sound. Appears to be extending range to former breeding area in cen. Florida.

Habitat: Coastal areas, generally associated with red mangroves. Usually on mangrove islands.

Nest: May be solitary, but usually in colonies, often with other species in crowded heronries. Commonly in shrub or tree up to 20 ft. (6.1 m) above ground or water. Varies from a flat platform to a thickness of 10 in. (25.4 cm) with cup of sticks, twigs, rootlets, and grasses. Territory is selected by the male, defended by both. Building is done by both sexes; material added throughout egg-laying. Outside diam. 12–26 in. (30.5–66.0 cm); inside diam. 3–4 in. (7.6–10.2 cm).

Eggs: 3–4, occasionally 5, rarely more; av. 51.0 x 37.6 mm. Oval to long-oval. Shell smooth, not glossy. Pale bluish green, unmarked. Incubation by both sexes; period unknown, probably 3–4 wks.

Notes: The former name, Peale's Egret, referred to the white phase of the Reddish Egret, which is pure white at all ages. Mated reddish birds may hatch white young. Species unreported in Florida from 1927 to 1937; recovery now seems assured. Age at 1st breeding not known.

MAGNIFICENT FRIGATEBIRD *Fregata magnificens*
(Man-o'-War-Bird)
(proper order after Anhinga, p. 7)

Breeding range: Marquesas Keys, Florida.

Habitat: Remote, little-disturbed coasts and islands in tropical and subtropical seas; dense mangrove areas favored.

Nest: In colonies; in homogeneous groups often, but not always, adjacent to colonies of other species. Usually on top of mangrove, sea grape, sea lavender, cactus, or gumbo-limbo. Loosely made platform of sticks and twigs, generally sparingly lined with dry grass. Nesting territory little more than area of nest; nest small for size of bird. Male chooses nest site, attracts female with spectacular display of red balloonlike gular sac. Male carries nest material collected in flight, torn from bushes or stolen from other birds; female builds. Outside diam. 10–15 in. (25.4–38.1 cm).

Eggs: 1; av. 68.4 x 46.5 mm. Long-oval. Shell smooth and luster-less, thin for a large egg. Pure white. Incubation by both sexes; period uncertain, probably about 6 wks.

Notes: Recently reported breeding in U.S. Site may have been used several years before discovered. 40 nests in 1970; 100 nests in 1971. Birds commonly seen most of the year along Florida and Gulf Coasts; stragglers to New England. Males display red gular sac in Florida roosting areas.

TRICOLORED (LOUISIANA) HERON *Hydranassa tricolor*

Breeding range: Coastal regions from Louisiana to Florida, north to New Jersey; casual to Massachusetts.

Habitat: Islands, ponds, sloughs, lakes, bayous, in fresh or salt-water environment; favors latter.

Nest: Typically in large colonies; sometimes solitary at periphery of range. Often nests in same shrubs and trees with other species or may be in homogeneous groups within larger colony. In mangroves, buttonwoods, willows, holly, and other low shrubs and trees, 2–12 ft. (0.6–3.7 m) above ground or water. Low, flat, round or elliptical nest of sticks, twigs; egg cavity sparingly lined with green leaves, grasses, weeds. Outside diam. 12–18 in. (30.5–45.7 cm).

Eggs: 4–5, sometimes 3, occasionally 6, rarely 7; av. 44.1 x 32.3 mm. Oval to long-oval. Shell smooth, not glossy. Pale greenish blue, unmarked. *Indistinguishable from eggs of Little Blue Heron or Snowy Egret.* Incubation by both sexes; 21 days. 1 brood.

Notes: Positive identification of nest and eggs not possible without seeing bird. Probably the most abundant heron in South, some colonies numbering thousands. Since only white plumes were in demand by millinery trade, Louisiana Heron escaped ravages of plume hunters during early 1900s.

CATTLE EGRET *Bulbulcus ibis*

Breeding range: All Florida and locally along Gulf Coast to Louisiana; north along Atlantic Coast to New England. 1st Wisconsin breeding record 1971. Species a recent arrival in U.S. from Africa; still extending range.

Habitat: Fresh and saltwater marshes, mangrove islands, cedar swamps, willow-buttonwood ponds.

Nest: Birds highly social. Many nests up to 30 ft. (9.1 m) above ground in willows, mangroves, buttonwoods, maples, cedars, etc., some only inches apart. A platform of sticks, twigs, and vines. Pilfering material from other nests common. Male carries materials; female builds, taking 3–6 days; roles occasionally reversed. One bird of pair remains at nest at all times. Building continues during incubation. Outside diam. 10–18 in. (25.4–45.7 cm); height 3–9 in. (7.6–22.9 cm).

Eggs: 3–6, probably laid every other day; av. 47.5 x 33.7 mm. Oval. Shell smooth, no gloss. Very pale blue or bluish white, unmarked; *paler than eggs of other herons.* Incubation by both sexes; 21–24 days. Occasional polygamous matings suspected. 1 brood.

Notes: First N. American nest found at Lake Okeechobee, Florida, May 5, 1953. Florida cattle industry has provided optimum feeding environment for this insect-eating species, which is more independent of water than other herons.

14

GREEN HERON *Butorides virescens*

Breeding range: All eastern states. Permanent resident from S. Carolina to Florida and along the Gulf Coast.

Habitat: Mostly in shrubs and trees near or overhanging water, but sometimes in orchards and groves far from water.

Nest: Typically a single nest or loose colony away from other species; occasionally on outskirts of heronry. In wide variety of trees and shrubs, usually 10–30 ft. (3.0–9.1 m) from ground. Flimsy to tightly woven platform of sticks and twigs; may or may not be lined with finer material. Male selects site, starts building. After pairing, male carries most material, female builds. Twigs, lining added after laying. Outside diam. 10–12 in. (25.4–30.5 cm); inside diam. 4–5 in. (10.2–12.7 cm).

Eggs: 4–5, 3–9 recorded; av. 38.0 x 29.5 mm. Oval. Shell smooth, without gloss. Pale greenish or bluish green, unmarked. Incubation by both sexes; 20 days. Sometimes 2 broods.

Notes: Some nests so shallow and flimsy eggs can be seen through the bottom. In rare cases nests are on ground, on muskrat houses, or in cattails or reeds. Author has seen an unusual situation: A loose colony of 5 nests scattered 30–50 ft. (9.1–15.2 m) from ground in maple woodlot inside the limits of a small Pennsylvania town.

BLACK-CROWNED NIGHT-HERON *Nycticorax nycticorax*

Breeding range: Florida and Gulf of Mexico north to Canada, except much of Appalachian region. Permanent resident coastal areas to New England.

Habitat: Extremely varied — in fresh, salt or brackish water areas; in trees, shrubs, groves, forests, thickets, reeds, cattails; even city parks. Most adaptable of all herons.

Nest: In small to very large colonies; close together, usually adjacent to nests of other heron species. Site from ground to 160 ft. (48.8 m) in trees, shrubs, cattails, *Phragmites*. Built of sticks, twigs, reeds with fine lining; varies with availability; very flimsy to substantial. Birds defend nest territory together; both sexes build; male most active in gathering material. Building time 2–5 days. Outside diam. about 2 ft. (61 cm); height to 18 in. (45.7 cm).

Eggs: 3–5, sometimes 1–2, occasionally 6; av. 51.5 x 37.0 mm. Oval  to long-oval. Shell smooth, no gloss. Pale blue or greenish blue, unmarked. Similar to Great Egret egg but slightly smaller. Difficult to distinguish from Yellow-crowned Night-Heron egg. Incubation by both sexes; 24–26 days. 2 broods occasionally suspected.

Notes: Breeds when 1–3 yrs. old, usually 2–3. Cape Cod colony had 2536 active nests in 854 low pitch pine trees in 1923.

16

YELLOW-CROWNED NIGHT-HERON *Nyctanassa violacea*

Breeding range: Chiefly southern states; sparingly north to Tennessee, Michigan, Pennsylvania, New Jersey; rarely Long I. and Massachusetts.

Habitat: Bayous, backwaters in cypress swamps, freshwater ponds, swamps, mangrove forests, isolated groves.

Nest: Usually in small to large colonies; single nests also occur, particularly at extremities of range. May nest with other herons, but isolated colonies common. Built 1–50 ft. (0.3–15.2 m) from ground or water in variety of trees and shrubs. Nest may be fragile or thick; built of sticks and lined with fine twigs, rootlets, and leaves. Both sexes build; continue to add material after young hatch. May reuse nest from previous season. Outside diam. about 20 in. (50.8 cm).

Eggs: 3–4 sometimes 5; av. 51.3 x 36.9 mm. Oval, long-oval, or cylindrical. Shell smooth, not glossy. Pale bluish green, unmarked. Difficult to distinguish from eggs of Black-crowned Night-Heron. Incubation by both sexes; length of period unknown.

Notes: More secretive in nesting habits than other herons except bitterns; less gregarious than Black-crowned Night-Heron. In May 1965 author visited loose colony of 7 pairs in wild cherry grove in New Jersey. 1 nest per tree, scattered 12–25 ft. (3.7–7.6 m); 4 nests of 5 eggs each, other clutches incomplete.

17

LEAST BITTERN *Ixobrychus exilis*

Breeding range: Florida and Gulf Coast north to s. Maine, Wisconsin. Permanent resident s. Florida.

Habitat: Principally freshwater marshes, sedgy bogs; also areas of brackish water; sometimes saltwater marshes.

Nest: Solitary, but high density noted in favorable habitat. Generally in cattails, tall grass, dense aquatic vegetation, bushes, woody growth; usually 1–8 ft. (0.3–2.4 m) above water or ground. Platform of dead plant material interwoven with living plants. Male probably chooses nest site; both sexes build. Outside diam. 6–10 in. (15.2–25.4 cm); height 5–6 in. (12.7–15.2 cm).

Eggs: 4–5, sometimes 3 or 6 (in about 50 nests, 70 percent contained 5 eggs); av. 31.0 x 23.5 mm. Oval, elliptical, or long-oval. Shell smooth, not glossy. Very pale bluish or greenish, unmarked. Incubation by both sexes; 17–20 days, starting with 1st or 2nd egg. 2 broods; 3 unlikely.

Notes: Our smallest heron; shy, solitary, retiring. Northern birds average larger egg clutches than southern birds. 15 nests in 2 acre (.8 ha) patch of rushes, Michigan; 1 nest per 2.5 acres (1 ha) for 26 nests; 19 nests in 44 acre (17.8 ha) marsh. During incubation adults do not fly directly to nest but land nearby and approach by walking quietly through the vegetation.

18

AMERICAN BITTERN *Botaurus lentiginosus*

Breeding range: All northern states; locally south from s. Illinois and Virginia to n. Florida and Gulf of Mexico.

Habitat: Freshwater marshes, bogs, swamps, especially cattail, bulrush environments; also grassy fields; brackish and saltwater tidal marshes and meadows.

Nest: In loose colonies in favorable habitat, but solitary nesting usual. On dry ground or on a mound 3–8 in. (7.6–20.3 cm) above water or mud among cattails, bulrushes, tall grasses. A scanty platform of available material: dried cattails, reeds, grasses. Nest becomes more hidden as surrounding green vegetation continues to grow. Female gathers material and builds. Outside diam. 10–16 in. (25.4–40.6 cm).

Eggs: 3–7, generally 4–5, probably laid at irregular intervals; av. 48.6 x 36.6 mm. Oval to long-oval. Shell smooth, slightly glossy. Plain buffy brown to olive-buff, unmarked; often blends with color of surrounding foliage. Incubation by female; 24–28 days, beginning with 1st egg.

Notes: Less gregarious, more retiring than other herons except Least Bittern. Species may be polygynous. When approached, female sits tight on nest, neck and bill pointed skyward; camouflage with surroundings effective.

19

WOOD STORK *Mycteria americana*   (American Wood-Ibis)

Breeding range: Presently s. and cen. Florida, sparingly north to Jacksonville; formerly coastal S. Carolina to Texas.
Habitat: Chiefly freshwater cypress ponds; also mangroves, buttonwoods, custard apples, dead oaks (in phosphate sludge ponds).
Nest: In colonies, 5–25 nests per tree. Large cypress trees standing in water preferred, nests in tops of tallest trees, 50–80 ft. (15.2–24.4 m) up. Frail platform of sticks, loosely made, sparingly lined with fine materials, green leaves, moss; built in about 3 days. Sticks added throughout the season. Outside diam. 2–3 ft. (61.0–91.4 cm).
Eggs: 3, sometimes 4, rarely 5; av. 67.9 x 46.0 mm. Oval to long-oval. Shell finely granulated or pitted. Dull or dirty white or cream-white, unmarked; occasionally blood-stained. Incubation by both sexes; 28–32 days (29.7 av. in 10 clutches). 1 brood.
Notes: Only true stork in U.S. Population declining; estimated at 6000 in 1973. Formerly 10,000 nests extended 1 mile (1.6 km) in Okaloacoochee Slough, s. Florida. Future of species tenuous; endangered species status urged by many. Entire colonies have skipped a year without nesting. Inadequate food supply may be a factor in this behavior.

ROSEATE SPOONBILL *Ajaia ajaja*
(proper order after White Ibis, p. 22)

Breeding range: At present confined to a few keys in Florida Bay; no inland breeding.
Habitat: Bay islands, mostly mangrove.
Nest: Formerly in large colonies with anhingas, herons, egrets, ibises; presently tend to nest by themselves in small colonies. Nests quite close together in small trees and shrubs, especially mangroves; typically 6–15 ft. (1.8–4.6 m) above water. Somewhat bulky, well built, of coarse sticks and twigs; lined with finer twigs and green and dry leaves; deeply hollowed. Male brings material; female does most building.
Eggs: 3, often 4, sometimes 2, rarely 5; not always laid on successive days; av. 65.0 x 43.9 mm. Oval to long-oval. Shell thick, roughly granulated, no gloss. Dirty white with evenly distributed spots or blotches in various shades of brown; markings occasionally concentrated around larger end. Incubation by both birds; about 23–24 days, beginning when clutch is complete. Probably 1 brood.
Notes: Earliest breeding, at least 3 yrs. old. Formerly abundant over much of s. Florida, north to Pelican I., Indian R., and Tarpon Springs on Gulf Coast. Until 1920 species seemed doomed. Under rigid protection appears to be increasing gradually.

GLOSSY IBIS *Plegadis falcinellus*

Breeding range: Florida and along Atlantic Coast locally from S. Carolina to Rhode Island (Gould I.) and Maine (Saco). Extending range northward. Permanent resident in s. Florida.

Habitat: Fresh, brackish, saltwater swamps, marshes, islands.

Nest: In small to large colonies, typically with nests of herons and other ibises. On or near ground in marsh vegetation or as high as 10 ft. (3 m) above ground or water in trees and shrubs. Fairly large substantial structure of sticks and dried plant material with well-cupped, well-lined egg cavity. Both sexes build in about 2 days; material added to nest until young leave.

Eggs: 3–4; av. 52.1 x 36.9 mm. Oval, elliptical, or long-oval. Shell smooth or finely pitted, little or no gloss. Dull blue, unmarked; much darker than pale blue eggs of herons. Incubation by both sexes, mostly by female, starting when clutch is complete; 21 days. 1 brood.

Notes: Nests observed by author in Florida and New Jersey have contained fewer sticks and more dry leafy vegetation than herons' nests. 4 Florida nests were substantially lined with dry leaves of swamp-lily (*Crinum*).

21

WHITE IBIS *Eudocimus albus*

Breeding range: N. Carolina (Moorehead City) to Florida and Gulf Coast. Permanent resident in much of its range.

Habitat: In salt, fresh, or brackish water environment, generally near coast, often on islands or in swamps.

Nest: White ibises highly sociable; nests sometimes touch each other. In cypress, mangrove, buttonwood, willow, custard apple, bay, myrtle, vines, etc., 8–15 ft. (2.4–4.6 m) above ground or water, often under active nests of other herons, cormorants, or pelicans. Of dead sticks, live twigs, and leaves broken from nearby vegetation, Spanish moss; deeply cupped. Male establishes territory and gathers material; female selects nest site and does most building. Nest size variable; material added throughout nesting season. Outside diam. 8–24 in. (20.3–61.0 cm).

Eggs: 4, sometimes 3 or 2, rarely 5; av. 57.6 x 38.3 mm. Oval to long-oval. Shell smooth or finely granulated, no gloss. Pale buff, bluish or greenish white, from almost immaculate to heavily spotted and blotched or splashed with shades of brown, markings often concentrated at large end. Incubation by both sexes; 21–23 days; begins when clutch complete.

Notes: Colonies desert one location to nest at another. 1st breeding in 2nd yr.

ROSEATE SPOONBILL
Ajaia ajaja p. 20
MUTE SWAN *Cygnus olor* p. 27

CANADA GOOSE *Branta canadensis*

Breeding range: Extensive stocking by man has made it difficult or impossible to distinguish between ranges of wild and semi-domestic birds. Formerly from Arctic Coast south to northern edge of U.S. Now, regularly in northern tier of states and locally to Alabama — 1000 miles (1609 km) south of main range.

Habitat: Considerable variation: shores of lakes, ponds, sloughs; in swamps, marshes, grassy fields; on rocky cliffs, in trees, often on islands in lakes; old beaver dams.

Nest: Usually on ground near water, often on a low stump, mound, or muskrat nest; sometimes an old hawk nest. Typically a depression in ground lined with sticks, cattails, reeds, and grasses gathered nearby; lined with soft gray down. Site selected and nest built principally by female. Av. outside diam. 25 in. (63.5 cm); av. inside diam. 9 in. (22.9 cm), av. depth 3³⁄₁₆ in. (8.1 cm).

Eggs: 4–10, commonly 5–6; av. 85.7 x 58.2 mm. Oval to long-oval. Shell smooth or slightly rough, not glossy. Creamy white or dirty white, unmarked when laid, becoming nest-stained. Incubation by female alone; 28 days. 1 brood.

Notes: Canada Geese mate for life. While gander does not incubate, he is always nearby guarding and defending nest and territory against intruders. To avoid detection on nest, goose will lie flat and motionless with long neck outstretched.

23

MALLARD *Anas platyrhynchos*

Breeding range: Wisconsin east through n. Illinois, Indiana, Ohio, w. Pennsylvania, New York; locally and sparingly south and east of main range.

Habitat: Edges of freshwater lakes, ponds, sloughs, reservoirs; open prairies (sometimes far from water).

Nest: Well concealed in tall grass, thick dead reeds, cultivated fields (alfalfa). Typically on dry ground (occasionally in trees) in a depression built up with cattails, reeds, grasses, and other locally available material. Lined with down and feathers from female's breast.

Eggs: 8–12, sometimes 6–15; laid 1 a day; av. 57.8 x 41.6 mm. Long-oval. Shell smooth, very little luster. Light greenish buff to light grayish buff or nearly white, unmarked; *indistinguishable from eggs of Black Duck.* Incubation by female alone; 23–29 days, usually 26, beginning with laying of last egg. Sometimes lays in nests of other ducks. Normally 1 brood.

Notes: Perhaps more than any other waterfowl, Mallards seek unnatural nesting sites: the rain gutter on roof of a 4-story building, incubating 7 eggs; in vines at the top of stone wall, 12 ft. (3.7 m) from ground, incubating 12 eggs; in accumulated leaves at bottom of window well, 4–5 ft. (1.2–1.5 m) below ground level; on brick floor of an open recess on side of a building, 35 ft. (10.7 m) from ground.

24

BLACK DUCK *Anas rubripes*

Breeding range: Northern border U.S. south to N. Carolina, W. Virginia, Ohio, n. Indiana, n. Illinois.

Habitat: Great variety of situations in thickets, briars, woodland borders, tall grass; islands, marshy borders of ponds, and marshes.

Nest: On dry ground, slightly elevated above level of marsh. Hollow in ground filled with dry grasses, leaves, available debris; sometimes in trees on old hawk or crow nests. Lined with olive-brown down from female's breast; down added as incubation advances. Outside diam. about 18 in. (45.7 cm); depth 3–4 in. (7.6–10.2 cm).

Eggs: 8–10, sometimes 6–12, laid 1 a day; av. 59.4 x 43.2 mm. Oval to long-oval. Shell smooth, very little luster. Dull or creamy white to shades of pale green or buff, unmarked. *Indistinguishable from eggs of Mallard.* Incubation by female; 26–28 days, beginning with laying of last egg.

Notes: Most abundant breeding duck in e. U.S., but diversity of nesting locations makes usual nest-finding methods unproductive. For example, author has found a nest buried in sphagnum moss in a bog in Maine, another built almost entirely of dry leaves on ground in a large heronry in New Jersey (see illus.). Nests have been found by accidentally flushing incubating bird.

MOTTLED DUCK *Anas fulvigula*
(Florida Duck, Dusky Duck)

Breeding range: Permanent resident in peninsular Florida (*A. f. fulvigula*); rare breeder in s. Alabama, s. Mississippi (*A. f. maculosa*).

Habitat: In very thick cover near freshwater ponds, marshes, sloughs, and canals, and in brushy open fields.

Nest: On ground well hidden in luxuriant growth of tall grasses, weeds, briars, vines, or saw grass; not always close to water. Built of weeds, grasses, and leaves; rim of nest and lining of egg cavity of brown down from female's breast.

Eggs: 5–12, generally 8–10, probably laid 1 a day; av. 57.0 x 44.3 mm (Florida Duck, *A. f. fulvigula*), 54.9 x 40.5 mm (Mottled Duck, *A. f. maculosa*). Oval to long-oval. Shell smooth, sometimes slightly glossy. Creamy white or greenish white, unmarked. Incubation by female alone; 26–28 days. 1 brood.

Notes: Most male ducks desert their mates when the incubation begins, but drake Mottled Duck remains in the nest area, feeding regularly with the female and flying with her to the nest area when she returns. The author suspects that Florida birds (*A. f. fulvigula*) mate for life. They are generally seen in pairs winter and summer and are rarely in flocks even when feeding.

26

GREEN-WINGED TEAL *Anas crecca*

Breeding range: Locally from n. Michigan to Massachusetts and Rhode Island, south to Maryland (Deal I., 1971).

Habitat: On islands and borders of freshwater lakes, ponds, and sloughs.

Nest: Usually in long grass at edge of lake or slough; sometimes a quarter mile (400 m) or more from water. Often concealed by tall grass at base of shrub or willow. Hollow on dry ground; foundation of grasses, weeds, and leaves; lined with very dark brown down. More down added during incubation.

Eggs: 6–18, usually 10–12; av. 45.8 x 34.2 mm. Oval or long-oval. Shell smooth, with slight gloss. Dull white, cream-white or pale olive-buff, unmarked. *Indistinguishable from eggs of Blue-winged Teal.* Incubation by female; 21–23 days. 1 brood.

GADWALL *Anas strepera*

Breeding range: Locally from s. Wisconsin east to New England, Long I., New York, coastal Delaware and N. Carolina. Increasing its range in Northeast.

Habitat: On islands; in meadows and open prairies.

Nest: Commonly on islands, well concealed in thick grasses or tall reeds, on dry ground; sometimes in meadows or prairies some distance from water, concealed by thick grass or small shrub. Hollow lined with material gathered from immediate surroundings: reeds, grasses, stems, roots, mixed with down from bird's breast. Down added during incubation.

Eggs: 7–13, generally 10–12; av. 55.3 x 39.7 mm. Nearly oval. Shell dull creamy white, unmarked (similar to American Wigeon eggs). Incubation by female; 24–27 days.

Notes: The down in Gadwall's nest is somewhat darker and larger than down in American Wigeon's nest.

MUTE SWAN *Cygnus olor*
(proper order after Roseate Spoonbill, p. 22)

Breeding range and Habitat: In many eastern states small colonies exist as semidomestic populations in large parks along borders of lakes and ponds. Originally a native of n. Europe. Domesticated in Great Britain before the 12th century. Stock introduced into N. America has gone wild, mainly along Northeast seaboard.

Nest: On ground close to open water in wild situations, where birds fiercely defend territory against intruders, including man. Huge structures of cattails, reeds, roots, and coarse aquatic vegetation lined with fine plant matter and some feathers and down. Outside diam. 5–6½ ft. (1.5–2.0 m), height 20 in. (50.8 cm); inside diam. 15–18 in. (38.1–45.7 cm).

Eggs: 5–7; older birds 9–12; av. 112.8 x 73.5 mm. Pale gray to bluish green, unmarked. Incubation by female with occasional help from male; 5 wks. or longer.

BLUE-WINGED TEAL *Anas discors*

Breeding range: Wisconsin, Illinois south to Tennessee, east to New England (Massachusetts, Rhode Island), New Jersey, and south along Atlantic Coast to N. Carolina; rarely in Florida and Alabama.

Habitat: Borders of freshwater sloughs, swamps, small ponds, moist meadows, cattail marshes, lakeshores, alfalfa fields.

Nest: On dry ground, sometimes on a muskrat house; not far from water. Well-built basketlike structure placed in hollow in ground; of fine dry grasses or pieces of dead cattail blades mixed with brown down from female's breast. Surrounding vegetation usually arched over nest; provides excellent concealment. Female builds; may take 2–7 days. Down added as incubation advances.

Eggs: 10–13, sometimes 6–15, laid 1 egg a day; av. 46.6 x 33.4 mm. Oval to long-oval. Shell smooth, slightly glossy. Dull white, light cream, or pale olive-white, unmarked. *Indistinguishable from eggs of Green-winged Teal.* Incubation by female; 23–24 days, beginning the day last egg is laid.

Notes: Eggs of larger ducks are sometimes found in teals' nests, but teals apparently seldom lay elsewhere. Migrant Blue-winged Teal habitually arrive on nesting grounds later than most ducks. Single nests; or loosely colonial in suitable habitat (large grassy marshes).

28

RING-NECKED DUCK *Aythya collaris*

Breeding range: Wisconsin, Michigan, ne. New York, n. Vermont, n. New Hampshire, Maine.
Habitat: Freshwater marshes, sedge meadows, wooded lakes, bogs, beaver ponds, sloughs; seldom saltwater environment.
Nest: On floating islands, hummocks, and clumps of bushes in open marshes, commonly where cove or inlet breaks into plants at edge of marsh, often near to same or other species. Nest building starts with egg laying. 1st egg laid on few bent-down strands of grass or sedge; down and grass, reeds, debris within reach of nest added daily. If water level rises, nest is built up as much as 2 ft. (61 cm) to avoid flooding. Outside dimensions variable, depending on surrounding cover. Inside diam. 5–7 in. (12.7–17.8 cm); depth 2–4 in. (5.1–10.2 cm).
Eggs: 6–14, usually 8–10, laid 1 a day; av. 57.5 x 39.8 mm. Long-oval. Olive-gray, olive-buff, unmarked. Incubation by female; 25–29 days, commonly 26–27, starting the day last egg laid. Drake accompanies hen when off nest. 1 brood.

COMMON GOLDENEYE *Bucephala clangula*
(proper order after Wood Duck, p. 30)

Breeding range: N. Michigan, n. New York, n. and cen. Maine.
Habitat: Mature forests near water.
Nest: In natural hole 6–60 ft. (1.8–18.3 m) above ground in large tree near or over water; no apparent preference for species of tree. Nest includes white down from female's breast and whatever debris has accumulated in cavity. Occupied hole often has down clinging to outside.
Eggs: 5–15, commonly 8–12; av. 59.7 x 43.4 mm. Oval to long-oval. Shell smooth, dull luster. Pale green to olivaceous, unmarked; often with various shades in same nest. Incubation by female; probably 28 days (20 days, Bent). 1 brood.

RUDDY DUCK *Oxyura jamaicensis*
(proper order after Red-breasted Merganser, p. 33)

Breeding range: Wisconsin, n. Illinois, se. Michigan; very locally from Great Lakes to New England and Long I., New York.
Habitat: Freshwater sloughs, lakes, ponds, marshes.
Nest: Concealed in bulrushes, sedges, and cattails growing in 10–12 in. (25.4–30.5 cm) of water. 7–8 in. (17.8–20.3 cm) above water level; attached to growing plants; woven of similar plant material. Outside diam. 8–16½ in. (20.3–41.9 cm); inside diam. 4–12 in. (10.2–30.5 cm).
Eggs: 6–10; av. 62.3 x 45.6 mm, remarkably large for so small a bird. Short to long-oval. Shell surprisingly rough and granular. Dull or creamy white, unmarked. Incubation by female; about 25–26 days. Male attentive during incubation and raising of young.

WOOD DUCK *Aix sponsa*

Breeding range: All eastern states; permanent resident in South.
Habitat: Wooded swamps, river forests, woodlots, lake borders, sloughs, marshes; along rivers, creeks, lakes.
Nest: 3–60 ft. (0.9–18.3 m) high in tree in a natural cavity lined with accumulated chips or bits of wood and pale mouse-gray down from female's breast; sometimes in old pileated woodpecker holes. Size of cavity varies greatly. Have successfully used man-made wood or metal nest boxes erected on poles in suitable habitat. Female adds down to man-placed wood shavings in box (see illus.). Cone-shaped tops or lids make boxes practically predatorproof.
Eggs: 10–15, sometimes 6–8, occasionally 18–40 ("dump nests" used by 2 or more females); usually 1 egg laid a day; av. 51.1 x 38.8 mm. Oval. Shell smooth, somewhat glossy. Creamy white, dull white, or pale buff, unmarked. Incubation by female alone; 28–31 days. Male attentive during incubation. Normally 1 brood; 2nd broods have been recorded.

Notes: Two females occasionally use same nest box, incubating in turns or simultaneously. Wood Duck boxes often attract other birds such as Tree Swallows, Northern House-Wrens, Common Starlings, Hooded Mergansers, and Common Grackles.

COMMON GOLDENEYE
Bucephala clangula   p. 29

COMMON EIDER *Somateria mollissima*

Breeding range: Common along Maine coast and isolated offshore islands.

Habitat: Usually on islands, wooded or treeless, with thick cover of tall grasses, weeds, briars (raspberry bushes); entirely saltwater environment.

Nest: Typically in large communities, territory between nests sometimes only a few yards or meters; near to gulls and cormorants. On dry ground, usually well concealed by surrounding vegetation. Made of grasses, seaweeds, mosses, small twigs, with thick lining of gray down.

Eggs: 4–6, sometimes 7–8; av. 76.0 x 50.7 mm. Oval. Shell smooth or slightly rough, without luster. Pale olive-green or brownish olive, unmarked. Incubation by female alone; 26–28 days. Male never approaches nest. 1 brood.

Notes: Female completely covers eggs with down when leaving nest. Down for commerce is collected from nests during incubation period. 35–40 nests required to produce 1 lb. (453.6 gm) eiderdown. Nests robbed of down usually not deserted. Predation by gulls main factor limiting nesting success. Community of 64 nests on Ship I., Blue Hill Bay, Maine: 8 in old stone foundation 15 x 15 ft. (4.6 x 4.6 m); 8 nests had 2 eggs; 12 nests, 3 eggs; 20 nests, 4 eggs; 20 nests, 5 eggs; 2 nests, 6 eggs; 1 nest, 7 eggs; 1 nest, 8 eggs.

31

HOODED MERGANSER *Lophodytes cucullatus*

Breeding range: Wisconsin to Maine and locally south; rare breeder in Alabama, Mississippi, N. Carolina, S. Carolina; absent from Georgia, Florida.

Habitat: Heavily wooded timber surrounding ponds, lakes, river bottomlands.

Nest: In natural tree cavity, usually near water. Quite variable; cavity size, shape, and height above ground or water and kind of tree apparently unimportant. May use hollow top of a stump or fallen hollow log. Uses man-made nest boxes erected primarily for Wood Ducks. Nest lined with down from female's breast mixed with debris in cavity. May use same site year after year.

Eggs: 10–12; sometimes 6–18; av. 53.5 x 44.9 mm. Oval or almost round. Shell thick, usually glossy. Pure white; resembles white egg of domestic chicken. Incubation by female alone; 31 days. Male deserts area after incubation starts, making 2nd brood unlikely. Eggs have been found in nests of Wood Duck and Common Goldeneye. Known to share incubation with Wood Duck hen.

Notes: Author observed 3 Wood Duck nest boxes in Union City, Pennsylvania, reservoir occupied by incubating Hooded Mergansers, April 16, 1966. Boxes held 11, 11, and 14 eggs (see illus.).

COMMON (AMERICAN) MERGANSER *Mergus merganser*

Breeding range: Northern edge of U.S., Maine to Wisconsin.
Habitat: Wooded areas, preferably near fresh water, lake borders, islands.
Nest: Usually in tree cavity, at any height; moderate elevation preferred; typically in hardwood, maple or ash, often a live tree. Also nests in holes in banks, cliffs, piles of rocks. Ground nest well concealed by overhanging rocks, logs, tangles of dense shrubs. Nest cavity lined with white breast feathers and grayish-white down from bird's body. Ground nest usually bulky; of dead weeds, fibrous roots, moss. Same site may be used year after year. Ground nest, inside diam. 7½ in. (19.1 cm).
Eggs: 6–17, commonly 6–10; av. 64.3 x 44.9 mm. Long-oval. Shell thick, little or no luster. Pale buff or ivory-yellow, unmarked; lighter than eggs of Red-breasted Merganser. Incubation by female alone; 28 days. 1 brood. Drake deserts after eggs are laid.
Notes: In flying from nest, female Common Merganser may be mistaken for very similar female Red-breasted Merganser. However, Red-breasted Merganser always nests on ground, Common Merganser rarely; color of feathers, down, and eggs of Red-breasted is darker. May or may not nest near others of same species. Availability of suitable nesting sites is probably major factor in distribution.

RED-BREASTED MERGANSER *Mergus serrator*

Breeding range: N. U.S., New England and New York west to Wisconsin; rarely along coast to S. Carolina (Charleston).
Habitat: Generally on borders of freshwater ponds, lakes, rivers in wooded areas; often near the seacoast; occasionally on coastal islands some distance from woods.
Nest: Usually within 25 ft. (7.6 m) of water. Sometimes built in open, but typically sheltered by tall grasses, overhanging willows, spruces, firs; among tree roots or piles of driftwood. Nest is scooped-out hole or natural hollow in ground profusely lined with brownish-gray down and whitish feathers with some plant material. Outside diam. 12–14 in. (30.5–35.6 cm); inside diam. 7–8 in. (17.8–20.3 cm).
Eggs: As many as 16, commonly 8–10; av. 64.5 x 45.0 mm. Elliptical to long-oval. Shell smooth, very little luster. Buff or more commonly various shades of olive, unmarked. Incubation by female alone; 26–28 days. Drake rarely seen in vicinity of nest. 1 brood.
Notes: May be confused with nest of Common Merganser, which occasionally is on ground. Common Merganser tends to build a much bulkier nest, and its feathers, down, and eggs are all lighter in color. Red-Breasted Merganser is solitary nester, rarely if ever near nests of others of same species.

RUDDY DUCK *Oxyura jamaicensis*   p. 29

TURKEY VULTURE *Cathartes aura*   (Buzzard)

Breeding range: Gulf of Mexico north to Connecticut, w. and cen. New York, and Wisconsin.

Habitat: Remote areas generally inaccessible to predators, such as precipitous cliffs, caves, hollow stumps or logs, dense shrubbery; saw palmetto (*Serenoa repens*) thickets favored in Florida.

Nest: Little or no nest; eggs laid on ground, on gravel of cliffs, or on rotted chips or sawdust in logs and stumps.

Eggs: Typically 2, rarely 1 or 3; av. 71.3 x 48.6 mm, smaller than Black Vulture eggs. Elliptical or long-oval. Shell smooth or finely granulated; little or no gloss. Dull white or creamy white; handsomely marked with irregular spots, blotches, and splashes of pale brown overlaid with spots, blotches, and splashes of bright brown. Incubation by both sexes; "very close to 30 days" (Jackson from Bent); "41 days" (Pennock from Bent); "between 5 and 6 wks." (Grossman and Hamlet).

Notes: Careful concealment from predators is imperative due to  strong odor when young are fed carrion. Unusual nesting sites recorded: abandoned pigsty in woods; floor of old, neglected barn; snag of dead tree with entrance 14 ft. (4.3 m) above nest; 6 ft. (1.8 m) below ground surface in rotted stump; natural cavity in live beech tree, 40 ft. (12.2 m) above ground.

34

BLACK VULTURE *Coragyps atratus*   (Buzzard)

Breeding range: Resident in s. U.S. north to Maryland, W. Virginia, Pennsylvania (rarely), s. Ohio, and s. Indiana.

Habitat: Hollow stumps, exposed roots of large trees, dense thickets of palmetto, yucca, saw grass; caves; under large boulders.

Nest: None. Eggs laid on bare ground, bottom of stump, or in hollow log; rarely in hollow trees.

Eggs: Usually 2, occasionally 1, rarely 3; av. 75.6 x 50.9 mm, larger than Turkey Vulture eggs. Oval to elliptical or long-oval. Shell smooth, not glossy. Gray-green, bluish white, or dull white with large blotches or spots of pale chocolate or lavender wreathed or clustered near large end, overlaid with dark brown blotches and spots. Some eggs almost without spots. Incubation by both sexes; 28–39 days. In 21 Florida nests incubation required 28–30 days.

Notes: Roger Tory Peterson found Louisiana nest in tree cavity 8 ft. (2.4 m) above ground. Author found nests on Kissimmee Prairie, Florida, in saw palmetto (*Serenoa repens*) thickets by thumping outside with stout club, flushing birds incubating inside. Sometimes gregarious; at least 12 pairs nested on bare ground under intertwining stems of yucca (Beaufort, S. Carolina). Decorate nest area with bright bits of trash — bottle caps, broken glass, piece of comb, etc.

35

OSPREY *Pandion haliaetus* (Fish Hawk)

Breeding range: Throughout e. U.S., principally Atlantic Coast; owing to hard pesticides in the food chain now rare, local, or absent in areas where formerly common. Permanent resident in s. U.S.

Habitat: Always near fresh or salt water; otherwise shows little or no preference.

Nest: Tends to be in small loose colonies. On ground to 60 ft. (18.3 m) high on dead snags, living trees, utility poles, duck blinds, fishing shacks, storage tanks, aerials, cranes, billboards, chimneys, windmills, fences, channel buoys. Foundation of small to huge sticks; lined with inner bark, sod, grasses, vines. Often used successive years. Height a few inches (or cm) to 10 ft. (3 m).

Eggs: 3, sometimes 2, rarely 4; av. 61.0 x 45.6 mm. Oval, short-oval, elliptical, or long-oval. Shell fairly smooth, finely granulated. White, pinkish white, pale pinkish cinnamon; generally heavily spotted or blotched with rich or reddish brown. Incubation entirely by female; probably about 35 days. 1 brood.

Notes: John Steinbeck found 3 shirts, 1 bath towel, 1 arrow, and his rake in nest in his garden. Also seen in nests: rope, broom, barrel staves, hoops, fishnet, toy boat, old shoes, fishlines, straw hat, rag doll, bottles, tin cans, shells, sponges, etc.

36

SWALLOW-TAILED KITE *Elanoides forficatus*

Breeding range: Florida, S. Carolina, rarely in Georgia's Oke-fenokee Swamp, Mississippi, and Alabama. Common in Big Cypress Swamp, Florida. Formerly more widespread in South.
Habitat: Cypress strands and slash pines in or near cypress swamps.
Nest: 60–130 ft. (18.3–39.6 m) from ground in treetops. Of cypress twigs, pine needles, Spanish moss; lined with mosses and lichens. Both sexes build; gather material in talons.
Eggs: Usually 2; sometimes 3; av. 46.7 x 37.4 mm. Short-oval or nearly oval. Shell smooth, not glossy. White or creamy white, boldly and irregularly blotched or spotted with shades of bright brown. Incubation by both sexes; 21–24 days.

SNAIL (EVERGLADE) KITE *Rostrhamus sociabilis*

Breeding range: Lake Okeechobee; Loxahatchee Marsh, Palm Beach Co., Florida.
Habitat: Permanent freshwater marshes.
Nest: Only a few yards (or meters) apart in colonies. 3–8 ft. (0.9–2.4 m) above water in clumps of saw grass or myrtle, or occasionally on dead tree stumps. Compact platform of sticks; lined with willow leaves, Spanish moss, and vines. Outside diam. 15 in. (38.1 cm), height 1 ft. (30.5 cm); depth 3½ in. (8.9 cm).
Eggs: 3–4, sometimes 2; av. 44.2 x 36.2 mm. Mostly oval. Shell smooth, without gloss. White, profusely blotched or spotted with shades of brown. Incubation by both sexes; length of period unknown.
Notes: Rare endangered population; less than 100 birds in U.S. but abundant in tropics. Continued existence probably dependent upon availability of favored food, freshwater snails (*Pomacea*).

MISSISSIPPI KITE *Ictinia misisippiensis*

Breeding range: Gulf states north to sw. Tennessee; also east to ne. Florida; rarely in S. Carolina.
Habitat: Local in tall timber of southern plantations and forests.
Nest: 12–130 ft. (3.7–39.6 m) in tops of tallest trees in area; sweet-gum, cottonwood, pines often chosen. Compact and well-built shallow saucer of twigs, sticks, sprigs of green leaves and moss; usually lined with green leaves. Same nest often used successive years. Both sexes build. Size varies with location. Outside diam. 10–25 in. (25.4–63.5 cm).
Eggs: Generally 1, occasionally 2, rarely 3; av. 41.3 x 34.0 mm. Oval to short-oval. Shell smooth, without gloss. Plain white or pale bluish white, usually unmarked. Incubation 31–32 days.

BALD EAGLE *Haliaeetus leucocephalus*

Breeding range: Locally throughout e. U.S.

Habitat: Open areas, forests, mountains, typically near lakes, rivers, seashores; sometimes in or close to populated areas.

Nest: An eyrie, built in fork near crown of giant tree; species of tree not so important as its size, shape, distance from other nesting eagles. Immense pile of large sticks, branches, cornstalks, rubbish; lined with grasses, moss, twigs, sod, weeds. Both birds build. Same nest used year after year, or may have 2 nests for use in alternate years. Nests, added to each year, eventually topple of own weight. New nest: outside diam. 5 ft. (1.5 m), height, 2 ft. (.6 m); inside diam. 20 in. (50.8 cm), depth 4–5 in. (10.2–12.7 cm).

Eggs: 2, sometimes 1, rarely 3, probably laid at intervals of 3–4 days; southern race, av. 70.5 x 54.2 mm; northern race, av. 74.4 x 57.1 mm; small for such a large bird. Short-oval to oval, bluntly rounded on ends. Shell rough or coarsely granulated. Dull white, unmarked. Incubation by both sexes; about 35 days.

Notes: Adult at 3 yrs., rarely breeds before. Florida population, although greatly diminished, probably highest in U.S. except Alaska. Endangered species e. U.S.

38

MARSH HAWK *Circus cyaneus* (Northern Harrier)

Breeding range: In favorable habitat locally throughout e. U.S.; rare in peninsular Florida.

Habitat: Prefers fresh or saltwater marshes, wet meadows, sloughs, and bogs; may nest in dry fields, prairies, usually not far from water.

Nest: On or near ground, sometimes built up over water. Flimsy to well-made structure of sticks, straws, grasses. Height of substructure varies from 1–2 in. (2.5–5.1 cm) in drier places to 18 in. (45.7 cm) in wet situations. Nests high in tidal marshes to avoid flooding. Built mostly by female; male often gathers material for mate. Outside diam. 15–30 in. (38.1–76.2 cm); inside diam. 8–9 in. (20.3–22.9 cm).

Eggs: 5, frequently 4 or 6, occasionally 7–9; may be day or more between layings; av. 46.6 x 36.4 mm. Oval to short-oval. Shell smooth, with little or no gloss. Dull white or pale bluish white, generally unmarked. Incubation mostly or entirely by female; about 24 days, often beginning with laying of 1st egg.

Notes: Polygyny reported occasionally (1 male defending nests of 2 females in same area). In Saskatchewan, 18 nests of waterfowl found within 100 yds. (91.4 m) of Marsh Hawk nest; no predation evident.

39

NORTHERN GOSHAWK *Accipiter gentilis*

Breeding range: N. and cen. New England, n. and cen. New York west to Wisconsin; Pennsylvania.

Habitat: Heavily wooded, remote wilderness areas, often mountain forests.

Nest: Usually in tall trees as high as 75 ft. (22.9 m) from ground, av. 30–40 ft. (9.1–12.2 m). Nest placed in crotch or on limb against trunk. Bulky nest of large sticks; slightly hollowed, lined with bark chips, evergreen sprigs; commonly feathers and down in and around nest. May use other hawk nests as base; often occupies same nest year after year. Outside diam. 3–4 ft. (91.4–121.9 cm), height 18–35 in. (45.7–88.9 cm).

Eggs: 3–4, sometimes 2, rarely 5; not always laid on successive days; av. 59.2 x 45.1 mm. Oval to long-oval. Shell rather rough, granulated or pitted. Pale bluish white or dirty white, typically unmarked. Occasionally eggs are sparsely brown-spotted. Incubation "said to be about 28 days" (Bent); "incubation (36–38 days), almost entirely by the hen, begins with the second or third egg" (Grossman and Hamlet).

Notes: Of 62 nesting records: 11 were in conifers — 7 in white pine, 2 in firs, 1 each in spruce, hemlock; 51 in deciduous trees — 18 in beeches, 14 in birches, 11 in poplars, 6 in maples, 1 each in oak, cottonwood (Bent). Goshawks fiercely defend nest; have been known to harass and even attack persons approaching or simply passing near a nest tree.

SHARP-SHINNED HAWK *Accipiter striatus*

Breeding range: E. U.S. south to Alabama and S. Carolina.

Habitat: Woodland, preferably coniferous.

Nest: Usually in conifer but occasionally in deciduous tree (oak). Bent reported 17 of 18 nests found in Massachusetts in white pine. 20–60 ft. (6.1–18.3 m) from ground, av. 30–35 ft. (9.1–10.7 m). A broad platform of sticks and twigs, built on limb against tree trunk; unlined or lined with chips of pine bark. Prefers new nest annually but sometimes repairs old one. Nest large in proportion to size of bird: outside diam. 24–26 in. (61–66 cm), height 7 in. (17.8 cm); inside diam. 6 in. (15.2 cm), depth 2–3 in. (5.1–7.6 cm).

Eggs: 4–5, often 3, rarely 6, 7, 8; av. 37.5 x 30.4 mm. Spherical or short-oval. Shell smooth, not glossy. Dull white or pale bluish white, with large blotches or splashes of bright rich brown concentrated at either end or forming a wreath midway. Incubation by both sexes, mostly female; 21–24 days.

Notes: Formerly eggs of this species heavily collected as "the most handsome of all hawk eggs." Some collections contained several hundred sets, the result of years of hunting.

COOPER'S HAWK *Accipiter cooperii*

Breeding range: All eastern states. Until recent years a common forest hawk; population now greatly reduced. Exact breeding range uncertain; may nest locally in most of area.

Habitat: Deciduous and coniferous woodlands.

Nest: Placed 20–60 ft. (6.1–18.3 m) from ground in upright crotch of deciduous tree or next to trunk on horizontal limbs of conifer, often white pine. Substantial structure of sticks and twigs always lined with chips or flakes of outer bark of oak or pine; not decorated with greenery as often as nest of buteo (see illus.). Usually builds a new nest annually but may repair old one or build on old squirrel or crow nest. Both sexes build. Outside diam. 24–28 in. (61.0–71.1 cm), height 7–8 in. (17.8–20.3 cm) (nests in crotches higher but not so wide); depth 2–4 in. (5.1–10.2 cm).

Eggs: 4–5, sometimes 3, rarely 6; deposited at intervals of 1–2 days; av. 49.0 x 38.5 mm. Short-oval to oval. Shell smooth, not glossy. Bluish white when fresh, fades to dirty white; sometimes scattered pale spots. Incubation by both sexes, mostly female; 24 days (Bent), 36 days (Heinz Meng in Grossman and Hamlet). May start before clutch complete.

Notes: Woods containing Cooper's Hawk nest may be heavily populated with nesting songbirds, but they are rarely disturbed. Species hunts away from nest area.

41

RED-SHOULDERED HAWK *Buteo lineatus*

Breeding range: Throughout e. U.S. Declining in New England.
Habitat: Moist woodlands, river timber, borders of swamps; open
pine woods, palmetto hammocks (Florida).
Nest: Often close to tree trunk, usually 20–60 ft. (6.1–18.3 m) from
ground, av. 35–45 ft. (10.7–13.7 m). No preference in kind of tree.
Well built of sticks and twigs; lined with strips of inner bark, fine
twigs, dry leaves, sprigs of evergreen, feathers, down. Resembles
nest of Red-tailed Hawk but smaller. Outside diam. 18–24 in.
(45.7–61.0 cm), height 8–12 in. (20.3–30.5 cm); inside diam. 8 in.
(20.3 cm), depth 2–3 in. (5.1–7.6 cm).
Eggs: Usually 3, sometimes 2 or 4; av. 54.7 x 43.9 mm. Oval to

short-oval. Shell smooth, no gloss. Dull white
or pale bluish with variety of shades and
arrangements of brown spots, blotches, or
streaks. Incubation by both sexes; 28 days.
1 brood, unless eggs destroyed or stolen; in this
case, 2nd nesting 3–4 wks. later in same territory.
Notes: Very consistent in returning to same
territory or nesting site annually. Bent tells
of birds in Massachusetts that returned to
same territory for 26 yrs. Permanent residents
in South generally repair old nests each year.
Of 177 nests in Massachusetts: 49 were in
chestnut, 46 red oak, 26 white pine, 19 white
oak, 15 swamp white oak, 13 scarlet oak, 8
maple, 1 ash (Bent).

BROAD-WINGED HAWK *Buteo platypterus* .

Breeding range: Throughout e. U.S.; rarely in s. Florida.
Habitat: Dry forests, wooded hillsides; mostly deciduous forests near small ponds, streams; occasionally in conifers.
Nest: Typically in main crotch or on supporting branches against the trunk of tree 24–40 ft. (7.3–12.2 m) from ground. Small, poorly built of sticks, dead leaves; lined with strips of inner bark, chips of outer bark (pine, oak); often decorated with green leaves and sprigs. Usually new yearly; occasionally a rebuilt crow, hawk, or squirrel nest. May take 3 wks. or more to build. Outside diam. 15–17 in. (38.1–43.2 cm), height 5–12 in. (12.7–30.5 cm); inside diam. 6–7 in. (15.2–17.8 cm), depth 1–3 in. (2.5–7.6 cm).
Eggs: 2–3, sometimes 1 or 4; av. 48.9 x 39.3 mm. Nearly oval to long-oval. Shell finely granulated. Dull white, creamy white, bluish white; many variations in color, shape, and size of blotches, splashes, and spots; mostly shades of brown. Incubation mostly by female; 30 days or more.
Notes: Broadwings probably mate for life; change nesting sites and territories regularly. Eggs in each of 406 clutches: 15 of 1, 183 of 2, 190 of 3, 18 of 4. Of 21 nesting trees: 7 oak, 6 white pine, 4 chestnut, 2 pitch pine, 1 maple, 1 gray birch (Bent).

SHORT-TAILED HAWK   p. 47
Buteo brachyurus

RED-TAILED HAWK *Buteo jamaicensis*

Breeding range: Throughout e. U.S. Permanent resident southern and central states.

Habitat: Dry woodlands, forests, farm woodlots, hilly woods; especially heavy patches of tall timber with oaks or white pines at edge.

Nest: Placed 35–90 ft. (10.7–27.4 m) above ground in tree. Flat and shallow, becoming thicker if added to from year to year. Well made of sticks and twigs; lined with inner bark of grapevine or cedar, moss, and evergreen sprigs. Green sprigs constantly renewed during incubation. Old nests sometimes repaired in autumn. Both sexes build. Larger than nest of Red-shouldered Hawk; outside diam. 28–30 in. (71.1–76.2 cm); inside diam. 14–15 in. (35.6–38.1 cm), depth 4–6 in. (10.2–15.2 cm).

Eggs: Typically 2 in eastern and southern portions of range, 3 in central and western areas; occasionally 4; rarely 1 or 5; av. 59 x 47 mm. Oval or long-oval. Shell finely granulated or smooth, without gloss. Dirty white or bluish white, usually with varying arrangements of spots or blotches in shades of brown. Incubation by female; 28–32 days, av. 30. Male brings food to nest for mate during incubation.

Notes: Difficult to approach closer than about 100 yds. (91.4 m) before incubating bird flushes. Pairs probably mate for life. Migratory birds arrive on breeding grounds mated.

44

CARACARA *Caracara cheriway*
(Audubon's or Crested Caracara)

Breeding range: Permanent resident cen. Florida prairies.

Habitat: Open prairies. Center of abundance Kissimmee Prairie north of Lake Okeechobee.

Nest: In tall trees in small groves or hammocks of cabbage palm and live oak. In a 1928 account of 40 nests found on the Kissimmee Prairie, 3 were in oak trees, 1 in pine, and the remainder in cabbage palm. Bulky nest of brush, vines, and briars broken off, piled in heap, and trampled to make hollow for eggs; unlined or sparingly lined with leaves, grapevine. Same nest site used successive years.

Eggs: 2–3, typically 2, rarely 4; av. 59.4 x 46.5 mm. Generally oval. Shell smooth or finely granulated. White or pinkish white; mostly concealed with covering of buff, cinnamon, or rust, with irregular dark brown blotches, scrawls, splashes, and spots. Incubation by both sexes; about 28 days. 1 brood.

Notes: Typical nest photographed by author was 36 ft. (11 m) above ground in cabbage palm in live oak hammock on Kissimmee Prairie — a thorny tangle of smilax and blackberry vines and some pond cypress built on remnants of an old nest. Could not be seen from ground. Incubating bird flushed; was not seen or heard during photography of nest. 4-yr. survey completed 1970 estimated less than 100 birds in state.

AMERICAN KESTREL *Falco sparverius* (Sparrow Hawk)

Breeding range: Throughout e. U.S.

Habitat: Open wooded areas, orchards; buildings on farms, in cities.

Nest: Natural tree cavities, old flicker and pileated woodpecker holes, man-made nest boxes; nooks, crannies in eaves of buildings; rarely in the open in old nests of other birds. Little or no nesting material added to cavity.

Eggs: 3–5, commonly 4–5, laid on alternate days; av. 35 x 29 mm. Oval, short-oval. Shell smooth, no gloss. White, pinkish white, or light cinnamon, rather evenly covered with small dots and spots of various shades of brown; markings sometimes concentrated at one end or in ring around egg. Incubation mostly by female; 29–31 days.

Notes: In Butler Co., Pennsylvania, author attracted Kestrels to man-made boxes and nail kegs; roofed, had 3-in. (7.6 cm) opening in side, placed 20–30 ft. (6.1–9.1 m) above ground on orchard trees and utility poles. Sawdust and chips placed in bottom of boxes

invariably pushed aside and eggs laid on bare wood; all clutches had 5 eggs (see illus.). Female vigorously resisted intrusion; occasionally had to be lifted bodily from nest box so eggs could be checked. Disturbance caused no desertions. 3 nests of Kestrels at one time in rafters of steel company plant in Aliquippa, Pennsylvania.

46

MERLIN *Falco columbarius* (Pigeon Hawk)

Breeding range: Northern edge of U.S. (Maine, Michigan).
Habitat: Open woods or heavy timber in wilderness areas; cliffs.
Nest: About 35–60 ft. (10.7–18.3 m) above ground on ledges, in natural cavities of trees, on old nests of other birds; rarely on ground or under roofs of deserted buildings. Sticks interwoven with moss; sparingly lined with fine twigs, lichens, conifer needles.
Eggs: 4–5, sometimes 3, rarely 6; av. 40.2 x 31.3 mm. Short-oval, oval, elliptical. Shell smooth, no gloss. Whitish, almost covered by fine dots or bold blotches of browns; sometimes wreathed. Like small Peregrine Falcon eggs. Incubation mostly by female; about 30 days.

PEREGRINE FALCON *Falco peregrinus* (Duck Hawk)

Breeding range: Present status uncertain. Formerly n. U.S., locally south to Georgia. Presumably extinct in e. U.S.
Habitat: Cliffs overlooking rivers, lakes, seacoasts; roofs, ledges of tall city buildings.
Nest: Scrape or slight hollow on ledge of high cliff; many records of nests on buildings. Site selected by female, who scratches out a hollow 1–2 in. (2.5–5.1 cm) deep. Same site may be used annually.
Eggs: 4, sometimes 3, occasionally 5; usually laid every other day, sometimes interval of 2 days between 3rd and 4th eggs; av. 52 x 41 mm. Short-oval to long-oval. Shell smooth or finely granulated. Creamy white to whitish pink, almost concealed by blotches and spots of brilliant rich browns; often overlaid. Sometimes markings concentrated at one end. Incubation mostly by female; 33–35 days. 1 brood.
Notes: Endangered species facing possible extinction in U.S.

SHORT-TAILED HAWK *Buteo brachyurus*
(proper order after Broad-winged Hawk, p. 43)

Breeding range: Florida from Everglades National Park north to Palatka, Gainesville, St. Marks.
Habitat: Cypress swamps, pinelands, cabbage palms; in hammocks.
Nest: In cypress, magnolia, gum, pine, mangrove, cabbage palm; 16–60 ft. (4.9–18.3 m) above ground, often far out from trunk. Twigs lined with moss and green leaves.
Eggs: 1–3, usually 2; av. 53.4 x 42.8 mm. Oval or short-oval. Shell finely granulated, not glossy. Pale bluish white in unmarked eggs; dirty white marked irregularly with brown spots and blotches. Incubation data unrecorded.

SPRUCE GROUSE *Canachites canadensis*

Breeding range: Extreme n. U.S., Maine to Wisconsin.

Habitat: Coniferous forests, tamarack swamps, cedar bogs, low-lands bordering sluggish streams.

Nest: In sheltered and well-concealed place in tangle of bushes, or most often under low overhanging spruce limb. Shallow hollow, commonly in moss on top of low mound; lined sparsely with dead leaves, grasses, spruce needles, a few feathers. Female builds.

Eggs: 4–10, typically 6–8, reportedly laid every other day; av. 43.2 x 31.1 mm. Oval to long-oval. Shell smooth, has slight gloss. Cinnamon to buff, usually boldly marked with large spots and blotches of rich browns; occasionally markings are finer and more scattered. Incubation by female alone; variously given as 17 and 24 days, beginning after last egg is laid. Female sits very tight, well camouflaged by surroundings. Male polygamous.

Notes: Breeding population constantly diminished by expansion of forest cutting and need for agricultural land. Last great strong-hold is in commercially useless bogs in remote wilderness areas. Bird's decline has been expedited by lack of fear of man, which has earned it the local name of "fool hen." Unlike the wary Ruffed Grouse, this "partridge" often exposes itself to a man with a gun.

SHARP-TAILED GROUSE *Pedioecetes phasianellus*
(proper order after Greater Prairie Chicken, p. 50)

Breeding range: N. Michigan, cen. Wisconsin; formerly farther south. Range more and more restricted as habitat is lost to development and cultivation.

Habitat: Prairie brushlands, woodland clearings, open forests with considerable brushy growth, often in or near marshy area.

Nest: Sites vary widely; under thick tufts of grass, thick weeds, bushes. Well-hidden hollow scraped in ground; sparingly lined with grasses, dry leaves and ferns, a few feathers. Female builds. Inside diam. of cup 7–8 in. (17.8–20.3 cm), depth 2½–4 in. (6.4–10.2 cm).

Eggs: 9–17, av. 12; av. 42.6 x 32.0 mm. Oval. Shell smooth, with slight gloss. Light brown to olive-buff, often with dark brown speckles, small spots, or dots; when 1st laid have darker brown color and purplish bloom, which quickly disappears. Incubation by female alone; about 21 days. 1 brood.

Notes: As with Prairie Chicken, courtship is community affair (dancing, stomping on booming grounds for promiscuous males). Females attracted to dancing grounds for mating, although mating also occurs elsewhere on territory. In cen. Wisconsin, most nests found within 1 mile (1.6 km) of dancing grounds. Female on nest well camouflaged in prairie grass; sits very tight.

RUFFED GROUSE *Bonasa umbellus*
("pheasant" in South, "partridge" in North)

Breeding range: Resident from Canada south to New Jersey, n. Indiana, s. Wisconsin; Appalachians to Georgia, Alabama; locally in s. Indiana, w. Illinois.

Habitat: Forested areas of conifers, deciduous trees, or mixed.

Nest: In thick woods and dense cover, female hollows site for nest at base of tree, under log, rock, or root, or in dense brush in dry situation. Lined with hardwood leaves, pine needles, available material, mixed with few grouse feathers. Size varies with situation.

Eggs: 9–12, occasionally less, sometimes to 14; 1 egg laid daily until clutch complete; av. 38.9 x 29.6 mm. Short-oval to long-oval. Shell smooth, slight gloss. Buffy; a few eggs speckled with brownish spots. Incubation by female alone; 21–24 days (affected by cold, wet weather, or by interruptions). Male promiscuous; no pair bond formed.

Notes: Female generally does not flush until intruder is close. Left front fender of author's parked automobile was 3 ft. (.9 m) from grouse nest in Pennsylvania on each of several days before bird finally flushed when author walked around car. The car, coming or leaving, failed to dislodge her from her 14 eggs (see illus.).

49

GREATER PRAIRIE CHICKEN *Tympanuchus cupido*

Breeding range: Local; Wisconsin, Michigan, Illinois, Indiana; formerly s. Maine south to Virginia and Kentucky (Heath Hen).
Habitat: Open meadows, prairies, haymarshes, brushy pastures, drained peat grasslands; sometimes adjacent to woodlands.
Nest: On ground among grasses, weeds, low bushes. Cover often includes sedges, goldenrod, dewberry, bluegrass, willow, sweet fern, blueberry, aspen. Natural cavity or hollow scraped by bird, concealed by heavy vegetation; sparsely lined with grass, sedges, small twigs, feathers. No roof built, but cover often naturally arched. Female builds. Inside diam. of cup about 7 in. (17.8 cm), depth 2–3 in. (5.1–7.6 cm).
Eggs: 5–17, av. 12, usually laid at irregular intervals; number of laying days about twice number of eggs laid; av. 44.86 x 33.59 mm. Oval. Shell smooth, slight gloss. Olive-buff or grayish olive, mostly dotted with fine (a few large) sepia spots. Incubation by female alone; 23–24 days. 1 brood.

Notes: Males are promiscuous. In early spring females are attracted to booming grounds where mating occurs; only a few dominant males take part. In Wisconsin, 9 of 25 nests were within ½ mile (.8 km) of booming grounds; most within 1 mile (1.6 km).

SHARP-TAILED GROUSE
Pediocetes phasianellus   p. 48
50

COMMON BOBWHITE *Colinus virginianus*

Breeding range: Resident over most of e. U.S. except more northern regions.

Habitat: Farm country, open meadows, weedy pastures, open woodlands. In one report of 602 nests, 97 were in woodlands, 336 in brown-sedge fields, 88 in fallow fields, and about 4 percent in cultivated fields.

Nest: Hollow in tussock of dead grass or among growing grasses; weeds often woven into arch over nest, completely concealing it; lined with dead or growing grass or other nearby material; built by both sexes, mostly female.

Eggs: 12–20, typically 14–16, as few as 7–8, as many as 30, 32, 37 (2 females?); av. 30 x 24 mm. Short-pyriform, sometimes quite pointed. Shell smooth, slightly glossy, hard, tough. Dull or creamy white, never spotted. Incubation by both sexes; 23–24 days. At least 2 broods, especially in South.

Notes: Birds may not build nest until several weeks after mating but are inseparable at this time. Nest seldom found except by accident; close-sitting female will not flush until almost stepped upon. Northern limits of Bobwhite's breeding range vary from year to year with fluctuations in weather. Hard winters cause widespread mortality; good years allow population to increase and move northward.

COMMON (RING-NECKED) PHEASANT
Phasianus colchicus

Breeding range: Mainly north of Mason-Dixon Line (Delaware, n. Maryland, s. Ohio, s. Indiana) and north only as far as deep snow permits (s. Maine, n. New York, s. Michigan, s. Wisconsin).

Habitat: Grain-growing farmlands, bushy pastures, hedgerows; rarely in woods or at any great distance from water.

Nest: On ground in open, weedy fields, bushy pastures, hayfields. Natural hollow, or one scraped by female, is lined with weed stalks, grasses, leaves. Surrounding vegetation helps concealment.

Eggs: 6–15, commonly 10–12; av. 41.85 x 33.50 mm. Oval to short-oval. Shell smooth, with slight gloss. Rich brownish olive or olive-buff, unmarked. Incubation by female alone; 23–25 days. Incubating female more protectively marked than exposed eggs; will not leave nest until almost stepped on. Males polygamous; pair bonds tenuous.

Notes: May use hayfields as nesting sites when preferred cover is not available to accommodate all breeding population of an area. When fields are mowed, females invariably desert hayfield nests regardless of stage of incubation. Known to lay in other birds' nests: Ruffed Grouse, domestic fowl, Common Bobwhite, Blue-winged Teal, Blue Grouse. Nest in Michigan contained 13 pheasant eggs, 8 Common Bobwhite eggs.

COMMON TURKEY *Meleagris gallopavo*

Breeding range: Resident in southern woodlands north to w. New York, Pennsylvania, e. Kentucky; most numerous in Appalachian highlands from Pennsylvania south.

Habitat: Forests, woodland clearings, mostly in hilly or mountainous regions. Distribution depends largely upon food supply from oaks, nut-bearing trees.

Nest: On dry ground; a simple depression in dead leaves in forested area, often under a log or concealing bush or at base of tree; lining almost entirely of leaves gathered nearby.

Eggs: 8–15 (smaller clutches by younger birds), sometimes 18, 20, or more (2 or more females?); av. 62.6 x 44.6 mm. Short-oval to long-oval, sometimes quite pointed. Shell smooth, little or no gloss. Pale buff or buffy white; rather evenly marked with reddish-brown or pinkish-buff spots or fine dots. Incubation by female alone; 28 days. 1 brood. Male polygamous, each gobbler consorts with harem of several hens.

Notes: While encroachment of civilization has greatly diminished the population of this shy gamebird, propagation by state conservation agencies has done much to stabilize the situation. In Pennsylvania, where a program of farm-rearing has been successful, there are more turkeys today than ever before.

53

SANDHILL CRANE *Grus canadensis*

Breeding range: Two distinct ranges 600 miles (967 km) apart: Florida Sandhill Crane (*G. c. pratensis*) breeds in Florida and s. Georgia (Okefenokee Swamp), a small population along Gulf Coast of Mississippi; Greater Sandhill Crane (*G. c. tabida*) breeds in Wisconsin and Michigan.

Habitat: Uninhabited open plains, wet meadows, saw grass sloughs, pine flatwoods, shallow marshes, along marshy borders of lakes and streams. Predominate plants in northern breeding range are cattails, sedges.

Nest: In marshes, bogs, prairie ponds. 6–8 in. (15.2–20.3 cm) above surrounding water usually on crane-built islands in thick vegetation knee- to shoulder-high. Nest is mound of sticks, mosses, dead reeds, rushes, tufts of grass. Outside diam. 3–5 ft. (0.9–1.5 m) or more.

Eggs: 2, sometimes 1, rarely 3; laid about every other day; av. 96.2 x 61.4 mm. Oval to long-oval. Shell smooth, little or no gloss. Drab buff or olive, with lavender spots overlaid with brown and olive spots. Incubation by both sexes; 31–32 days.

Notes: Much nesting habitat has been lost to constant encroachment of civilization. Except in protected areas (state and national parks and sanctuaries) the wilderness demanded by this shy bird is fast disappearing.

KING RAIL *Rallus elegans*
(proper order after Limpkin, p. 55)

Breeding range: Florida and Gulf of Mexico north to Massachusetts (rarely), s. Wisconsin. Permanent resident in South.

Habitat: Freshwater marshes, ponds, rice plantations, sloughs, marshy edges of sluggish streams, roadside ditches. Not known to breed in coastal saltmarshes.

Nest: 6–18 in. (15.2–45.7 cm) above water in a hummock, clump of cattails, among marsh grasses, rushes, other aquatic vegetation; generally with natural canopy. A basketlike structure of dead rushes, grasses, cattails, built mostly by male. Outside diam. about 8 in. (20.3 cm).

Eggs: 6–15, typically 10–12, laid 1 per day; av. 41 x 30 mm. Oval. Shell smooth, has very slight gloss. Pale buff, sparingly and irregularly spotted with shades of brown; overlaid appearance. Incubation by both sexes; 21–23 days. Eggs may be laid before nest completed. Normally 1 brood; may have 2 in South.

Notes: Incubating birds seldom flush until an intruder is within 10 ft. (3 m) or less of nest. Habitat of the freshwater King Rail and the saltwater Clapper Rail meet where water becomes brackish in marshes of tidal rivers and creeks along Atlantic and Gulf Coasts. Mixed pairs have been noted.

LIMPKIN *Aramus guarauna*

Breeding range: Florida, s. Georgia (Okefenokee Swamp).
Habitat: Freshwater marshes, bayous, cypress swamps, sloughs, marsh-bordered streams in timbered regions. Restricted to habitat of favorite food, freshwater snails (*Pomacea*).
Nest: In loose colonies where food abundant. As high as 45 ft. (13.7 m) above water in bushes or trees along banks of streams and lakes; at base of bushes a few inches or centimeters above water; or most often among clumps of tall grass or other aquatic plants growing in shallow water. Of reeds and grasses interwoven with growing plants; tree nests of green twigs which could be reached and broken off from nest site. Both sexes build; building initiated by male.
Eggs: 3–8, commonly 5–6, probably laid at irregular intervals; av. 59.4 x 43.8 mm. Oval or short-oval. Shell smooth, has slight gloss. Olive-buff, cream-buff, usually boldly marked with overlaid spots and blotches of light brown, occasionally somewhat concentrated at large end. Incubation by both sexes; duration unrecorded. Typically 2 broods: 3 are possible.
Notes: Little if any material brought to nesting sites in water hemlock in Ocala National Forest, Florida. Surrounding vegetation bent and trampled; eggs laid on flat surface (see illus.).

KING RAIL p. 54
Rallus elegans

55

CLAPPER RAIL *Rallus longirostris*

Breeding range: Saltmarshes along Atlantic and Gulf Coasts north to Connecticut.

Habitat: Saltwater and brackish marshes.

Nest: Higher and drier portions of saltmarsh usually not flooded by tide. Elevated 8–12 in. (20.3–30.5 cm) in clumps of marsh grass, arched over by surrounding grass. Platform built between stems of plants; constructed of dead plant material collected at site (mostly *Spartina*); well cupped. In New Jersey study, 48 of 63 nests were in salt grass (*Spartina*); 45 were within 12 ft. (3.7 m) of a tidal ditch; 43 nests had ramps or runways constructed from nests to ground (see illus.). Outside diam. 7–10 in. (17.8–25.4 cm); inside diam. 5–6 in. (12.7–15.2 cm).

Eggs: 4–12, generally 8–11, laid 1 per day; av. 42.5 x 30.0 mm. Oval. Shell smooth, slightly glossy. Yellowish cream to pale olive-buff, irregularly marked with small blotches and spots of brown. Incubation by both sexes; 18–22 days, av. 20. Normally 1 brood, but 2 have been recorded in South.

Notes: In New Jersey study, most nests more than 150 ft. (45.7 m) apart; closest were 75 ft. (22.9 m), highest 16 in. (40.6 cm) above ground. Flooding by high tides causes most nest mortality.

56

VIRGINIA RAIL *Rallus limicola*

Breeding range: Canada south to Kentucky and e. N. Carolina.
Habitat: Freshwater marshes; rarely, in upper reaches of saltwater marshes.
Nest: Generally well concealed in marsh vegetation in drier area or over water. Built of cattails, coarse grass stems, or other available plant material; may use only rushes. May be entirely of coarse material or have lining of finer material. Usually has canopy of live sedges and rushes. Outside diam. 6¾ in. (17.1 cm), height 3 in. (7.6 cm); inside diam. 4¼ in. (10.8 cm), depth 1½ in. (3.8 cm).
Eggs: 6–13, usually 8–10, laid 1 per day; av. 32.0 x 24.5 mm. Oval to long-oval. Shell smooth, little or no gloss. Pale buff to nearly white, sparingly and irregularly spotted with shades of brown, often concentrated around larger end. Incubation by both sexes; 19 days, starting when last or next to last egg laid. 1 brood.
Notes: Virginia Rails and Soras nest in same habitat, often in close proximity. Before eggs are laid, nests are difficult to distinguish. The Virginia nests generally in drier areas than Sora. Virginia Rail's eggs are lighter colored, less heavily marked, and less glossy than Sora's.

SORA *Porzana carolina*

Breeding range: Canada south to Maryland, s. Ohio, s. Illinois.
Habitat: Freshwater marshes, swamps, bogs, borders of sloughs, wet grassy meadows; shows preference for sedges or cattails where mud and water are quite deep.
Nest: Built about 6 in. (15.2 cm) above water level, supported and arched over by surrounding growing vegetation, commonly cattails or bulrushes. Nest difficult to see, even when standing over it. A well-made basket of dead cattail blades, bulrushes, grasses; finely lined. Sometimes runway made of nest material leads to nest. Av. outside diam. 6 in. (15.2 cm), height 5 in. (12.7 cm); inside diam. 3 in. (7.6 cm); depth 2 in. (5.1 cm).
Eggs: 6–13, av. 10–12, laid 1 per day; av. 31.5 x 22.5 mm. Oval. Shell smooth, glossy. Rich buff, irregularly spotted with shades of brown. Incubation by both sexes; 16–19 days, starting after laying of 1st few eggs. At one time nest may contain young just hatched, others hatching, and eggs in various stages of development. While one bird incubates, the other cares for young, which leave nest soon after hatching. 1 brood.

Notes: Sora eggs more richly colored (olive-buff), more heavily spotted, glossier than those of Virginia Rail. Empty nests nearly indistinguishable; but Sora nest more likely over deep water than Virginia, and more substantially built.

BLACK RAIL *Laterallus jamaicensis*

Breeding range: Florida north along coast to Massachusetts.

Habitat: Saltmarsh meadows overgrown with salt grass and sedge.

Nest: At edge of saltmeadow in heavy growth of fine grass 18–24 in. (45.7–61.0 cm) high bent over by wind, rain. Hidden under tuft of matted dead marsh grass, arch of growing green grass, or a mixture of dead and green plants. A deep cup loosely woven of fine grasses in a depression in the ground, lightly resting on damp ground, or held above water or ground by mat of dry grass; supported by and interwoven with surrounding vegetation. Nest arched over with entrance on side (resembles nest of Meadowlark). Outside diam. 4½ in. (11.4 cm); height 3½ in. (8.9 cm); inside diam. 3¼ in. (8.3 cm), depth 2½ in. (6.4 cm).

Eggs: 6–10; 13 recorded; av. 25.6 x 19.8 mm. Oval. Shell smooth, has little or no gloss. Buffy white or pinkish white, marked with evenly distributed fine brown dots. Incubation data unrecorded; probably by both sexes.

Notes: Like most rails, this smallest of the Rallidae is elusive and seldom seen. It is probably more abundant than nesting records indicate, but its shyness makes observation and study difficult. There are reports of incubating birds sitting so closely that they have been caught in the hand.

YELLOW RAIL *Coturnicops noveboracensis*

Breeding range: Uncertain in e. U.S.; breeds locally in Wisconsin, Michigan (Upper Peninsula).

Habitat: Drier parts of freshwater marshes of grass and sedge; damp hayfields.

Nest: Lightly resting on wet ground or on flattened plants; completely concealed under dense flattened mass of dead rushes or grasses; or naturally hidden by canopy of growing vegetation. Some nests, supported by surrounding plant stems, are suspended above water 1–4 in. (2.5–10.2 cm) deep. Made almost entirely of dead marsh grass coiled to form a small cup; lined with fine bits of sedge and grass, sometimes moss. 1 nest: outside measurements 5⅜ x 4⅞ in. (13.7 x 12.4 cm), height 3⅜ in. (8.6 cm); walls 1½ in. (3.8 cm) thick. 2nd nest: outside diam. 3¾ in. (9.5 cm); inside diam. 2¾ in. (7 cm); cup 1 in. (2.5 cm) thick.

Eggs: 8–10; av. 28.3 x 20.7 mm. Oval or short-oval. Shell smooth. Creamy buff (paler than eggs of Sora, darker than eggs of Virginia Rail), capped at larger end with large reddish-brown spots. Incubation data unknown.

Notes: Shy, elusive, and seldom seen, even leaving nest. Yellow Rail's life history least known of rails; very few nest studies recorded.

COMMON (FLORIDA) GALLINULE *Gallinula chloropus*

Breeding range: Gulf of Mexico and Florida to Vermont, Massachusetts, New York, west to Wisconsin. Permanent resident in South.

Habitat: Large or small freshwater marshes, canals, ponds, and reservoirs.

Nest: Typically over water (often covered with duckweed) anchored in clump of vegetation; occasionally in shrub (willow, alder, wild rose, dogwood) in or near water. Same overall habitat as Purple Gallinule; generally shallower water and lower nest site preferred. Well-made cup of dead cattails, rushes, stems of aquatic plants; often has incline or ramp from water to elevated nest. Incomplete nestlike platforms nearby (roosting, loafing, brooding areas). Size of 1 nest: outside diam. 15 in. (38.1 cm), height 8 in. (20.3 cm); inside diam. 8 in., depth 3 in. (7.6 cm).

Eggs: 6–17, typically 10–12; av. 44 x 31 mm. Oval. Shell smooth, little or no gloss. Cinnamon to buff, irregularly marked with brownish spots, fine dots. Incubation by both sexes; 21 days, said to begin with laying of 1st egg.

Notes: Eggs differ from Purple Gallinule's: larger, ground color slightly darker; spots larger, more irregular, less evenly distributed.

PURPLE GALLINULE *Porphyrula martinica*

Breeding range: Florida north to S. Carolina, Tennessee.
Habitat: Freshwater swamps, river marshes, marshy borders of ponds, lakes; lagoons, rice plantations; especially in areas of dense pickerelweed, spatterdock, water lettuce, cattails.
Nest: Usually surrounded by water 4–10 ft. (1.2–3.0 m) deep. A few inches (cm) to 4–5 ft. (1.2–1.5 m) above water in thick willows, bushes, reeds; often in herbaceous plants of floating islands, or in pickerelweed, where purple flowers afford camouflage. A mass of dead flags, green or decaying leaves, plant stalks, interwoven with and held up by surrounding plants; vegetation usually arched over top. Measurements of 1 nest: outside diam. 15 in. (38.1 cm); inside diam. 8–10 in. (20.3–25.4 cm), depth 3 in. (7.6 cm).
Eggs: 5–15, commonly 6–8; av. 39.2 x 28.8 mm. Oval. Shell smooth, has little or no gloss. Pale pinkish buff, with a few unevenly scattered small brown spots or tiny dots; may be somewhat wreathed. Incubation reported to require 23–25 days, probably by both sexes.

Notes: Incomplete nests of this species often in vicinity of nest in use. Nest in illus. in maiden cane surrounded by water. Eggs of Common Gallinule somewhat larger, color darker, spots larger and more irregular in size and distribution.

61

AMERICAN COOT *Fulica americana*

Breeding range: Wisconsin, Michigan, south to Tennessee (Reelfoot Lake), Massachusetts (Plum I.), New York, New Jersey, occasionally south to Florida.

Habitat: Freshwater marshes, ponds, lakes, wet meadows.

Nest: Quite variable, but typically floating in 1–4 ft. (0.3–1.2 m) water attached firmly to surrounding growing plants (often cattails). A cupped platform of dead or rotted bulrushes, cattails, reeds, or grasses, preferably dry, placed several inches (or cm) above surface of water. Both sexes carry material and build. Av. outside diam. 14–18 in. (35.6–45.7 cm); inside diam. 7 in. (17.8 cm).

Eggs: 6–22, usually 8–12 (excess of 12 may be laid by 2 or more females); laid at intervals of slightly more than 24 hours; av. 49.0 x 33.5 mm. Oval, sometimes quite pointed. Shell smooth, has slight gloss. Buff; dense covering of evenly distributed small spots and minute dots of dark brown. Incubation by both sexes; 23–24 days; generally starts after laying of 3rd or 4th egg.

Notes: Platform construction on territory noted in most nesting pairs, except where muskrat houses or other structures are available for resting, copulating, and brooding young. Nest building normally delayed until marsh vegetation is high enough to conceal structure.

62

AMERICAN OYSTERCATCHER *Haematopus palliatus*

Breeding range: Atlantic Coast from Massachusetts, New York (Long I.), and New Jersey to Florida; locally on Gulf Coast to Louisiana. Permanent resident from Virginia south.

Habitat: Sandy or shell beaches; rubble above high-water mark.

Nest: Generally solitary; in loose colonies, where ideal nesting conditions prevail. On higher parts of sandy beaches among scattered bits of shell. Simple hollow in sand or shells; usually not lined, but may have rim of broken shells.

Eggs: 2–3, sometimes 4; 2 known records of 5 from same female; av. 55.7 x 38.7 mm. Oval to long-oval. Shell smooth, has slight gloss. Buff or olive-buff; irregularly marked and overlaid with spots and blotches of light and dark brown. Incubation by both sexes; about 27 days.

Notes: Apparently limited in northern expansion by scarcity of suitable nesting sites: large expanses of undisturbed coastal beaches. Also limited because of occupation of sites by other species (gulls, terns). Since 1st nesting on Long I. in 1957, species has expanded its range to 4 or more locations. Nests of American Oystercatcher on New Jersey saltmarsh island without sand may indicate that greater habitat flexibility is developing.

63

PIPING PLOVER *Charadrius melodus*

Breeding range: Atlantic Coast, Maine to N. Carolina; locally west along shores of Great Lakes to Wisconsin.

Habitat: Dry sandy outer beaches; on upper stretches near dunes, usually large open grassless sand areas, but sometimes with sparse scattering of beach grass.

Nest: Solitary; in favorable habitat seldom less than 100 ft. (30.5 m) from another nesting pair; generally 200 ft. (61 m) or more apart. Well above high-tide mark. Slight hollow in sand, rimmed or often lined with pebbles or bits of broken shell.

Eggs: Almost always 4 in 1st nesting attempt of season; laid every other day until clutch is complete; may be 3 in 2nd nesting attempt; av. 31.4 x 24.2 mm. Oval to pyriform. Light buff, evenly and lightly marked with fine spots of dark brown. Shell smooth, has no gloss. Last egg of clutch tends to be longest, often widest and heaviest. Incubation by both sexes; 27–28 days, occasionally longer; may sometimes start with laying of 3rd egg. 1 brood.

Notes: Banded adults often return annually to same nesting area. Some are known to have had same mates in consecutive years.

In examination of 526 nests on Long I. beaches: 448 observed with 4 eggs, 70 with 3, 8 with 2 (evidence indicated incomplete clutches or nests suffered predation).

64

SNOWY PLOVER *Charadrius alexandrinus*

Breeding range: Gulf Coast, Florida to Louisiana.
Habitat: Broad stretches of dry coastal sand flats above beach, often near sand dunes.
Nest: May be in loose colonies where habitat is suitable, but single nests not uncommon; sometimes near tern colony. Slight hollow in ground lined with pieces of shell or debris.
Eggs: 3, sometimes 2 (record of 44 sets: 3 eggs in 33, 2 in 11); av. 30.4 x 22.3 mm. Oval to pyriform. Shell smooth, has no gloss. Light buff (sand colored), more or less evenly covered with small spots, dots, little scrawls of black. Incubation by both sexes; 24 days. Eggs said to be laid 3 days apart (Bent). Probably 1 brood.
Notes: All nests found by author in Florida have been at the perimeter of nesting colonies of Least Terns. The fact that the eggs of these two species are very similar in size, color, markings, and number laid, and that nesting scrapes are also much alike causes speculation: Could survival percentage increase for single nest among hundreds of tern nests over solitary nesting elsewhere? As with similar Piping Plover, color and markings of eggs, young, and adult birds provide excellent camouflage with sand and shell surroundings.

KILLDEER *Charadrius vociferus*

Breeding range: Throughout e. U.S., except southern tip of Florida peninsula and the keys.

Habitat: Typically far from water, often in close proximity to human habitation: lawns, airports, cemeteries, driveways, roadsides, parking lots, cultivated fields, etc. Availability of suitable ground cover (gravel, cinders, stones, rubble) to afford camouflage for eggs and incubating bird appears to be important factor in choice of habitat.

Nest: In open where incubating bird has extended view. Male makes various scrapes in ground; one is later accepted by female as nest site. Depression in ground may be unlined or lined with pebbles, wood chips, grass, assorted debris. Outside diam. 5–7 in. (12.7–17.8 cm); inside depth 1–1½ in. (2.5–3.8 cm).

Eggs: 4, rarely 3 or 5; av. 36.3 x 26.6 mm. Oval to pyriform, typically quite pointed. Shell smooth, has no gloss. Shades of buff with bold black or brown spots, scrawls, blotches, sometimes wreathed or capped. Incubation by both sexes; 24–26 days. Interval between laying of each egg often varies. Sometimes 2 broods.

Notes: Nests with eggs have been found in heaps of broken glass, on roof of racetrack grandstand 50 ft. (15.2 m) above ground, between ties of railroad tracks in use.

66

WILSON'S PLOVER *Charadrius wilsonia*

Breeding range: Coastal beaches and islands from New Jersey to Louisiana.

Habitat: Open areas on sandy islands, edges of sand dunes, open shell beaches with scattered vegetation above high-water mark; generally within short distance of salt or brackish water.

Nest: In loose colonies although not close together, 60 ft. (18.3 m) being minimum. Usually in open, sometimes concealed by beach grass arching overhead. Simple hollow in sand or shell, generally lined with bits of broken shells. Nests often placed near conspicuous object on territory: piece of driftwood, mangrove seedling, stump, clump of short grass, pile of debris, etc.

Eggs: 3, sometimes 2, rarely 4; av. 35.7 x 26.2 mm. Oval to pyriform. Shell smooth, without gloss. Shades of buff, quite evenly blotched, spotted, and scrawled with black or dark brown. Incubation by both sexes; 24 days. Occasionally, 2 days may intervene between egg-layings. 1 brood.

Notes: Scrapes in sand or shell made by male within bounds of territory during courtship are undoubtedly invitations to female to mate and accept his territory for actual nest. After pair bond is formed, female accepts one site previously proffered by male. Often found nesting in same general area as Least Terns.

67

WILLET *Catoptrophorus semipalmatus*

Breeding range: Atlantic Coast, Maine (York Co.), New Jersey to Florida; Gulf Coast to Louisiana.

Habitat: Low or sparse vegetation on open saltmarshes a short distance from feeding area.

Nest: In colonies, normally 200 ft. (61 m) or farther apart. On ground, generally well concealed in short, thick grass; sometimes on open beach. Grass blades bent to form thin base in natural hollow; lined with fine grass. Female selects site. Outside diam. 6–7 in. (15.2–17.8 cm).

Eggs: 4, rarely 5, laid at intervals of 1 or more days; av. 52.5 x 38.0 mm. Oval to pyriform. Shell smooth, has slight gloss. Grayish, greenish, or olive-buff, boldly marked with an overlay of small to large spots and blotches of brown shades. Incubation by female (possibly male at night); 22–29 days, probably starting before clutch complete. 1 brood.

Notes: Since eggs are laid at varying intervals and incubation starts before clutch is complete, hatching period is prolonged, perhaps several days. It is characteristic of this species to desert eggs that have not hatched by time 1st-hatched young ready to leave nest. Abandoned eggs generally have well-formed embryos. Nest loss to high tides significant survival factor. May or may not initiate 2nd nesting if 1st nest lost.

68

SPOTTED SANDPIPER *Actitis macularia*

Breeding range: Wisconsin to Maine, south to N. Carolina and Alabama.

Habitat: Open terrain: prairies, dry fields, pastures, edges of freshwater ponds, sloughs, lakes; weed-choked shoulders of roads.

Nest: Solitary or in loose colonies, 244 nests per 100 acres (40.5 ha) recorded. Grass-lined depression in ground under rank weeds, bushes, or in grass 6–30 in. (15.2–76.2 cm) high. Often remote from water. Both sexes build. Diam. 4½–5 in. (11.4–12.7 cm).

Eggs: 4, occasionally 3, rarely 5 (of 37 nests, 33 had 4 eggs, 3 had 3, 1 had 5); typically 1 egg laid per day, but day may occasionally be skipped; av. 32 x 23 mm. Oval to pyriform. Shell smooth, slight gloss. Buff, heavily spotted and blotched with brown shades. Incubation by male; 20–22, usually 21.

Notes: Females often polyandrous. One observer watched 5 females initiate 12 nests: 2 were monogamous, 2 had 2 mates, 1 had 4 mates. Females shared incubation with males only in final clutches. In another situation 12 females were observed with 19 clutches for 14 males. Variant behavior of females seems to indicate that polyandry is still in process of evolving.

69

UPLAND SANDPIPER *Bartramia longicauda*
(Upland Plover)

Breeding range: Wisconsin to s. Maine, south to s. Illinois and n. Virginia.

Habitat: Inland pastures, hayfields (alfalfa, clover), openings in forests; large expanses of open territory.

Nest: In loosely spaced colonies; density varies from 1½–15 acres (0.6–6.1 ha) per nest. Well hidden in depression in thick clump of grass arched over top; invisible from above. Grass twisted in circle to form neat cup. Outside diam. 4–5 in. (10.2–12.7 cm); inside depth 2–3 in. (5.1–7.6 cm).

Eggs: 4, rarely 5; av. 45.0 x 32.5 mm, large egg for size of bird.

Oval to pyriform. Shell smooth, has slight gloss. Creamy or pinkish buff, speckled, spotted, overlaid with light reddish brown. Incubation by both sexes; 21 days. 1 brood.

Notes: Like Prairie Horned Lark, this species took advantage of man's openings in eastern forests to increase its range. During the period 1895–1920, overshooting and loss of habitat to agriculture almost exterminated the species. Today, hunting forbidden, but extensive agriculture still a factor in slowing its comeback. Each incubating bird has own flushing distance: some flush with intruder 6 ft. (1.8 m) away, others permit back-stroking on nest. Flushing does not cause desertion.

AMERICAN WOODCOCK *Philohela minor*

Breeding range: Principally Wisconsin, Michigan; New York and New England south to ne. W. Virginia and n. Virginia. Locally in South except Gulf Coast and s. Florida.

Habitat: Damp woods near water; near foraging territory, open dry woods, abandoned fields, conifer plantations, brushy areas, mixed forests.

Nest: At least 300 ft. (91 m) from nearest singing grounds. No attempt at concealment; a slight depression on the ground in dead leaves, sometimes rimmed with twigs, lined with pine needles.

Eggs: 4 (late nests, 3), 1 egg a day until clutch complete; av. 38 x 29 mm; large for such a small bird. Oval. Shell smooth, has slight gloss. Pinkish buff to cinnamon, covered with light brown spots or blotches overlaid with darker brown markings. Incubation by female alone; 20–21 days. Male promiscuous, probably polygamous. Female disturbed during early stages of incubation may abandon nest. 1 brood.

Notes: Female attracted to singing ground (site of male's courtship performance), where mating occurs. Most crepuscular and nocturnal of N. American shorebirds. Solitary nester but may share feeding grounds with other Woodcocks. Incubating bird sometimes permits stroking by hand. Close sitting and effective camouflage of bird's plumage make nests difficult to find.

71

COMMON (WILSON'S) SNIPE
Gallinago [Capella] gallinago

Breeding range: Northern U.S. south to Illinois, Ohio, Pennsylvania, New Jersey.

Habitat: Freshwater marshes, wet meadows, bogs; sometimes in dense low woody growth with open terrain nearby.

Nest: In or at edge of marsh or bog, concealed in tussock of grass projecting above water; sometimes buried in sphagnum; neat, well-cupped structure generally built of grasses; sometimes with overstory of living plants woven into a protective canopy. Outside diam. 5–6 in. (12.7–15.2 cm), height 2¼ in. (5.7 cm); inside diam. 3–4 in. (7.6–10.2 cm), depth 1¼ in. (3.2 cm).

Eggs: 4, rarely 5; av. 38.6 x 28.1 mm. Pyriform. Shell smooth, has slight gloss. 2 color types: light buff or dark brown. Both types spotted, heavily blotched, scrawled, overlaid with deep brown. Incubation by female; 18–20 days. Male monogamous, helps care for young. 1 brood.

Notes: Male "winnows" in spectacular aerial performance until territory is established. Display attracts female and pair bond is formed. Incubating bird is close sitter; records of persons stroking back of bird or even lifting from nest not uncommon. Late clutches of fresh eggs (Aug.) are believed to be from females hatched previous year.

72

BLACK-NECKED STILT *Himantopus mexicanus*

Breeding range: Florida north locally along coast to N. Carolina and Delaware.

Habitat: Ponds, sloughs, canals, fresh or brackish marshes, wet meadows, mud flats, rice plantations, shores of drainage ditches.

Nest: In small colonies (6–10 nests). Dry site near water or mound built up above shallow water level (see illus.). No nest (eggs on bare ground), or a scrape in ground lined with bits of shell; or elaborate mound of mud, sticks, shells, debris, hollowed in center. Outside diam. 6–10 in. (15.2–25.4 cm); inside diam. 4 in. (10.2 cm).

Eggs: 4, occasionally 3, rarely 5; av. 44.0 x 30.5 mm. Oval to pyriform, typically quite pointed. Shell smooth, has little or no gloss. Buffy or sandy, blotched with brownish black or black, sometimes with dots and spots; often stained with mud. Incubation by both sexes; probably about 25 days.

Notes: Assumed to be single-brooded, but fresh eggs are found over a long span of time (April–July). Rising water prompts birds hurriedly to add material to nest, elevating eggs above water. Many nests abandoned annually when early nesters mistake temporary pools for permanent water. Nesting birds gang up to distract intruder in breeding area; fly overhead in sweeping circles uttering loud, harsh, shrill, monotonous cries.

73

RING-BILLED GULL *Larus delawarensis*
(proper order after Herring Gull, p. 76)

Breeding range: Generally restricted to interior; Great Lakes, New York, nw. Vermont (Lake Champlain), Michigan, Wisconsin (Door Co.).
Habitat: On islands, rocky reefs, freshwater marshes.
Nest: In colonies, often near nests of other gulls, terns, ducks, cormorants. In open situations on the ground on matted vegetation or at upper edges of beaches among rocks. Made of dried grasses, mosses, weeds, rubbish; lined with finer grasses, some feathers. Outside diam. 10–12 in. (25.4–30.5 cm), height 3–4 in. (7.6–10.2 cm); inside diam. 6–9 in. (15.2–22.9 cm), depth 2 in. (5.1 cm).
Eggs: 3, often 2, rarely 4; av. 59.3 x 42.3 mm. Oval or short-oval. Shell smooth, lusterless. Buffy to whitish with spots, speckles, irregular scrawls, splashes, blotches in shades of brown; markings appear overlaid. Incubation by both sexes, 21 days. 1 brood.
Notes: Colonies not always stationary; from year to year may shift from one island to another. In May 1955 there were estimated to be 45,000 Ring-billed Gull nests on a 20 acre (8.1 ha) tract on Little Galloo I., Lake Ontario, a density of about 2000 nests per acre (.4 ha). Ring-bill nests may be intermingled with other species (terns), sometimes 3 or 4 nests within 1 sq. yd. (.8 sq. m).

CASPIAN TERN *Hydroprogne caspia*
(proper order after Gull-billed Tern, p. 79)

Breeding range: Local and widely scattered along Great Lakes, Atlantic Coast of Virginia to n. Florida, Gulf Coast.
Habitat: Low, flat, marine and lake islands; also mainland beaches.
Nest: In compact colonies, generally near nests of other species of terns and gulls, but typically in segregated groups. May also nest singly. Nests vary greatly in different localities; some shallow hollows in ground, sparingly lined, with very little material added; others large deep hollows, lined with sticks, straws, rubbish, shells; rim generally built up more like gull nest than usual tern nest.
Eggs: Normally 2 in South, 3 in North; rarely 4; av. 64.5 x 45.0 mm. Oval or long-oval. Shell somewhat rough, lusterless. Buffy, sparingly marked, and overlaid with small or large brown spots, irregular blotches, occasional scrawls. Look more like gull eggs than typical tern eggs. Similar to Royal Tern eggs. Incubation by both sexes; 20–22 days. 1 brood.
Notes: In nesting areas, Ring-billed Gull is most likely neighbor. Although formerly robbed of its eggs for food, this species has generally escaped depletion by hunters owing to its extreme shyness. Unlike most terns, Caspians do not normally attack human intruders who enter nesting colonies.

GREAT BLACK-BACKED GULL *Larus marinus*

Breeding range: Atlantic Coast from Maine, Massachusetts, New York (Long I.) locally to Virginia (Fisherman I.). Extending range.
Habitat: Mostly offshore rocky or grassy islands; also saltmarshes, rocky driftwood-strewn shores along coastal mainland.
Nest: In colonies, often near colonies, but not mingled with nests, of other species (Herring Gulls, Double-crested Cormorants, Common Eiders, various species of terns). May be unlined hollow in short grass or large pile of coarse grasses, seaweeds, sod, mosses, rubbish; lined with finer grasses. Outside diam. 20–54 in. (50.8–137.2 cm); inside diam. about 10 in. (25.4 cm), deeply hollowed.
Eggs: 3, sometimes 2, laid every other day; av. 77.9 x 54.2 mm. Oval to long-oval. Shell slightly rough, no gloss. Olive-buff to brown, typically spotted or blotched heavily with shades of brown overlaid on shades of pale lilac or lavender-gray. Incubation by both sexes; 26–29 days, beginning before clutch complete. 1 brood.
Notes: Great Black-backed Gulls are notorious nest robbers, eating both eggs and young of other species. There is speculation that this characteristic may change distribution of species upon which they are heavily preda-tory (eiders and terns). Many fishermen who take eider eggs for food do not bother nearby gulls, believing eiders will not nest when gulls are absent.

75

HERRING GULL *Larus argentatus*

Breeding range: Atlantic Coast south locally to New Jersey, Maryland, Virginia, and N. Carolina (range extending steadily southward); inland along large northern lakes.

Habitat: Coastal islands, rocky hillsides, cliffs, saltmarshes; invariably near water.

Nest: In large or small colonies. Almost anywhere on or near ground; occasionally in trees, especially where disturbed by man; on ledges of rocky cliffs. Built of grasses, mosses, debris; lined with finer grasses, some feathers. Shape and size vary with site. Outside diam. 13–24 in. (33–61 cm), height 5–10 in. (12.7–25.4 cm); inside diam. 8–10 in. (20.3–25.4 cm), depth 3–4 in. (7.6–10.2 cm).

Eggs: 3, sometimes 2, laid every other day; av. 72.3 x 50.5 mm. Shape varies considerably, short-oval to cylindrical, mostly long-oval. Shell slightly rough, very slight gloss. Olive-drab, light blue to cinnamon; marked with grayish spots and blotches of irregular size overlaid with brown spots and blotches. Incubation by both sexes, mainly by female; 24–28 days, starting with 1st egg. 1 brood.

Notes: Birds tend to return to same nesting sites in successive years. Monogamous; pairs often mated for many years. Nests of 150 pairs on tar-and-gravel roof, Boston waterfront. 4 successive sets erythristic eggs recorded.

RING-BILLED GULL p. 74
Larus delawarensis

RING-BILLED GULL p. 74

76

LAUGHING GULL *Larus atricilla*

Breeding range: Atlantic and Gulf Coasts.

Habitat: Saltmeadows interspersed with tidal creeks; grassy islands.

Nest: In compact breeding colonies, sometimes containing thousands of nests; may be with colonies of terns, Black Skimmers. In beach grass 2 ft. (61 cm) or more high, beach peas, under bayberry bushes; between and among low sandy dunes, generally well concealed by surrounding vegetation. Nest may be mere hollow in sand lined with dry grass, sticks, debris; or a well-made, bulky structure of grass, stems, firmly interwoven and built up several inches above ground; lining of fine grasses. Both birds build. Av. outside diam. 18 in. (45.7 cm); long stems forming base may project farther.

Eggs: 3, frequently 4, sometimes 2, rarely 5; av. 53.5 x 38.5 mm. Typically oval, some short-oval or long-oval. Shell slightly rough, has very slight gloss. Olive-buff or olive-brown, rather evenly spotted, blotched, scrawled with brown shades. Incubation by both sexes; about 20 days. Monogamous. 1 brood.

Notes: Greatest nest mortality probably from summer high tides that sweep over saltmarshes and sometimes inundate entire colonies. Herring Gulls are predators on both eggs and young where 2 species nest close together.

BLACK TERN *Chlidonias niger*

Breeding range: Maine, n. Vermont west to Wisconsin, n. Illinois, south to Tennessee, Ohio, Pennsylvania.

Habitat: Inland marshes, prairie sloughs, wet meadows.

Nest: In very loose colonies in favorable marsh areas. Typically on low, thin, wet islands of dead and fallen floating vegetation. 197 nests av. 1⅓ in. (3.4 cm) above water; some elaborately built; more often a few pieces of weed stems, dead reeds, cane, cattails, loosely cup-shaped. Sometimes eggs laid in slight depression in floating rubbish with no attempt at nest building; eggs often wet.

Eggs: 3, occasionally 2, rarely 4–5 (av. clutch in 151 nests, 2.6 eggs; 63 percent contained 3 eggs); av. 34 x 24 mm. Oval to pyriform. Shell smooth, dull luster. Deep olive or buff, heavily spotted, blotched, overlaid with black or dark brown, frequently wreathed. Incubation by both sexes; 21–24 days. 1 brood; 2nd brood suspected in southern portion of range.

Notes: Hordes of Black Terns and Forster's Terns may breed in same marsh; Forster's favor higher, drier areas (tops of muskrat houses typical), Blacks prefer lower, wetter sites (mats or platforms of floating, rotting, wet vegetation).

GULL-BILLED TERN *Gelochelidon nilotica*

Breeding range: Coastal, locally from New Jersey to Louisiana; inland in Florida.

Habitat: Sand and shell beaches.

Nest: Typically in segregated groups among or near nests of other species (terns most frequently). High, dry sand flats behind outer beaches above high-tide line, often among large quantities of washed-up shells. Slight hollow in sand where eggs are well camouflaged by surrounding shells; sometimes elaborate piles of dead sedges gathered from nearby marshes. For 1 nest, outside diam. 18 in. (45.7 cm).

Eggs: 2–3, occasionally 4; av. 47 x 34 mm. Oval or short-oval, well rounded at small end (rounder and lighter colored than eggs of any other medium-sized tern). Shell smooth, has no gloss. Light buff, spotted, blotched, overlaid irregularly with shades of brown. Incubation by both sexes; 22–23 days. 1 brood.

Notes: Formerly a typical marsh breeder until population was greatly reduced by eggers and millinery trade. Present population status uncertain; appears to be slowly returning to former haunts.

CASPIAN TERN   p. 74
Hydroprogne caspia

COMMON TERN *Sterna hirundo*

Breeding range: Coastal, Maine to Louisiana; inland, Wisconsin, Michigan, n. Pennsylvania.

Habitat: Sand and shell beaches; grassy uplands or rocky shores of islands.

Nest: In loose colonies, with and among nests of other species of terns (Roseate, Least, Gull-billed), Black Skimmers, Laughing Gulls. May be no nest, merely a slight hollow in sand, shells, or pebbles; depression in windrow of seaweed and trash above high-water mark. Some material may be added: seaweed, dried grasses, small twigs, bits of rubbish (see illus.).

Eggs: 3, sometimes 2 or 4, typically laid 1 a day until clutch is complete but occasionally at irregular intervals; av. 41.5 x 30.0 mm. Oval, short-oval, long-oval. Shell smooth, no gloss. Pale buff to cinnamon-brown, generally heavily spotted and overlaid with shades of dark brown; tend to be wreathed. Incubation by both sexes; av. 24–26 days, minimum 21 days. 1 brood.

Notes: Future growth or decline of Common Tern population in e. U.S. depends largely upon availability of suitable nesting sites. Constant encroachment of civilization upon beach environment critical. Increase in Herring Gull populations on offshore islands crowds terns, causing desertion. Terns have resorted in some areas to nesting on spoil banks.

80

SONG SPARROW *Melospiza melodia*

Breeding range: Wisconsin to Maine, south to s. Illinois, se. Tennessee, n. Georgia.

Habitat: Farms, cities, suburbs, gardens, yards, roadsides, brushy fields, thickets, swamps, hedgerows, woodland edges.

Nest: Well hidden on ground under tuft of grass, bush, brush pile, or in low bush, tree, as high as 12 ft. (3.7 m), generally 2–3 ft. (.6–.9 m). Cup of grasses, weed stems, leaves, bark fibers; lined with fine grasses, rootlets, hair. Female builds in 5–10 days. Outside diam. 5–9 in. (12.7–22.9 cm), height 4½ in. (11.4 cm); inside diam. 2½ in. (6.4 cm), depth 1½ in. (3.8 cm).

Eggs: 3–5, rarely 6; av. 19.9 x 15.5 mm. Oval to short-oval. Shell smooth, has slight gloss. Greenish white; heavily dotted, spotted, blotched with reddish brown, purple; some underlaid with gray. Markings commonly over entire egg, often obscuring ground color, making egg appear light brown. Considerable variety in size, shape. Incubation by female; 12–13 days. 2 broods, sometimes 3.

Notes: Except for Yellow Warbler, most frequently reported host of Brown-headed Cowbird. As many as 7 Cowbird eggs reported in 1 nest. 1 female known to have had 5 nestings in 1 season, although not all succeeded. Nests recorded from sea level to 6300 ft. (1920 m) on Mt. Mitchell, N. Carolina.

SWAMP SPARROW *Melospiza georgiana*

Breeding range: Northern border of U.S. south to n. Illinois, n. Indiana, cen. Ohio, s. and cen. W. Virginia, Maryland, Delaware.
Habitat: Freshwater marshes, wet brushy fields, meadows, lake-shores.
Nest: In loose colonies where habitat is particularly suitable; also single. In tussock of grass, sedge, or in low bush, commonly over water 2 ft. (.6 m) or more deep, built about 1 ft. (.3 m) above surface. Female builds large bulky foundation entirely of grass and lines inner cup with finer grass. Outside diam. 4 in. (10.2 cm); inside diam. 2⅜ in. (6 cm), depth 1½ in. (3.8 cm).
Eggs: 3–6, commonly 4–5; av. 19.4 x 14.6 mm. Oval. Shell smooth, has slight gloss. Pale green when fresh, fading to greenish white during incubation; heavily dotted, spotted, blotched with browns, gray. Markings vary but usually heavy. Practically indistinguishable from eggs of Song Sparrow, except blotching and clouding typically heavier. Incubation by female; 12–13 days. 1 brood, sometimes 2.
Notes: Author has found favorite nesting habitat in Pennsylvania and Wisconsin to be marshes of cattails, spirea, sedges, alders, with scattering of saplings throughout. Although nearby nests of Red-winged Blackbirds rarely parasitized by Brown-headed Cowbird, Swamp Sparrow was found by author to be frequent victim.

249

ARCTIC TERN *Sterna paradisaea*

Breeding range: Coast and islands, Maine to Massachusetts (Monomoy I.).

Habitat: Rock, moss, sand, grass-covered marine islands.

Nest: In colonies of own species or with nests of other terns (Common, Roseate). Nests thickly scattered on ground; typically simple hollows in sand, moss, or among rocks, often containing a few dry grasses or pieces of shells. Outside diam. 5 in. (12.7 cm); inside depth 1 in. (2.5 cm).

Eggs: 1 or 2, sometimes 3 (census of 279 nests: 181 had 2 eggs, 95 had 1 egg, 3 had 3 eggs); av. 41.0 x 29.5 mm. Oval to short-oval. Shell smooth, no gloss. Pale buff to brown, irregularly spotted or blotched with darker shades of brown. Both sexes incubate; 21–22 days. 1 brood. *Indistinguishable from eggs of Common Tern;* bird must be seen at nest for positive identification of eggs.

Notes: As with other small terns, number of Arctics has recovered with protection from millinery trade. Strictly an inhabitant of colder regions; has shown very little range extension in e. U.S. Breeding season short, arriving mid-May to early June, leaving for Antarctic winter home as early as Aug. 1. Unlike Common and Roseate Terns, which usually alight near their nests and walk to them, Arctic Terns fly directly to their nests.

FORSTER'S TERN *Sterna forsteri*

Breeding range: Atlantic and Gulf Coasts, Maryland to Louisiana; Great Lakes, ne. Illinois, Wisconsin, Michigan.

Habitat: Extensive inland marshes and marshy borders of lakes, large ponds; coastal saltmarshes behind open sandy beaches.

Nest: In colonies, close together; birds very social. Inland nests often on muskrat houses, feeding platforms, floating material. Placed higher and drier than Black Tern nests often found in same marshes; 107 nests averaged 8½ in. (21.6 cm) above water. Cupped depressions with a few pieces of emergent vegetation added. Coastal nests large, elaborate; well-built piles of dead grasses, sedges; lined with fine grass, reeds. Outside diam. 20–30 in. (50.8–76.2 cm); inside diam. 7–8 in. (17.8–20.3 cm), depth 1–1½ in. (2.5–3.8 cm).

Eggs: 3, sometimes 2 or 4, rarely 5; av. 43 x 31 mm. Oval, short-oval, long-oval. Shell smooth, no luster. Olive or grayish or pinkish buff marked and overlaid with small brownish spots; often wreathed near large end; sometimes boldly marked with large brownish blotches or irregular scrawls. Incubation by both sexes; 23–24 days. 1 brood. *Eggs indistinguishable from those of Common Tern.*

Notes: On Wreck I., Virginia, 12 nests were observed in area 10 x 3 yds. (9.1 x 2.7 m); 1 nest within 3 ft. (.9 m) of Clapper Rail nest.

ROSEATE TERN *Sterna dougallii*   p. 86

SOOTY TERN *Sterna fuscata*

Breeding range: Dry Tortugas, Florida.

Habitat: Remote oceanic islands with scattered cover of shrubby tropical plants (bay cedar, *Suriana maritima*).

Nest: In immense colonies with ground nests placed so close together that each nesting pair occupies a space only 14–24 in. (35.6–61.0 cm) in diam. Territory acquired and held through constant fighting with intruding neighbors. Nest is slight depression scratched in sand, occasionally rimmed with a few bay cedar leaves.

Eggs: 1, rarely 2; av. 50 x 35 mm. Oval. Shell smooth, has slight luster. Whitish with brown spots and small blotches scattered rather evenly over egg. Incubation by both sexes; 26 days.

Notes: Sooty Tern colony on Dry Tortugas, 68 miles (109.4 km) west of Key West in the Gulf of Mexico, is one of the largest concentrations of birds in N. America. In 1949–51, nesting population was estimated at 100,000 birds on Bush and Garden Keys. Disastrous storms, hurricanes occasionally deplete the population; but since its discovery in 1516 it has continued to exist. Such a disaster in 1969 was followed with more than 30,000 young produced in 1970. Nesting birds are unusually tame, probably because there is little human predation. The colony is in Tortugas National Monument under protection of U.S. Dept. of Interior, headquarters, Fort Jefferson, Garden Key.

82

LEAST TERN *Sterna albifrons*

Breeding range: Coastal, Maine to Louisiana; inland, in Mississippi R. system to Ohio. Populations shift and fluctuate from year to year.

Habitat: Broad, flat, open sand or gravel beaches of islands or mainland; river sandbars; newly cleared land (housing developments, spoil banks).

Nest: In large or small colonies; sometimes segregated from, sometimes among or near nests of Common Terns, Black Skimmers, Piping Plovers; may be solitary. A hollow scraped in sand, shell, or gravel; some nests sparingly lined with plant material.

Eggs: 2, occasionally 3; av. 31.0 x 23.5 mm. Oval to short-oval. Shell smooth, lusterless. Pale olive-buff to whitish, unevenly sprinkled with small or large brown spots or blotches; protectively colored, matching surroundings. Incubation by both sexes; 20–21 days; 14–16 days (Bent). 1 brood, 2 doubtful.

Notes: On hot days it is typical of incubating bird to leave nest, plunge into water, and return to nest and shake water drops onto eggs. 20 pairs nested on roof of city auditorium, Pensacola, Florida, 1957; have continued to do so annually. Flocks vociferous and active in protecting nests; dive at intruder's head. Millinery trade depleted population in early years.

ROYAL TERN *Thalasseus maximus*

Breeding range: Coast, Maryland to n. Florida and Louisiana. Permanent resident in much of range.

Habitat: Coastal islands and mainland beaches.

Nest: In very dense colonies (see notes); hollow scraped in sand or shell on upper beaches or sandbars; no lining.

Eggs: 1–2, occasionally 3; av. 63.0 x 44.5 mm. Oval, long-oval, cylindrical. Shell smooth, lusterless. Buffy or whitish with scattered brown dots, spots, often blotches, sometimes overlaid on spots or washed-out splashes of light brown. Incubation probably by both sexes; 20 days (Sprunt). 1 brood.

Notes: Eggs laid just far enough from each other that incubating birds do not touch. Almost impossible to walk through colony without stepping on eggs. In island colony of 3500 nests, 100 were in space 16 sq. yds. (13.4 sq. m). June 4, 1947, Sprunt estimated 11,000 nests on Cape I., S. Carolina. In a colony of 3000 nests on St. Helena Sound, S. Carolina, all were sets of 1 egg except 300 sets of 2, and 29 sets of 3. Nests are often destroyed by storms and high tides, so 2nd nestings are common, and prolong the breeding season into Aug. Royal Terns were too large to be in

demand by millinery trade in bygone years, but eggs were collected in large quantities for food. Royals tolerate close relatives, Sandwich Terns, nesting in their colonies.

84

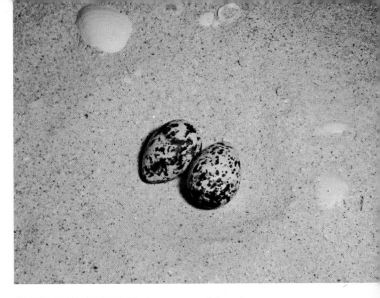

SANDWICH TERN *Thalasseus sandvicensis*
(including Cabot's Tern)

Breeding range: Coast, locally from Virginia to n. Florida and Louisiana.

Habitat: Coastal islands and mainland beaches.

Nest: In colonies, typically among nests of Royal Terns. Mere scrape in sand or shell, generally unlined.

Eggs: 1–2, occasionally 3; av. 51.1 x 36.0 mm. Oval to long-oval. Shell smooth, lusterless. Pale pinkish buff to olive-buff, with wide variety of markings: uniformly covered with small dark brown dots or spots, densely or sparingly; others boldly marked with heavy blotches or irregular scrawls. Incubation by both sexes; about 21 days.

Notes: So close is the Sandwich Tern's association with the Royal Tern that generally when the latter is not present in a breeding colony neither is the Sandwich. Nests are seldom if ever scattered singly among those of Royal Tern; small colonies are grouped together in sections by themselves, although generally surrounded by Royal nests. Each sitting bird is just beyond reach of its neighbor. Eggs of Sandwich Tern are similar to those of the Royal but are smaller and often bear characteristic scrawls that are unusual on tern eggs. Royal and Sandwich Terns associate throughout year and return to breeding areas together.

BROWN NODDY *Anous stolidus*

Breeding range: Dry Tortugas, Florida.
Habitat: Remote oceanic islands with scattered cover of tropical shrubs.
Nest: In loose colonies. Shallow, bulky nests in bay cedar bushes (*Suriana maritima*) or in branches of cacti. Constructed of bay cedar branches, seaweed; lined with seashells, coral. Old nests repaired and added to each year, resulting in some very high structures. Both birds build. Unlike Sooty Terns with which they share Garden and Bush Keys, Noddies rarely nest on the ground.
Eggs: 1; av. 52 x 35 mm. Oval or long-oval. Shell smooth, without luster. Buffy white, sparingly marked with small brownish spots overlaid on spots and blotches of pale brown or lavender; tend to be capped. Incubation by both sexes; 35–36 days (Bent).
Notes: Population of several hundred pairs of Noddy Terns on Dry Tortugas only a small fraction of vast hordes of Sooty Terns that breed there. Noddies show no fear of humans; will attack when unduly bothered; incubating bird typically refuses to leave nest even when touched. Birds migrating to keys arrive at night; do not land until ready to lay egg a week or two later.

ROSEATE TERN *Sterna dougallii*
(proper order after Forster's Tern, p. 81)

Breeding range: Maine to Louisiana in widely separated coastal areas; most common in s. New England, e. Long I., New York.
Habitat: Marine islands; sandy beaches with sparse vegetation.
Nest: In colonies as separate groups but near other terns, or scattered among nests of other species, most generally Common Terns. Nest may be bare depression in sand or may be lined with few pieces of grass or rubbish.
Eggs: 1–2, sometimes 3; av. 42 x 30 mm. Oval to long-oval, generally quite pointed. Shell smooth, no luster. Buff or pale olive-buff, evenly sprinkled, overlaid with spots or dots on entire surface (sometimes wreathed), with or without some small blotches. Incubation by both sexes; 21 days or more.
Notes: Visitors to colonies where Common, Roseate, and Arctic Terns are nesting indiscriminately have difficulty identifying nests and eggs. Adults, all similar in appearance, mill overhead in screaming hordes, usually refusing to return to nests while intruder is in sight. Arctic and Common Tern eggs are indistinguishable; but Roseate Tern eggs tend to be paler, to have finer, less blotchy, and more numerous markings, and to be more pointed.

BLACK SKIMMER *Rynchops niger*

Breeding range: Coast, Massachusetts to Louisiana. Permanent resident in South.

Habitat: Marine beaches, bays, islands, pebbly sand flats, spoil banks.

Nest: In compact colonies; individual colonies often close to other birds: various species of terns, gulls, plovers. In Georgia colony of 200 pairs, nests averaged 3 ft. (.9 m) apart. Unlined, well-defined hollow in sand or shell on open beaches above high-tide line. Diam. 5–10 in. (12.7–25.4 cm); depth 1–2 in. (2.5–5.1 cm).

Eggs: 4–5, sometimes 3, rarely 6; av. 45.0 x 33.5 mm. Short-oval, oval, occasionally long-oval. Shell smooth, lusterless. Bluish white, creamy white, pale buff or pinkish buff, heavily marked, overlaid with dark brown spots, blotches, scrawls. Incubation probably by both sexes, mostly by female; male (?) typically stands guard close to nest as mate incubates; 21–23 days. 1 brood, but season generally prolonged; destruction by storms and high tides necessitates renesting.

Notes: Birds defend colony by flying and "barking" at intruders. Nests were once heavily robbed of eggs for food; today winds and tides are chief enemies. In 30 minutes wind can almost cover unattended eggs; returning bird scoops sand from around eggs reforming nest hollow.

87

BLACK GUILLEMOT *Cepphus grylle*

Breeding range: Islands off coast of Maine.
Habitat: Perimeters of rockbound islands.
Nest: In colonies. Crevice under or between loose rocks or boulders above high-water mark on cliffs or beaches. Eggs laid on bare ground or rock or on shallow bed of pebbles, broken stones, bits of moss, straws.
Eggs: 2, occasionally 1, rarely 3; laid at various intervals; 54 eggs in U.S. National Museum av. 59.5 x 40.0 mm; 77 eggs on Kent I., New Brunswick, av. 57.7 x 38.9 mm. Oval to long-oval. Shell smooth, lusterless. Dull white, cream, or creamy buff; with light brown spots and blotches overlaid with large brown blotches grouped around the larger end; often wreathed. Incubation by both sexes; usually about 28 days (from 27 to 33 days reported). Incubation begins 1–5 days after laying of last egg. Often one bird sits outside nest while other incubates. 1 brood.

Notes: On Kent I., New Brunswick, in 13 nests eggs were laid 3 days apart; in 2 nests, 2 days apart; in 1 nest, 4 days apart. 39 nests held 2 eggs each; 9 nests held 1 egg each; 1 nest had 3 eggs. 2 destroyed clutches were replaced in 14 and 16 days. Author lifted fearless birds from nests on Little Duck I., Maine, to count eggs. In this colony of over 100 pairs, only 1 nest had 3 eggs.

COMMON PUFFIN *Fratercula arctica*

Breeding range: Reaches southern extremity of range in Maine (Matinicus Rock).

Habitat: Oceanic islands where soil and rocks are suitable for building and maintaining nest burrows.

Nest: In colonies, often near nests of Leach's Storm-Petrels, Arctic Terns, and Black Guillemots; typically crowded into available sites on few islands. At end of tunnel in friable soil of open area or in hole under rock, generally the latter for Maine. Burrows curve and slant downward to about 12 in. (30.5 cm) below surface. Old colony a labyrinth of interconnecting passages, but each pair has own entrance. Nest cavity may be unlined or sparingly lined with a loose mass of withered grass, leaves, feathers, stones. Burrows 2-4 ft. (0.6-1.2 m) long.

Eggs: 1, occasionally 2; av. 63.0 x 44.2 mm. Oval to elliptical. Shell dull white, soon becomes soiled. Has limy surface sometimes with faded lilac or dull brown spots at larger end. Incubation by both sexes, mostly by female; 40-43 days (Lockley). 1 brood.

Notes: Male digs burrow, using bill as tool for loosening earth; shovels and ejects it backward with webbed feet. Strong, curved, sharp inner toenail on each foot may indicate adaption for digging. Adult has 2 brood spots, 1 on each side (well removed from each other); incubates on its side. Faded markings on egg, 2 brood spots, and occasional laying of 2 eggs in a burrow would indicate evolution from a time when puffins laid 2 colored eggs in open situations. Some other auks have 2 brood spots but lay only 1 egg (Razorbill and Dovekie).

WHITE-CROWNED PIGEON *Columba leucocephala*

Breeding range: Florida Keys.

Habitat: Small brushy keys edged with mangrove.

Nest: Often in congested colonies, not with or near nests of other colonial species. At heights from ground to 15 ft. (4.6 m) or more. Sometimes in shrub or on cactus; often in mangrove, usually high, but occasionally low, overhanging the water. Reported about 50 ft. (15.2 m) apart. Compact platform of small sticks or twigs, more substantial than Mourning Dove nest; generally well lined with grasses and fibrous roots. "The nest is placed high or low, according to circumstances, but there are never two on the same tree." (Audubon, from Bent)

Eggs: Commonly 2, sometimes 1; av. 36.8 x 27.0 mm. Elliptical to nearly oval. Shell smooth, quite glossy. Pure white. Incubation by both sexes; probably 17-19 days. Number of broods unrecorded.

Notes: Nesting colonies generally on small keys in Gulf of Mexico or Florida Bay away from main keys of Overseas Highway. Adults often fly to highway keys from nest areas to procure food. Adults, young, and eggs once in much use as food by natives.

ROCK DOVE *Columba livia* (Domestic Pigeon)

Breeding range: Feral birds firmly established throughout e. U.S.

Habitat: Wild birds typically on cliffs, in caves, generally near water; feral birds generally in populated areas, farms, suburbs, and cities.

Nest: In colonies or singly. On window ledges, crevices in buildings, under bridges, in barns. Shallow, flimsy platform of carelessly arranged grasses, straws, debris.

Eggs: 1–2, normally 2; av. 38.1 x 27.9 mm. Oval to elliptical. Shell smooth, glossy. White, unmarked. Incubation by both sexes; 17–19 days. Several broods annually; breeding season extends most of year.

Notes: Thousands of domestic pigeons, introduced from Europe, have escaped and live as wild birds. The A.O.U. recognizes this species and lists it under ancestral name from Old World. Feral birds in e. U.S. have rarely reverted to rocky cliffs (as does species in Britain); many in Oregon now live on coastal cliffs. Since the species is so prolific that it generally breeds to the limit of its food supply, it is likely that local populations in urban areas are controlled to a great extent by the generous handouts of pigeon feeders.

90

MOURNING DOVE *Zenaida (Zenaidura) macroura*

Breeding range: Throughout e. U.S.; rare in n. Maine.
Habitat: Open woods, evergreen plantations (Christmas trees), orchards; roadside trees, suburban gardens. Avoids dense woods.
Nest: As high as 50 ft. (15.2 m), av. 10–25 ft. (3.0–7.6 m), in trees, typically evergreens; in tangles of shrubs or vines; rarely on ground. Platform of sticks, surprisingly strong for frail appearance; little if any lining of grass, weeds, rootlets. Eggs often visible from ground through loosely placed twigs. Sometimes uses nest of American Robin, Gray Catbird, Common Grackle, or other species as foundation for its twig platform.
Eggs: 2, occasionally 3, rarely 4; av. 28.4 x 21.5 mm. Oval to elliptical. Shell smooth, has slight gloss. White, unmarked. Incubation by both sexes; 13–14 days. Female normally incubates from dusk to dawn, when male replaces her. 2 or more broods.
Notes: In Michigan study of 736 nests, it was observed that deserted Robins' nests were used 11 times, Common Grackles' nests 3 times, 1 built on ground. In 1953 a Mourning Dove was found brooding 2 young in Black-crowned Night-Heron nest (occupied nests of herons were nearby); in same part of colony, a dove was incubating 2 eggs in Black-crowned Night-Heron nest. In Michigan, 8 young were raised in 4 broods in 1 nest from June to Sept. 1961.

COMMON GROUND-DOVE *Columbina passerina*

Breeding range: Gulf Coast, Florida, Georgia, S. Carolina.
Habitat: Open woods, beaches, farms, grasslands, gardens, dikes, brushy fields, highway shoulders.
Nest: Wide range of nesting sites: bushes, stumps, vines, cacti, horizontal limbs (often conifers), palm fronds, frequently on ground; may be high as 10 ft. (3 m). Shallow cup of grasses, rootlets, thin palm fibers, arranged in circular form. Nests of other species frequently used as foundation (Cardinal, Brown Thrasher). With renovation, same nest may be used for subsequent broods. Outside diam. 2½–3 in. (6.4–7.6 cm); very little depression (eggs show over rim).
Eggs: 2, rarely 3; av. 21.9 x 16.2 mm. Oval to elliptical. Shell smooth, little or no gloss. White, unmarked. Incubation by both sexes; 12–14 days. Breeding season prolonged, Feb.–Nov.; 2, 3, or more broods.
Notes: Of 45 nests examined by author on Sanibel I., Florida, 38 were built in V-shaped center of dead fronds of cabbage palm (see illus.); 4 in live fronds of cabbage palm; 1 each in sea grape, casuarina, and cajeput. None was on the ground. All 45 nests contained 2 eggs or 2 young each.

MANGROVE CUCKOO   p. 95
Coccyzus minor

YELLOW-BILLED CUCKOO *Coccyzus americanus*

Breeding range: Throughout e. U.S.

Habitat: Dense thickets in open woods (rarely in heavy woods), roadsides, streambanks, rural orchards, brushy overgrown fields with copse of small trees (crabapple), vines.

Nest: In tree, vine, shrub as high as 20 ft. (6.1 m) above ground, av. 4–10 ft. (1.2–3.0 m). Thick bushes overgrown with wild grape favored. Small, shallow, frail platform of sticks, vines, twigs, rootlets; thinly lined with bits of moss, grass, pine needles, catkins. Very little depression to contain eggs. Outside diam. about 5 in. (12.7 cm), depth about 1½ in. (3.8 cm).

Eggs: 3–4, sometimes 1–2, rarely 5; av. 30.4 x 23.0 mm; larger than eggs of Black-billed Cuckoo. Elliptical to cylindrical. Shell smooth, no gloss. Unmarked. Pale greenish blue, fading to greenish yellow during incubation (lighter than eggs of Black-billed). Incubation by both sexes, mostly by female, "said to be about 14 days" (Bent). Eggs laid at irregular intervals; incubation may start before clutch complete.

Notes: Eggs often can be seen through bottom of slightly built nest. Yellow-billed Cuckoo and Black-billed Cuckoo often lay eggs in each other's nests (see illus.). Former's eggs also found in nests of American Robin, Gray Catbird, Dickcissel, Cedar Waxwing, Cardinal, Wood Thrush, Mourning Dove, Red-winged Blackbird.

BLACK-BILLED CUCKOO *Coccyzus erythropthalmus*

Breeding range: Northern border of U.S. south to se. Kentucky, cen. Tennessee, S. Carolina, n. Georgia (mountains).

Habitat: Groves of trees, forest edges, thickets; prefers more wooded areas than Yellow-billed Cuckoo.

Nest: Well concealed by leaves and branches in deciduous or evergreen trees, 2–20 ft. (0.6–6.1 m), av. about 6 ft. (1.8 m) above ground. Platform of small twigs loosely interwoven; lined with catkins, cottony fibers, dry leaves, pine needles (generally more substantially lined than nest of Yellow-billed Cuckoo). Outside diam. 8 in. (20.3 cm); inside diam. 3–3½ in. (7.6–8.9 cm), depth ¾–1 in. (1.9–2.5 cm).

Eggs: 2–4, occasionally 5; av. 27.18 x 20.57 mm (smaller than eggs of Yellow-billed). Elliptical. Shell smooth, no gloss. Greenish blue (darker than eggs of Yellow-billed); occasionally have marbled appearance. Eggs laid at intervals of 1–3 days. Incubation by both sexes; reported as 14 days and 10–11 days. Incubation starts after laying of 1st egg.

Notes: Both Black-billed Cuckoo and Yellow-billed Cuckoo lay eggs in each other's nests. Black-billed also known to lay in nests of Yellow Warbler, Chipping Sparrow, Eastern Wood-Pewee, Cardinal, Cedar Waxwing, Gray Catbird, Wood Thrush. Characteristic of species to leave eggshells in nest after young hatch.

SMOOTH-BILLED ANI *Crotophaga ani*

Breeding range: Permanent resident s. Florida as far north as Sebastian (Indian River Co.) on east coast; Lee Co. on west coast.
Habitat: Gardens, roadside thickets, low, overgrown marshes, pastures; thick woods in cities, villages, or farm country.
Nest: In tree or dense shrub 6–30 ft. (1.8–9.1 m) above ground. Loosely constructed of a mass of twigs broken from trees, never picked up from ground; lined entirely with leaves. Built by single pairs or by community of several individuals (probably members of same flock). Both sexes build. Individuals gather material singly or simultaneously. Building may stop abruptly and be resumed in a day or more. Nests may be started and suddenly abandoned. Outside diam. 12 in. (30.5 cm); inside depth to 6 in. (15.2 cm).
Eggs: Number of eggs depends upon number of females laying in 1 nest; 4–21 have been reported. 1 female lays 4–7, usually 6. Av. 35.03 x 26.27 mm. Oval to long-oval. Shell bluish, overlaid and hidden by white chalky deposit, which becomes scratched as incubation progresses. In communal nests, eggs are often in layers with leaves separating each layer. Presumably, when top layer hatches and young are fledged (within a week) the other eggs are incubated. Incubation by both sexes, singly or to 4 individuals incubating simultaneously; period unrecorded. Monogamy, polyandry, or polygyny may exist in 1 flock.
Notes: It is questionable whether laying eggs in layers between leaves is intentional. When birds arrive to incubate, they bring leaves or twigs. If dropped into the nest, these may form unintended layers between groups of eggs.

MANGROVE CUCKOO *Coccyzus minor*
(proper order after Common Ground-Dove, p. 92)

Breeding range: Sw. coast of Florida and the keys.
Habitat: Mangrove swamps and thickets.
Nest: Typically built on horizontal branch of a mangrove. *Indistinguishable from nest of Yellow-billed Cuckoo.* A frail platform of dry twigs, unlined or sparingly lined with bits of fine plant material.
Eggs: 2, sometimes 3; av. 30.77 x 23.18 mm. Elliptical to cylindrical. Shell smooth, no gloss. Pale greenish blue, unmarked. Eggs indistinguishable from eggs of Yellow-billed Cuckoo. Incubation data unrecorded; probably about 14 days. 2 broods (Sprunt).
Notes: Positive identification of nesting species not possible without seeing bird since breeding range of similar Yellow-billed Cuckoo overlaps. Few nests have been found and little study has been made of nesting habits. Although species is typically migratory, arriving in March and departing in Sept., it is occasionally seen in winter in s. Florida, the northern extremity of its range.

BARN OWL *Tyto alba*

Breeding range: S. Wisconsin, s. Michigan, s. New England south to Florida and Gulf states.

Habitat: May be found almost anywhere, but especially open areas of farms, villages.

Nest: In barns, church steeples, silos, sides of old wells, abandoned mine shafts, underground burrows, natural cavities in trees, duck blinds, artificial nesting sites (boxes, barrels, baskets). No nest built. Owl castings (disgorged pellets) generally form base for eggs.

Eggs: 3–11, generally 5–7, laid at intervals of 2–3 days; av. 43.1 x 33.0 mm. Mostly elliptical, not so round as typical owl eggs. Shell finely granulated, little or no gloss. Pure white, becoming yellow stained. Incubation by female (fed regularly by male); reported as 32–34 days or 21–24 days, starts with laying of 1st egg. Variation of reports probably due to different methods of determination. Shorter period presumably indicates hatching time of single egg; longer period, time required to incubate full clutch. 1st owlet hatched may be 2 wks. old when last egg hatches. 2 broods probable.

Notes: Known to nest throughout the year; March–Sept. height of breeding period. Available food supply controlling factor in survival of last hatchlings.

96

COMMON SCREECH-OWL *Otus asio*

Breeding range: Throughout most of e. U.S.

Habitat: Forests, farm woodlots, orchards, stream edges, urban shade trees.

Nest: In natural cavities in many kinds of trees; abandoned nesting holes of Common Flicker, Pileated Woodpecker; crevices in buildings; birdhouses (see illus.); av. 5–30 ft. (1.5–9.1 m) above ground. No nest built, no material carried. Eggs laid in rotted chips, leaves, rubble contained in cavity, which often includes owl feathers or fur and feathers of prey.

Eggs: 2–7, generally 4–5, laid at intervals of 2–3 days; av. 35.5 x 30.0 mm. Elliptical to nearly spherical. Shell very finely granulated, moderately glossy. Pure white. Incubation entirely or mostly by female; reported 21–30 days, av. probably about 26; may start with 1st, 2nd, or 3rd egg.

Notes: Not uncommon to find both of a pair of owls together in nest cavity during day. Throughout incubation male brings food to female at night. Female generally sits tight on eggs when disturbed, may have to be lifted from cavity for eggs to be seen. Owl noted nesting in compartment of Purple Martin house while other compartments occupied by martins. Birds apparently undisturbed by one another.

97

GREAT HORNED OWL *Bubo virginianus*

Breeding range: Resident throughout e. U.S.
Habitat: Heavy forests, large farm woodlots; remote wilderness, rarely in populated areas.
Nest: Generally in old nest of large bird: Red-tailed Hawk (often), Osprey, Bald Eagle, Great Blue Heron, Common Crow. Sometimes squirrel's nest. Also in natural tree cavities, stumps, on rocky ledges, in caves; rarely on ground in logs, among rocks, or under palmetto (Florida). Very little if any material added; central hollow cleared, down from breast and feathers added (see illus.).
Eggs: 1–3, typically 2; av. 56.1 x 47.0 mm. Elliptical to nearly spherical. Shell coarsely granulated (feels rough to touch), has little or no gloss. Dull white, unmarked. Incubation mostly by female (male brings food); variously reported to be about 28 days, about 35 days, about 30 days; begins with 1st egg. Incubating bird often covered by snow in Jan.–March nesting. 1 brood.

Notes: Florida nests, found early as Dec., often contain 1 egg. Of 29 Wisconsin nests: 13 in Red-tailed Hawk nests; 8 in Common Crow nests; 3 in hollow trees; 2 in unidentified nests; 2 in holes or rocky crevices; 1 in Fox Squirrel nest. Breeding pair often will attack person climbing to nest, raking head or back with talons.

BURROWING OWL *Speotyto cunicularia*

Breeding range: Resident in cen. and s. Florida.

Habitat: Prairies, flat grassy plains, high sandy islands; canal dikes, airports, golf courses, large vacant urban lots; broad road shoulders.

Nest: Single or well separated in scattered colonies. Burrows in high ground, dug by owls; rarely in abandoned gopher tortoise burrows. Tunnel extends downward at slight angle, straight or curved, 4–8 ft. (1.2–2.4 m), terminating in circular nest cavity. Entrance 5 in. (12.7 cm) wide, 3½ in. (8.9 cm) high. Earth scratched out of burrow makes large mound at entrance, a lookout point for pair. Egg chamber unlined or more often lined with dry cow or horse manure or nearby plant material.

Eggs: 3–8, generally 5–6; av. 32.4 x 26.9 mm. Elliptical to short-oval. Shell typically smooth, quite glossy. Pure white when laid but soon badly nest-stained. Incubation by both sexes; probably about 3 wks. 1 brood.

Notes: Author found 2 burrows on island in Gulf of Mexico, Lee Co., Florida, with eggs laid on bare sand, no lining. Near Lake Kissimmee, Osceola Co., Florida, author found 3 nests with egg cavity lined with dried leaves of water hyacinth, probably carried from lake (see illus.). Extensive open space offered by airports has favorably influenced Florida nesting population.

99

BARRED OWL *Strix varia*

Breeding range: Resident throughout e. U.S. Distribution often coincides with that of Red-shouldered Hawk.

Habitat: Forests; mainly swampy woodlands.

Nest: Typically a tree cavity; hollow in top of broken tree stub; abandoned nest of hawks (generally Red-shouldered Hawk) or crows; rarely on ground. No lining in cavity nests except debris already present; open nests may be sparingly lined with green sprigs of pine.

Eggs: 2–3, rarely 4; av. 49 x 42 mm. Oval or elliptical. Shell granulated (slightly rough to touch), no gloss. Pure white. Incubation, possibly both sexes, mostly by female, begins with 1st egg; 28–33 days. 1 brood.

Notes: Pair shows strong attachment to same nest area from year to year. One pair in Massachusetts known to nest in same pine woods for 34 yrs., another pair 26 yrs. Often in alternate years will use same nest as Red-shouldered Hawks. 2 nests found in different years contained incubated eggs of both species at same time; in one nest, owl incubating; other nest hawk incubating. Not determined whether owl and hawk alternated on same nest. In one woods, nests of 2 species found 24 yds. (21.9 m) apart. Of 38 nests, 18 in old hawk nests, 15 in hollow trees, 5 in squirrel nests.

LONG-EARED OWL *Asio otus*

Breeding range: Resident Maine to Wisconsin, south to n. Virginia, Indiana, Illinois.

Habitat: Dense or open coniferous or deciduous forests (conifers preferred); wooded parks, orchards, farm woodlots.

Nest: Typically in old nests of crows (very often), hawks, squirrels; occasionally in tree cavities, tops of broken stubs; rarely on ground. Nests unlined or lined sparingly with grass, green twigs, leaves, feathers. Rarely construct own nest. May evict owner of occupied nest (broken eggs of crow found on ground beneath incubating owl).

Eggs: 3-8, normally 4-5, laid every other day; av. 40.0 x 32.5 mm. Oval. Shell smooth, glossy. Pure white. Incubation probably by female only, usually starting after 1st egg laid; 21 days. Oldest owlet may be 8-10 days old when last egg hatches.

Notes: One of most nocturnal of owls, seldom observed during day. Female sits very tight on nest; generally will not flush when tree is tapped. Male roosts near nest, carries food at night to incubating mate. Nest in shallow depression on the ground, concealed by tall grasses and broken-down branch of scrub oak, was found in 1950 in Michigan. It contained 6 eggs. Breeding range may be greater than recorded since species is easily overlooked (nocturnal habits, shyness, protective coloration).

SHORT-EARED OWL *Asio flammeus*

Breeding range: Maine to Wisconsin, south to n. New Jersey, n. Ohio, Indiana, Illinois.

Habitat: Found in open country, shuns woodlands; on fresh or saltwater marshes, plains, dunes.

Nest: Generally in a slight depression on the ground, sparsely lined with grasses, weed stalks, stubble, feathers. Occasionally just flattened vegetation of spot chosen. Slight hollow in sand, exposed or hidden by grass, weed clumps; rarely in excavated burrow. Same site may be used in successive years. Diam. 9-12 in. (22.9-30.5 cm); height 1½-2 in. (3.8-5.1 cm).

Eggs: 4-9, typically 5, 6, 7; av. 39 x 31 mm. Oval to elliptical. Shell smooth or finely granulated, little or no gloss. White or faintly creamy white; becomes quite nest-soiled. Incubation mostly or entirely by female; about 21 days. Male feeds mate on nest.

Notes: One of few owls that construct their own nests — such as it is. There is some evidence that Short-eared Owls nesting in New Jersey saltmarshes may move eggs or helpless young to escape unusually high tides. Frequently nests near Marsh Hawk, apparently without friction. Both species hunt in same area. Short-eared Owl often hunts by day. Permanent resident in more temperate parts of range.

NORTHERN SAW-WHET OWL *Aegolius acadicus*

Breeding range: Wisconsin to Maine, south to n. Indiana, mountains of W. Virginia, New Jersey.
Habitat: Coniferous or deciduous forests, woodlots, swamps, occasionally shade trees.
Nest: In cavity in dead stub, 14–60 ft. (4.3–18.3 m) above ground, usually an abandoned hole of Common Flicker, occasionally Pileated Woodpecker; birdhouses. No material added except breast feathers.
Eggs: 4–7, generally 5–6, laid at intervals of 1–3 days; av. 29.9 x 25.0 mm. Oval to nearly spherical. Shell smooth, little or no gloss. Pure white. Incubation mostly by female; estimated 21–28 days, beginning with laying of 1st egg and resulting in various-sized young in nest.
Notes: Unlike Common Screech-Owl, this species usually appears at cavity opening when tree is tapped. Disturbed while incubating, will not leave cavity until lifted out. Birdhouses erected for Saw-whet Owls by Massachusetts Audubon Society have been successful. Species so nocturnal and retiring it is seldom seen. May be more common than supposed. 1st nest, Mt. Desert I., Maine, discovered by Ralph Long, who observed mosquitoes swarming around cavity entrance, indicating warm-blooded prey inside.

GRAY (CANADA) JAY *Perisoreus canadensis*
(proper order after Purple Martin, p. 134)

Breeding range: N. New England, n. New York, n. Michigan, n. Wisconsin.
Habitat: Coniferous woodlands, swamps, mainly spruce forests.
Nest: On branch near trunk or in upright crotch of conifer 4–30 ft. (1.2–9.1 m) above ground, commonly 6–8 ft. (1.8–2.4 m). A bulky, compact structure; strips of bark, sticks, twigs, grasses, spider webbing, cocoons, catkins; heavily lined with bark, fine grasses, feathers (grouse), hair, fur; thick, insulating walls. Outside diam. 7–8 in. (17.8–20.3 cm), height 3–5 in. (7.6–12.7 cm); inside diam. 3–3½ in. (7.6–8.9 cm), depth 2–2½ in. (5.1–6.4 cm).
Eggs: 2–5, typically 3–4; av. 29.4 x 21.3 mm. Oval, rarely short-oval. Shell smooth, somewhat glossy, occasionally quite glossy. Pale gray to pale greenish, evenly spotted or peppered with dark olive-green. Incubation by female; 16–18 days. 1 brood.
Notes: Nests so early in snowbound northern woods (Feb.–March) that few nests have been studied. Birds are suspected of hoarding or storing nest material (deer hair) before use in nesting. Good insulation is needed to protect eggs and young from temperatures which may drop below 0°F (−17.8°C). Noisy, tame, and sociable at other seasons, Gray Jays are quiet and retiring during nesting period.

CHUCK-WILL'S-WIDOW *Caprimulgus carolinensis*

Breeding range: Florida and Gulf Coast north to s. New Jersey, s. Ohio, s. Indiana, s. Illinois.

Habitat: Oak and pine woodlands, edges of clearings and roads in southern forests.

Nest: None; eggs laid on ground on dead leaves (often oak) or pine needles. Incubating bird very well camouflaged. Eggs conspicuous when exposed.

Eggs: 2, laid on succeeding days; av. 35.56 x 25.57 mm. Oval to elliptical. Shell smooth, moderately glossy. Creamy white, profusely blotched, marbled, spotted, with shades of brown, overlaid on and mixed with lavender and gray. Incubation by both sexes; 20 days, starting with 1st egg.

Notes: May place eggs in nearly same spot year after year. Observer in Mississippi, returning after 12-yr. interval, found eggs laid in same small area. Audubon's tale of disturbed Chuck-will's-widow carrying eggs in mouth to new location is doubted by reputable ornithologists. Although transfer not observed, there have been instances where clutches of eggs were found moved several feet (or a few meters) from original nest site. Further study seems indicated now that oral egg transportation has been observed in other species (see Pile-  ated Woodpecker). Evidently depending upon camouflage, incubating bird sometimes permits close approach before flushing.

103

WHIP-POOR-WILL *Caprimulgus vociferus*

Breeding range: Maine to Wisconsin, south to n. Georgia, n. Alabama, n. Mississippi.

Habitat: Open woods, mixed growth oak, beech, pine; younger, drier hardwood areas preferred rather than mature forests.

Nest: None; eggs laid on ground on dead leaves. typically where light and shadow filter through trees, blending incubating bird with surroundings. As incubation progresses, a depression is formed around eggs by female's body.

Eggs: 2, laid on alternate days; av. 29.0 x 21.3 mm. Oval to elliptical, typically equal-ended. Shell smooth, somewhat glossy. White, irregularly spotted and blotched with gray, overlaid with brown. Incubation by female; probably 19 days or more, starting with laying of 1st egg. 1 brood.

Notes: Pair attached to a nesting locality will return year after year. Incubating bird sits close; when flushed, flies silently away like a moth. Occasionally will try to decoy intruder by feigning a broken wing. Eggs usually discovered by accident rather than by search. Friend of author flushed female from 2 eggs, and returning later to point out nest was unable to find it. After careful study, author detected nearly invisible female incubating 4 ft. (1.2 m) away. No proof that adults ever remove eggs or young when unduly disturbed.

COMMON NIGHTHAWK *Chordeiles minor*

Breeding range: Throughout e. U.S.

Habitat: Plains, dikes, burned-over areas, plowed fields, railroad right-of-ways, cities; rarely on stump, log, debris.

Nest: None. Eggs laid on ground, often gravelly, sparsely vegetated; on graveled roofs of city buildings.

Eggs: 2, laid successive days; av. 29.97 x 21.84 mm. Oval or elliptical. Shell close-grained, moderately glossy. Cream to pale gray, dotted with brown and gray, so densely on some eggs that ground color is almost obscured. Incubation by female; 19 days, beginning with laying of 2nd egg. 1 brood.

Notes: In Brunswick, Maine, banded female returned 2 successive yrs. to same gravel roof, although mates were different. Existence of adequate nesting site, not gregariousness, believed to explain occasional loose colonies; for instance, 16 nests on coral flat, Key Largo, Florida, av. 80 yds. (73.2 m) apart. Observations indicate that incubating bird keeps sun at back all day; has no orientation on cloudy days. 1 egg purposely moved 3 in. (7.6 cm) from nest site was retrieved by female through pushing with bill, feet, breast feathers. An egg moved 36 in. (91.4 cm) from nest site was ignored and single egg incubated until other egg was returned to within 12 in. (30.5 cm), when female brought it back in same way and continued to incubate both eggs.

105

CHIMNEY SWIFT *Chaetura pelagica*

Breeding range: Throughout e. U.S. except Florida Keys.

Habitat: Cities, towns, villages, farms; formerly hollow trees and caves.

Nest: In chimneys, air shafts, sometimes silos, barns, attics, old wells, garages. A frail, thin, half-saucer platform of twigs attached to inside of chimney by adults' glutinous saliva, which hardens and binds material. In flight, birds break twigs from ends of dead tree branches with feet; transfer them to bill before reaching nest. Building, by both sexes, requires 3–6 days. Nest 4 in. (10.2 cm) wide, 3 in. (7.6 cm) from front edge to wall.

Eggs: 3–6, generally 4–5, laid every other day; av. 20.10 x 13.24 mm. Long-oval to cylindrical. Shell smooth, moderately glossy. Pure white. Incubation by both sexes (may both occasionally occupy nest at same time); 18–21 days, and may start with laying of next to last egg. 1 brood.

Notes: One of few N. American birds favorably affected by white man's arrival. Hazards of chimney nesting include use of fireplaces on cold days and loosening of nests from walls by rains. On Kent State University campus, 1 banded male lost nests in same air shaft to rainstorms 4 successive yrs. In 85 nests at Kent, av. distance from top of chimney was 20⅝ ft. (6.3 m).

RUBY-THROATED HUMMINGBIRD *Archilochus colubris*

Breeding range: Throughout e. U.S.
Habitat: Mixed woodlands, orchards, shade trees.
Nest: Solitary; in variety of trees, 6–50 ft. (1.8–15.2 m), av. 10–20 ft. (3.0–6.1 m), above ground, attached to twig or small branch that slants downward from tree, usually sheltered above by leafy branches, open to ground beneath. Nest of plant down, fibers, bud scales, attached to limb with spider silk; lined with soft plant down and covered outside with greenish-gray lichens. Viewed from ground, nest looks like mossy knot on limb. Building is entirely by female, requires about 5 days; some construction continues throughout life of nest. Outside diam. 1–1¾ in. (2.5–4.4 cm), height 1–2 in. (2.5–5.1 cm); inside diam. ¾–1 in. (1.9–2.5 cm), depth ¾ in. (1.9 cm).
Eggs: 2; av. 12.9 x 8.5 mm. Elliptical, one end slightly more pointed. Shell smooth, no gloss. Pure white. Incubation by female alone, variously reported 14 or 16 days. Eggs sometimes laid before nest complete. Possibly 2 broods.
Notes: Male takes no part in nesting activity; suspected of polygamy. In Michigan, 1 female observed alternately feeding 1 young in 1 nest, incubating 2 eggs in 2nd nest 4 ft. (1.2 m) away. Both nests successfully fledged young.

BELTED KINGFISHER *Megaceryle alcyon*

Breeding range: Throughout e. U.S. except Florida Keys.
Habitat: Fresh and saltwater sandbanks, river bluffs, road and railroad cuts, sand and gravel pits.
Nest: Burrow in bank excavated by birds themselves, preferably near water. Generally 1–3 ft. (.3–.9 m) from top of bank, extending inward, curved or uncurved, sloping slightly upward, 3–6 ft. (0.9–1.8 m), rarely 10–15 ft. (3.0–4.6 m). Both sexes take turns digging. Excavation time depends on nature of soil, 2–3 wks. or less. Same burrow may be used succeeding years. Nest cavity enlarged circular dome-shaped chamber at end of tunnel; diam. 10–12 in. (25.4–30.5 cm); height 6–7 in. (15.2–17.8 cm). Tunnel entrance width 3½–4 in. (8.9–10.2 cm); height 3–3½ in. (7.6–8.9 cm).
Eggs: 5–8, commonly 6–7; av. 33.9 x 26.7 mm. Short-oval to elliptical. Shell smooth, rather glossy. Pure white. Incubation by both sexes; 23–24 days. 1 brood.

Notes: In new burrow eggs are laid on bare ground. Succeeding years, eggs laid on base of fish scales, residue from feeding young in previous years. Male may excavate roosting burrow for himself near burrow where female incubates at night. Bird arriving to relieve mate calls from nearby perch; bird on eggs leaves before mate enters tunnel.

COMMON (YELLOW-SHAFTED) FLICKER
Colaptes auratus

Breeding range: Throughout e. U.S.

Habitat: Open deciduous, coniferous, and mixed woods; orchards, farm woodlots, roadsides, yards.

Nest: Hole dug by both sexes in side of live tree (preferably one with partially decayed heart), dead tree or stub; utility pole, fencepost, side of building; 2–60 ft. (0.6–18.3 m) above ground. No material added. Building time 1–2 wks. Old cavity may be repaired. Entrance width 2–4 in. (5.1–10.2 cm), av. 3 in. (7.6 cm); depth of cavity 10–36 in. (25.4–91.4 cm). Birdhouses often used if built to suitable specifications.

Eggs: 3–10, typically 6–8, laid 1 a day; av. 26.85 x 20.58 mm. Oval to short-oval. Smooth, has brilliant gloss. Pure white. Incubation by both sexes; mostly by male at night, shared during day; 11–12 days.

Notes: By removing 1 egg a day, leaving 1 egg as a "nest egg," 71 eggs were removed from 1 flicker nest in 73 days. The female missed only 2 days in over 2 months of laying. Flicker eggs have been found in nests of Eastern Bluebird, Tree Swallow, House Sparrow, Red-headed Woodpecker, Pileated Woodpecker. In 169 nests the following were recorded: 11 sets of 4, 16 of 5, 35 of 6, 34 of 7, 38 of 8, 17 of 9, 13 of 10, 3 of 12, 1 each of 13 and 14.

109

PILEATED WOODPECKER *Dryocopus pileatus*

Breeding range: Throughout e. U.S.

Habitat: Mature coniferous, deciduous forests; large tracts of mixed woodlands.

Nest: A new hole excavated annually for each brood; in same nest area, often in dead stub (hole typically faces east or south), though may be in live tree; 15–70 ft. (4.6–21.3 m) above ground, av. 45 ft. (13.7 m). Both sexes build; no nest material brought in. Entrance hole sometimes circular, but tends to be oval or triangular, peaked above, leveled below. Inner chamber ordinarily conical, tapering from domed top downward to bowllike bottom. Entrance 3¼ in. (8.3 cm) horizontally, 3½ in. (8.9 cm) vertically; depth of cavity from bottom of entrance 10–24 in. (25.4–61.0 cm), av. 19 in. (48.3 cm).

Eggs: 3–4, av. 33.16 x 25.21 mm, for northern race; 3–5, av. 32.90 x 24.72 mm, for southern race. Oval to elliptical, some quite pointed. Shell smooth, decidedly glossy. China-white. Incubation by both sexes, male probably at night, both by day; 18 days. May start before clutch complete. 1 brood.

Notes: In 17 sets of northern race, 13 had 4 eggs, 4 had 3. On April 16, 1966, in Everglades National Park, Frederick Kent Truslow photographed a female Pileated Woodpecker carrying each of 3 eggs lengthwise in her bill from a stub (which had shattered at the nest cavity) to an unknown destination.

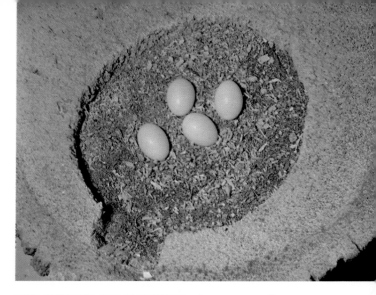

RED-BELLIED WOODPECKER *Centurus carolinus*

Breeding range: Florida and Gulf Coast north to New York (rarely east to Long I.), Pennsylvania, s. Wisconsin, s. Michigan.

Habitat: Coniferous, deciduous forests, orchards, gardens, and yards.

Nest: A hole dug in live tree (cabbage palm, a favorite in Florida), dead tree, stump, utility pole, wooden building; 5–70 ft. (1.5–21.3 m) above ground, usually under 40 ft. (12.2 m). May be in deserted nesting hole of other woodpecker or frequently in birdhouse. Both sexes build, mostly male. Entrance diam. 1¾–2¼ in. (4.4–5.7 cm); depth 12 in. (30.5 cm).

Eggs: 3–8, generally 4–5, laid 1 a day; av. 25.06 x 18.78 mm. Mostly oval. Shell fine-grained, has no gloss when laid but becomes moderately glossy during incubation. Pure white. Incubation by both sexes; said to be 14 days. Probably 1 brood in North, 2 broods in South.

Notes: Common Starlings are aggressive competitors of Red-bellied Woodpeckers, often forcing them to abandon excavations after completion. Author has pair of banded birds on his grounds in Florida that raises 2 broods in birdhouses each year, but only after Common Starlings are forcibly ejected early in season. This pair had 4 fresh eggs July 18, 1967, July 22, 1969, July 17, 1972.

111

RED-HEADED WOODPECKER *Melanerpes erythrocephalus*

Breeding range: Florida and Gulf Coast north to s. New England (rarely), New York, s. Michigan, and s. Wisconsin. Permanent resident in South.

Habitat: Open deciduous and coniferous forests, farm woodlots, towns, gardens, parks.

Nest: Hole dug in live tree, dead stub, utility pole, fencepost, 8–80 ft. (2.4–24.4 m) from ground; no material added. Both sexes excavate. Diam. of entrance 1¾ in. (4.4 cm); depth of cavity 8–24 in. (20.3–61.0 cm).

Eggs: 4–7, commonly 5, laid 1 per day; av. 25.14 x 19.17 mm. Oval to short-oval. Shell smooth, somewhat glossy when incubated. Pure white. Incubation by both sexes, said to be about 14 days, and may start before clutch complete. 1 brood, probably 2 in South.

Notes: Six sets of eggs, 28 in all, taken from same nest in 1 season, after which the pair drilled a new hole in same tree and raised 4 young (total 32 eggs). Migrant and late nester in North; arrives from South usually in early May. Like other medium-sized woodpeckers, the Redhead is victimized by Common Starlings, which are capable of ousting birds from cavities they have dug. Unlike some other woodpeckers, this species appears to shun birdhouses as nesting sites. Utility poles treated with creosote have been lethal to the eggs and young.

YELLOW-BELLIED SAPSUCKER *Sphyrapicus varius*

Breeding range: Wisconsin to Maine, south to nw. Indiana, n. Ohio, New York, w. Massachusetts; in mountains to N. Carolina.

Habitat: Coniferous and deciduous forests, orchards, woodlots.

Nest: Hole dug in live or dead tree or stub, 8–40 ft. (2.4–12.2 m) above ground. Cavity gourd–shaped, sides smoothly chiseled. May use same tree annually, digging new cavities for 5–6 years; rarely use old nest hole. Both sexes build, requiring 1 week or more depending on hardness of wood. May start several excavations before completing nest hole. Diam of entrance 1¼–1⅜ in. (3.2–4.1 cm); depth of cavity about 14 in. (35.6 cm); width of cavity 5 in. (12.7 cm).

Eggs: 4–7, commonly 5–6; av. 22.44 x 16.92 mm. Oval to elliptical. Shell smooth, has little or no gloss. Pure white. Incubation by both sexes; 12–13 days.

Notes: Nests easily discovered since adults become vocally alarmed when intruder is in vicinity. Aspen and a few other trees affected with tinder fungus (*Fomes igniarius*) are especially favored by the Yellow-bellied as nest trees. Fungus attacks heartwood; creates a center of soft decay that can be excavated readily. Outer surface, unaffected, is tough living shell, a deterrent to predators, especially raccoons. Author watched pair in Maine complete a nest cavity in live aspen in June 1968, which remained unused until eggs laid in May 1969.

HAIRY WOODPECKER *Dendrocopos villosus*

Breeding range: Resident throughout e. U.S.

Habitat: Coniferous and deciduous forests, wooded swamps, orchards.

Nest: Hole dug in dead or live tree or stub, 5–30 ft. (1.5–9.1 m) or more above ground. Both sexes excavate, taking 1–3 weeks, depending on hardness of wood. Aspens or other trees with decayed centers favored. Normally a new nesting cavity excavated annually; male may also dig roosting cavity. No material carried in; eggs laid on chips. Typical entrance hole somewhat elongated: 2½ in. (6.4 cm) high, 2 in. (5.1 cm) wide; cavity 10–12 in. (25.4–30.5 cm) or more deep; base inside 4½ in. (11.4 cm) diam.

Eggs: 3–6, commonly 4; av. 23.81 x 18.04 mm. Oval to elliptical. Shell smooth, quite glossy. Pure white. Both sexes incubate; male at night, alternately in day; 11–12 days. 1 brood.

Notes: Female permanent resident in breeding territory, male joins her at start of breeding season in late winter. Pair formation, courtship occur as much as 3 months before start of breeding season (April). Male initiates cavity excavation and may do large part of work, or reverse may occur. Male's aggressiveness toward predators (raccoons) could explain night occupancy of nest.

DOWNY WOODPECKER *Dendrocopos pubescens*

Breeding range: Resident throughout e. U.S.

Habitat: Open forests of mixed growth, orchards, swamps.

Nest: Hole in live or dead tree, stump or stub, fencepost, often in rotting wood, 3–50 ft. (0.9–15.2 m) above ground. Both birds excavate, but mostly female. Cavity opening perfect circle, about 1¼ in. (3.2 cm) diam.; goes straight in for several inches (or cm) before turning downward 8–10 in. (20.3–25.4 cm); cavity narrows from 3 in. (7.6 cm) at top to 2 in. (5.1 cm) at bottom.

Eggs: 3–6, generally 4–5; av. 19.35 x 15.05 mm. Oval to short-oval. Shell smooth, little or no gloss. Pure white. Incubation by both sexes during day, by male at night; 12 days. 1 brood in North, probably 2 broods in South.

Notes: Pair formation and courtship occur in late winter, often several months before nesting. It has been suggested that some degree of pair formation takes place among Downy Woodpeckers in fall (Oct.–Nov.), after which they separate until late winter. Each bird excavates a winter-roost hole. Birdhouses may be used as winter roosts but are rarely if ever occupied as nesting sites. Characteristic of Downy is placement of cavity entrance hole on underside of an exposed limb. If branch is protected from above by an overhanging limb, the entrance hole may be on top.

114

RED-COCKADED WOODPECKER *Dendrocopos borealis*

Breeding range: Resident in southern states; north in small numbers to s. Maryland, se. Virginia, w. Kentucky, Tennessee.
Habitat: Open, parklike pine woods.
Nest: A cavity dug invariably, according to recent studies, in a live pine affected by fungal disease (*Fomes pini*) called "red heart," which attacks heart of tree and causes it to become soft, pithy. Nest cavity 18–100 ft. (5.5–30.5 m) above ground, bored slightly upward through solid wood into soft center, then downward, creating gourd-shaped structure 8–12 in. (20.3–30.5 cm) deep. Birds chip holes through bark into sapwood several feet above and below nest entrance; this causes resin to flow freely (see illus.); reason unknown. Same nest used annually until tree dies or resin no longer exudes from punctures. One of roost holes dug by pair, generally male, becomes nest cavity later.
Eggs: 3–5; av. 24.04 x 17.86 mm. Elliptical to oval. Shell smooth, glossy, sticky from pine gum carried on breast of incubating bird. Pure white. Incubation by both sexes during day, male at night; believed to be 10 days, and begins after laying of 2nd egg. 1 brood.
Notes: On federal list of endangered species because of habitat depletion. Loosely colonial where favorable nesting sites are available. Pairs mate for life.

115

BLACK-BACKED THREE-TOED WOODPECKER
(Arctic Three-toed Woodpecker) *Picoides arcticus*

Breeding range: Ne. Wisconsin, n. and cen. Michigan, n. New York, Vermont, New Hampshire, n. Maine.

Habitat: Boreal coniferous forests, swamps; fire-killed areas are favored.

Nest: Hole in live (generally with dead heart) or dead tree, stub, fencepost, utility pole at low height, atypical for woodpecker: 26 nest holes 2–15 ft. (0.6–4.6 m) above ground. Both sexes excavate, usually a new cavity each year. Entrance about 1½ in. (3.8 cm) high, 1¾ in. (4.4 cm) wide; strongly beveled at lower edge, forming "doorstep." Cavity 9–11 in. (22.9–27.9 cm) deep.

Eggs: 2–6, commonly 4; av. 21.32 x 18.94 mm. Oval to elliptical. Shell smooth, dull or slightly glossy. Pure white. Eggs indistinguishable from those of Northern Three-toed Woodpecker. Incubation by both sexes; about 14 days. 1 brood.

Notes: *Positive identification of nesting species not possible without seeing bird.* Although Hairy Woodpecker sometimes bevels bottom of nest entrance, this feature plus usual lower height are helpful criteria in quickly identifying Three-toed cavity. Birds unusually tame around nesting site. Frequently visit nest while observer is near.

NORTHERN THREE-TOED WOODPECKER
(American Three-toed Woodpecker) *Picoides tridactylus*

Breeding range: N. New England, n. New York, n. Wisconsin.

Habitat: Coniferous forests.

Nest: Hole 5–12 ft. (1.5–3.7 m) above ground, rarely as high as 40 ft. (12.2 m), dug in live or dead coniferous tree or in utility pole by both sexes. Burned tracts of woods preferred. Entrance hole has lower edge chiseled to a slope resulting in irregularly shaped opening 1¾ in. (4.4 cm) wide, 2 in. (5.1 cm) high. Inward, ½ in. (1.3 cm) from trunk surface, hole becomes round, diam. 1½ in. (3.8 cm). Interior irregularly gourd-shaped, diam. about 4½ in. (11.4 cm); depth 10–12 in. (25.4–30.5 cm).

Eggs: 4; av. 23.32 x 18.01 mm. Oval. Shell smooth, moderately glossy. Pure white. Eggs indistinguishable from eggs of Black-backed Three-toed Woodpecker. Incubation by both sexes; about 14 days. 1 brood.

Notes: *Positive identification of nesting species not possible without seeing bird.* Little known about nesting habits of this species; probably quite similar to those of closely related Black-backed Three-toed Woodpecker. Ranges overlap, but Black-backed is more common. Northern is loosely colonial where nesting habitat is particularly suitable and food supply abundant. At nest, birds are unsuspicious and quite tame; usually will enter or leave nest cavity while intruder is close by.

EASTERN KINGBIRD *Tyrannus tyrannus*

Breeding range: Throughout e. U.S.

Habitat: Open woods, orchards (often apple trees), shade trees, forest edges, fencerows; dead stumps and snags in swamps and marshes, shrubby streambanks.

Nest: Generally on tree limb well out from trunk, 2–60 ft. (0.6–18.3 m), av. 10–20 ft. (3.0–6.1 m), above ground; sometimes in crotch of dead stub, often over water. Bulky cup (large for size of bird), rough, unkempt exterior of weed stalks, grasses, mosses; lined with fine grasses, plant down. Both sexes build. Outside diam. 5½ in. (14 cm), height 3¼ in. (8.3 cm); inside diam. 3 in. (7.6 cm), depth 1¾ in. (4.4 cm).

Eggs: 3–5; av. 24.2 x 17.7 mm. Vary from short- to long-oval. Shell smooth, slightly glossy. Creamy white; heavily and irregularly spotted with brown, black, lavender; sometimes wreathed. Incubation by female; 12–13 days, perhaps longer. 1 brood.

Notes: Sometimes nests in tree with other species, often Northern Oriole. Author found apple tree with occupied nests of Eastern Kingbird, Northern Oriole, and Yellow Warbler. Nest reported within 14 in. (35.6 cm) of occupied American Robin's nest. Many reports of strange nest sites for Eastern Kingbird including inside gourd in Purple Martin colony, in reflector of electric street light, inside confiscated Northern Oriole's nest, on top of 4 ft. (1.2 m) fencepost. Fearless and pugnacious with known enemies.

117

GRAY KINGBIRD *Tyrannus dominicensis*

Breeding range: Both coasts of Florida, common on keys; rarely in coastal Georgia, S. Carolina, Alabama.

Habitat: Islands, behind beaches; roadsides, woodlands, groves, and yards in urban or rural coastal areas. Indicates preference for mangroves.

Nest: In fork, or saddled to horizontal limb of tree or shrub 5–17 ft. (1.5–5.2 m), av. 12 ft. (3.7 m), above ground. Frail, poorly constructed shallow cup of coarse twigs; lined with rootlets or fine grass; sometimes has thin floor.

Eggs: 2–3, sometimes 4; av. 25.1 x 18.2 mm. Oval to long-oval. Shell smooth, slightly glossy. Rich salmon or "seashell pink," irregularly spotted and blotched or splashed and overlaid with shades of brown, lavender. Tend to be wreathed or capped. Incubation by female; probably 12–13 days, perhaps longer. 2 broods suspected.

Notes: Quite localized in Florida nestings. Many places that seem suitable in coastal areas are shunned. Species abundant on Sanibel I., where author has found it nesting in acacia, sea grape, casuarina, cabbage palm (where numerous), as well as red mangrove. Species indicates strong attachment to nesting site, returning yearly to same tree or clump of trees. No inland nests of Gray Kingbird have been found in Florida, and bird is rarely observed far from coast.

118

GREAT-CRESTED FLYCATCHER *Myiarchus crinitus*

Breeding range: Throughout e. U.S.

Habitat: Woodlands, old orchards, swamps, parks, edges of clearings.

Nest: In natural cavity or abandoned woodpecker hole in live or dead tree 3–75 ft. (0.9–22.9 m) above ground, av. 10–20 ft. (3.0–6.1 m). Often uses birdhouses. A bulky mass of twigs, leaves, hair, feathers, bark fibers, rope, other trash. Almost always includes cast-off snakeskin or piece of cellophane (see illus.). Small cup for eggs formed in trashy surroundings; lined with finer material, feathers. Both sexes build, taking as long as 2 wks. Cup diam. 2¾–3½ in. (7.0–8.9 cm); depth 1½–2 in. (3.8–5.1 cm).

Eggs: 4–8, generally 5; av. 22.6 x 17.2 mm. Oval to short-oval. Shell smooth, slightly glossy. Yellowish or pinkish white; scratched, lined, streaked, blotched with dark brown, purple. Markings often so dense ground color almost obliterated. Some scratches or fine hairlines as if drawn by pen. Incubation by female; 13–15 days.

Notes: Theory that snakeskins are used in nest to frighten away predators unacceptable. Probable that bird does not recognize snakeskin as such, that it is used along with other available trash as desirable material. Other species, such as Tufted Titmouse, also habitually add snakeskins to nests.

119

EASTERN PHOEBE *Sayornis phoebe*

Breeding range: Wisconsin to Maine, south to n. Mississippi, n. Alabama, n. Georgia, w. S. Carolina.

Habitat: Rocky woodland ravines, cliffs; farmlands, suburban areas.

Nest: On shelflike projections: windows, rafters of farm buildings, girders under bridges, trestles; plastered to rocky ledges, concrete and wooden walls. Large, well constructed of weeds, grasses, fibers, mud; covered with mosses, lined with finer grasses and hair. Semicircular when attached to wall, circular when flat on beam or rafter — less mud used when circular. Built mostly or entirely by female, 3–13 days. Outside diam. 4½ in. (11.4 cm), height 4 in. (10.2 cm); inside diam. 2½ in. (6.4 cm), depth 1¾ in. (4.4 cm).

Eggs: 3–6, commonly 5, rarely more; av. 19.0 x 14.7 mm. Oval. Shell smooth, little or no gloss. White, except 1 or 2 eggs sparsely spotted. Incubation by female alone; 15–16 days. Usually 2 broods.

Notes: Heavily parasitized by Brown-headed Cowbird; often deserts if Cowbird lays in nest first. Author found long periods (as much as 3 wks.) between completion of nest and egg-laying. Lack of orientation may cause female to build many nests side by side on long beam or girder. Author found 6 complete, 22 partly built nests on a bridge beam; 3 eggs in 1 nest, 1 egg in another.

YELLOW-BELLIED FLYCATCHER *Empidonax flaviventris*

Breeding range: Cen. Wisconsin, n. Michigan, n. Pennsylvania (rarely), n. New York, n. Vermont, n. New Hampshire, n. Maine.
Habitat: Coniferous forests, boreal bogs (often cedar, spruce, tamarack).
Nest: Built on or near ground in cavity among roots of fallen tree, in hummock of dense sphagnum moss, at base of coniferous tree. Well-hidden deep cup of mosses; lined with black hairlike rootlets, pine needles, fine grasses, moss stems; built by female alone. Outside diam. 3¼ x 4 in. (8.3 x 10.2 cm); inside diam. 2 in. (5.1 cm), depth 1 in. (2.5 cm).
Eggs: 3–4, occasionally 5 (in 200 nests, 25 contained 5 eggs); av. 17.4 x 13.4 mm. Oval to short-oval. Shell smooth, lusterless. Dull white, sparingly spotted over entire egg with fine brown dots, often heaviest at larger end. Incubation by female alone; 15 days.
Notes: Of 5 nests found by author on Mt. Desert I., Maine, 4 were in cavities of upturned roots of fallen trees; 1 was on ground at base of dead spruce (see illus.). 3 held 4 eggs; 2 had 3 eggs. Female, well hidden, sits very tight until intruder is within 1 ft. (30.5 cm) or so of nest; leaves silently, makes no fuss. Author has never seen male at or near nest except when feeding young. Shyness and silence of birds plus remarkable concealment make nest very difficult to find.

121

ACADIAN FLYCATCHER *Empidonax virescens*

Breeding range: Florida and Gulf Coast north to s. Wisconsin, s. Michigan, ne. Pennsylvania, s. New York, s. New England (casually). Only *Empidonax* species nesting in the South.

Habitat: Deciduous woodlands, shaded ravines, heavily wooded bottomlands, river swamps, hammocks of cypress ponds.

Nest: On lower branch of a large tree, far out from trunk; usually shaded by leafy branches; 8–20 ft. (2.4–6.1 m) above ground; av. for 44 nests 10½ ft (3.2 m). Frail, saucer-shaped, shallow basket swung hammocklike between horizontal twigs of a slender limb. Built of fine, dry plant stems, plant fibers, tendrils, catkins, Spanish moss (in South); by female alone. Slight lining of grass stems, fine rootlets, plant down, spider webs. Invariably long streamers of dried grass, grapevine, fibrous material hang below nest 1–2 ft. (.3–.6 m), giving it misleading trashy appearance from below (see illus.). Outside diam. 3½ in. (8.9 cm); inside diam. 1½ in. (3.8 cm), depth ⅞ in. (2.2 cm).

Eggs: 2–4, generally 3; av. 18.4 x 13.8 mm. Oval to long-oval. Shell smooth, very little or no gloss. Creamy to buffy white, sparingly marked with small brown spots or dots, mainly near large end. Incubation by female alone; 13–14 days. 1 brood.

Notes: Unique nest; cannot be mistaken for any other species. Occasionally parasitized by Brown-headed Cowbird.

122

WILLOW FLYCATCHER *Empidonax traillii*
(Traill's Flycatcher, in part)

Breeding range: S. Wisconsin, Illinois, Indiana, Ohio, Kentucky, W. Virginia, w. Pennsylvania, cen. and e. New York, New Jersey. More southern and western, but range expanding eastward and overlapping that of *E. alnorum.*

Habitat: Dry brushy fields, willow thickets, margins of mixed deciduous woods with water or low damp ground nearby.

Nest: In fork or on horizontal limb of shrub: dogwood, elderberry, blackberry, viburnum, willow, hawthorn, etc.; 3½–15 ft. (1.1–4.6 m) above ground (usually higher than *E. alnorum*). Av. height above ground in 2 studies 49½ in. (125.7 cm) and 55⅝ in. (141.3 cm). Tends to be compact cup of weed bark and fiber, bleached grass; lined with thin layer of fine grass, cottony and silky plant materials; has silvery appearance; typically with feathers in rim. Similar to Yellow Warbler nest. May have plant material dangling from bottom. 1 nest: outside diam. 3 in. (7.6 cm), height 2⅝ in. (6.7 cm); inside diam. 2 in. (5.1 cm), depth 1⅜ in. (3.5 cm).

Eggs: 3–4; av. 17.91 x 13.70 mm. Oval. Shell smooth, dull or slightly glossy. Often buffy (*E. alnorum* eggs are white) or sometimes creamy white; blotched, spotted with shades of brown, markings mostly at large end. Incubation by female; 12–15 days.

Notes: Male's song (*fitz-bew*) diagnostic in nest identification.

ALDER FLYCATCHER *Empidonax alnorum*
(Traill's Flycatcher, in part)

Breeding range: Boreal bog and swamp areas of n. Wisconsin, n. Michigan, w. Pennsylvania, New York, Vermont, New Hampshire, Maine. Typically more boreal, but range expanding, overlapping that of *E. traillii.*

Habitat: Edges of boreal bogs and alder thickets, brushy swamp and marsh borders.

Nest: In shrub, dogwood, blackberry, hawthorn, viburnum, willow, spirea; under 6 ft. (1.8 m), av. 22⅜ in. (56.9 cm) above ground. Tends to be loosely built; like nest of Song Sparrow or Indigo Bunting. Of coarse grass, moss, cattail down, rootlets, bark, twiglets; a small amount of cottony or silky material; untidy, regularly has plant strips dangling from bottom. Nest found by author in n. Wisconsin: upright fork of alder; compact (see illus.); like Yellow Warbler nest but bulkier, untidy beneath; no feathers. 1

nest: outside diam. 3⅛ in. (7.9 cm), height 2⅞ in. (7.3 cm); inside diam. 2 in. (5.1 cm), depth 1⅜ in. (3.5 cm).

Eggs: 3–4; av. 18.51 x 14.06 mm. Oval. Shell smooth, dull or slightly glossy. White (*E. traillii* eggs usually buffy), speckled and dotted with shades of brown, heaviest around large end. Incubation by female; 12–14 days.

Notes: Speciation not as evident in nest and eggs as in song (*fee-bee'-o*).

LEAST FLYCATCHER *Empidonax minimus*

Breeding range: Wisconsin to Maine, south to cen. Illinois, Indiana, n. Ohio, Pennsylvania, New Jersey; in mountains to n. Georgia.

Habitat: Open woodlands, old orchards (apple), city parks, suburban gardens, shade trees.

Nest: In crotch or fastened to limb of deciduous or coniferous tree 2-60 ft. (0.6-18.3 m) from ground, commonly 10-20 ft. (3.0-6.1 m). Compact, deep cup, well made of bark, weed stems, grasses, lined with plant down (thistle), feathers, hair, plant fibers. Built by female in 6-8 days. Resembles nests of American Redstart and Yellow Warbler. Outside diam. 2½-3 in. (6.4-7.6 cm), height 1¾-2½ in. (4.4-6.4 cm); inside diam. 1¾-2 in. (4.4-5.1 cm), depth 1¼-1½ in. (3.2-3.8 cm).

Eggs: 3-6, commonly 4; av. 16.1 x 12.9 mm. Oval to short-oval. Shell smooth, no gloss. Creamy white, unmarked. Incubation by female alone; about 14 days. 1 brood in North, possibly 2 broods in South.

Notes: Male defends nesting territory; female defends small area around nest. Definite colonies sometimes formed. At Mountain Lake, Va., 9 nests in 19 acre (7.7 ha) area. Location of 44 nests studied at Douglas Lake, Mich.: 20 at edge of clearing; 18 less than 10 ft. (3 m) from edge; 6 slightly over 20 ft. (6.1 m) from edge. Sex determined by *che-bek′* call which only male utters.

125

EASTERN WOOD-PEWEE *Contopus virens*

Breeding range: Wisconsin to Maine, south to Gulf Coast and cen. Florida.

Habitat: Mature forests, farm woodlots, orchards, parks, yards, borders of fields, clearings, roadsides.

Nest: On horizontal tree limb, live or dead, typically far out from trunk, 15–65 ft. (4.6–19.8 m) above ground. Dainty, shallow, thick-walled cup of grasses, weed stems, plant fibers, spider webs, hair; lined with finer pieces of same materials, covered on outside with lichens. From below looks like lichen-covered knot or piece of fungus on limb; small for size of bird. Built entirely by female. Outside diam. 2¾ in. (7 cm), height 1¾ in. (4.4 cm); inside diam. 1¾ in., depth 1¼ in. (3.2 cm).

Eggs: 3, occasionally 2, rarely 4; av. 18.24 x 13.65 mm. Oval to short-oval. Shell smooth, no gloss. Creamy white, wreathed with brown blotches, spots. Incubation by female; 12–13 days.

Notes: Of 18 nests found by author in w. Pennsylvania, 14 in oak, 1 each in maple, pine, sassafras, beech. All but 1 inaccessible for close study or photography; all far from trunk on horizontal limbs, many of which were dead. Lowest 15 ft. (4.6 m), highest 65 ft. (19.8 m), av. 35 ft. (10.7 m) above ground. Unusual Tennessee nest: when almost complete, ⅓ of material was green leaves, mainly elm, woven into structure.

126

OLIVE-SIDED FLYCATCHER
Contopus (Nuttallornis) borealis

Breeding range: N. Wisconsin, n. Michigan, New York, New England; mountains to e. Tennessee, N. Carolina.

Habitat: Cool coniferous forests, open woodlands, forest burns, boreal bogs, muskegs.

Nest: Well concealed on horizontal branch of conifer (usually well out from trunk), hidden among needles in cluster of upright twigs, 7–50 ft. (2.1–15.2 m) above ground. Flat saucer-shaped platform of twigs, rootlets, lichens; lined with needles, fine rootlets, and *Usnea.* Outside diam. 5–6 in. (12.7–15.2 cm), height 2⅛ in. (5.4 cm); inside diam. 2½ in. (6.4 cm), depth 1 in. (2.5 cm).

Eggs: 3, rarely 2 or 4; av. 21.7 x 16.1 mm. Oval, occasionally short-oval. Shell smooth, lusterless. Creamy white to light buff, wreathed at larger end with blotches, spots of brown shades. Incubation by female; 16–17 days. 1 brood.

Notes: Pair demands large nesting territory (several acres), which is patrolled by loud, vociferous male. Author found nests in Maine by playing tape of male's voice, arousing pair, then following female to nest. Author found nest with 3 eggs which was destroyed on June 28; 12 days later, female had built new nest and was incubating 3 eggs. This nest also destroyed. 16 days later same female incubating 3 eggs in new nest, which was successful. Male vigorous in defense of nest.

127

HORNED LARK *Eremophila alpestris*

Breeding range: Wisconsin to Maine, south to n. Mississippi, n. Georgia, N. Carolina.

Habitat: Grasslands, meadows, prairies, golf courses, cemeteries, parklands, mowed playgrounds, airports, athletic fields.

Nest: In hollow in ground, typically next to or partially under grass tuft. Shallow cup of coarse stems, leaves; lined with fine grasses. One side of nest rim often lined with "paving" of small pebbles or clods forming "patio" or "doorstep." Female alone builds; 2–4 days. Outside diam. 3¼ x 4 in. (8.3 x 10.2 cm), height 2 in. (5.1 cm); inside diam. 2 x 2½ in. (5.1 x 6.4 cm), depth 1½ in. (3.8 cm).

Eggs: 3–5, usually 4 (fewer in early nests); av. 21.6 x 15.7 mm. Commonly oval. Shell smooth, little or no gloss. Pale gray or grayish white, occasionally with greenish tinge; blotched and spotted with browns (salt-and-pepper appearance). Incubation by female alone; 11 days. 2 broods.

Notes: Often nests in Feb., March; many nests destroyed by heavy snows, freezing weather. Nest rarely well concealed from above but fits into environment so closely that search for nest without observing birds' behavior is usually fruitless. Incubating female leaves nest while intruder is 25–100 yds. (22.9–91.4 m) or more away; called nest concealment by abandonment.

128

TREE SWALLOW *Tachycineta (Iridoprocne) bicolor*

Breeding range: Wisconsin to Maine, south to nw. Tennessee, s. Illinois, cen. Indiana, cen. Ohio, n. W. Virginia, Virginia.

Habitat: Wooded swamps, open woods, fields near water.

Nest: Commonly solitary; also in groups where suitable tree cavities or birdhouses are available; in old woodpecker holes, fenceposts, rural mailboxes, holes in buildings. Material is accumulation of dry grass, hollowed in center or in corner; lined with feathers, often placed so curved tips curl over eggs. Female builds, taking a few days to 2 wks.

Eggs: 4–6; av. 18.7 x 13.2 mm. Oval to long-oval. Shell smooth, without gloss. Pure white. Incubation by female alone; 13–16 days. 1 brood.

Notes: All kinds and sizes of birdhouses have been boon to population. On Cape Cod, 98 wooden boxes increased population from 4 to 60 pairs; following year, over 400 boxes held 113 pairs (all boxes used were in open). Apartment houses for Purple Martins and large boxes for Wood Ducks attract nesting pairs. On Cape Cod, 3300 feathers were counted in 46 nest boxes; maximum in 1 box, 147; 99 percent Herring Gull feathers. Author noted almost all mailboxes on rural route near Oconto, Wisconsin, used for nesting; people generally left birds undisturbed. Nest reported with 8 eggs incubated alternately by 2 females; successfully hatched 8 young. 1 male defended territory.

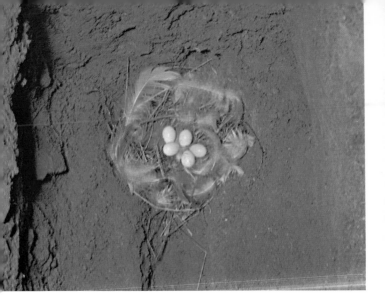

BANK SWALLOW *Riparia riparia*

Breeding range: Wisconsin to Maine, south to n. Alabama, cen. W. Virginia, e. Virginia.

Habitat: Sandbanks, gravel pits, road cuts.

Nest: Dense colonies (up to several hundred nests); burrows dug by both sexes, using feet and bill, at rate of about 5 in. (12.7 cm) per day. Birds kick earth out of tunnel as they dig in vertical side of bank, generally near top. Straws, grass stalks gathered by both sexes and placed in nest cavity after burrow complete; feathers added after incubation under way (see illus.). Burrows 15–47 in. (38.1–119.4 cm) deep, av. 28 in. (71.1 cm); 4–12 in. (10.2–30.5 cm) apart; outside opening 1½ x 2¼ in. (3.8 x 5.7 cm). Floor flat, ceiling arched; nest cavity 3 x 4½ x 6 in. (7.6 x 11.4 x 15.2 cm).

Eggs: 4–6, commonly 5; av. 17.9 x 12.7 mm. Oval to short-oval. Shell smooth, no gloss. Pure white. Incubation by both sexes; 15 days, beginning 2 or 3 days before clutch complete. 2nd brood, if ever, rare.

Notes: More burrows dug in colony than actually occupied. Obstacles (rocks) often terminate first efforts. Unmated or young birds start, never finish tunnels. Colonies have been recorded in sawdust piles and in dry well walls. Banding studies show majority of breeding birds reassemble in same colony season after season. Same nest holes may be refurbished and reused.

130

ROUGH-WINGED SWALLOW *Stelgidopteryx ruficollis*

Breeding range: Cen. Wisconsin, Michigan, cen. Vermont, New Hampshire, s. Maine south to Gulf Coast and n. Florida.

Habitat: Variety of open areas; streambanks, irrigation ditches; often in colony of Bank Swallows.

Nest: Generally solitary; favorable nest site may attract several pairs. Typically a burrow in exposed bank but may be in many other situations: side of building, cave, quarry; cranny under bridge, culvert, wharf; in drainpipe or gutter. Nest at end of cavity is bulky, built on foundation of twigs, bark, roots, weeds; lined with fine grasses. Unlike Bank Swallow, does not use feathers in nest lining (see illus.).

Eggs: 4–8, commonly 6–7 (average clutch larger than that of similar Bank Swallow); av. 18.3 x 13.2 mm. Long-oval (longer than Bank Swallow eggs). Shell smooth, has slight gloss. Pure white. Incubation by both sexes, probably mostly by female; 16 days. 1 brood.

Notes: Observers differ on whether birds dig own burrows. No nest site found by author was excavated by birds themselves; most in abandoned Belted Kingfisher holes. Nest built on buttress of steamboat that made daily trips across Tennessee R. from Gunterville to Hobbs I., distance of 24 miles (38.6 km). Parent birds followed boat to feed young.

131

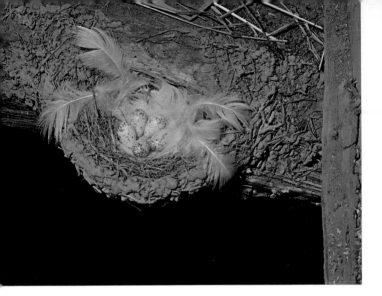

BARN SWALLOW *Hirundo rustica*

Breeding range: Wisconsin to Maine, south to n. Alabama, Tennessee, locally along Gulf Coast, n. Florida, coastal N. Carolina.
Habitat: Farmlands, rural, suburban areas, villages.
Nest: Often in colonies around many kinds of structures, especially barns and other farm outbuildings; under bridges, wharves, boat-houses, culverts. Formerly, now rarely, on cliffs, in caves and niches in rocks. Built of mud, straw, plastered to beams, upright walls, eaves; profusely lined with poultry feathers, especially white (see illus.). Both birds build, carrying mud pellets in beaks; female more active in lining. Top of nest is semicircle, tapering downward in cone shape. Building requires 6–8 days. May be delay in egg-laying after nest complete. Old nest often repaired for new brood. Outside diam. about 5 in. (12.7 cm); inside diam. 3 in. (7.6 cm).

Eggs: 4–5, sometimes 6; av. 18.8 x 13.5 mm. Oval to long-oval. Shell smooth, has no gloss. White, spotted and dotted with shades of brown. *Indistinguishable from eggs of Cliff Swallow.* Both sexes incubate, changing often (about every 15 minutes) during day; female at night with male perched nearby; about 15 days. Incubation starts before entire clutch is laid. 1 and 2 broods reported.
Notes: As many as 55 nests reported in 1 barn; 6–8 usual. Several instances of nesting on moving boats reported.

CLIFF SWALLOW *Petrochelidon pyrrhonota*

Breeding range: Wisconsin to Maine, south locally to cen. Tennessee, n. Alabama, s. S. Carolina, n. Georgia.

Habitat: Farmlands, villages, cliffs, fresh or saltwater areas.

Nest: In dense colonies; hundreds of nests may occupy side of barn (up to 800 reported). Gourd-shaped structure built of pellets of mud and clay; plastered to sides of buildings, bridges; under eaves of barns, houses, public buildings; sides of cliffs (formerly common, now rare). Nest chamber globular, extending forward into a tubular entrance tunnel with opening directed downward. Tube may be 5–6 in. (12.7–15.2 cm) long; may be absent. Nest chamber lined sparingly with grasses, hair, feathers. Both sexes build, gathering mud simultaneously with other pairs at shared puddle; pellets carried in mouth. Building requires 1–2 wks., av. about 1 in. (2.5 cm) per day. Typical nest contains 900–1200 mud pellets. Av. 15 nests: overall length 7¾ in. (19.7 cm); width at base 6⁵⁄₁₆ in. (16 cm); opening 1¾ in. (4.4 cm) high, 2 in. (5.1 cm) wide.

Eggs: 3–6, commonly 4–5; av. 20.3 x 13.9 mm. Oval to long-oval. Shell smooth, without gloss. White, spotted and dotted with shades of brown. *Indistinguishable from eggs of Barn Swallow.* Incubation by both sexes; about 15 days. Sometimes 2 broods.

Notes: Occasionally build mud front to old Bank Swallow tunnel and use as nest; attach nest to tree trunk.

133

PURPLE MARTIN *Progne subis*

Breeding range: Throughout e. U.S.

Habitat: Farmlands, parks, suburban yards, town squares; preferably near water.

Nest: In dense colonies; usually in dooryards in multiple-roomed houses set on poles, 15–20 ft. (4.6–6.1 m) above ground. Hollowed gourds with holes 2 in. (5.1 cm) in diam. cut in side, hung in clusters on poles (old Indian custom), attract birds, especially in South. Also old woodpecker holes near water; crevices under roofs of buildings. Nest built of grasses, twigs, bark, paper, leaves, string; by both sexes. Egg cup lined with fine grasses, decorated with fresh, green leaves (see illus.). Males arrive before females, establish territory. Female later selects male-nestbox combination, not one or the other. Nest generally started about 1 month before eggs laid.

Eggs: 3–8, commonly 4–5; av. 24.5 x 17.5 mm. Oval to long-oval. Shell smooth, has slight gloss. Pure white. Incubation by female alone; probably 15–16 days. 1 brood, rarely 2.

Notes: Nest boxes may contain from 1–200 apartments, often 10–30. Individual compartments 6 x 6 x 6 in. (15.2 cm³); entrance 2⅛ in. (5.4 cm) in diam., 1½ in. (3.8 cm) above floor.

GRAY (CANADA) JAY
Perisoreus canadensis p. 102

134

BLUE JAY *Cyanocitta cristata*

Breeding range: Resident throughout e. U.S.
Habitat: Forests, farms, parks, cities, suburbs.
Nest: Bulky, well hidden in crotch or outer branch of coniferous or deciduous tree, 5-50 ft. (1.5-15.2 m) above ground, commonly 10-25 ft. (3.0-7.6 m). Built by both sexes of thorny twigs, bark, mosses, string, leaves; lined with rootlets. Outside diam. 7-8 in. (17.8-20.3 cm), height, 4-4½ in. (10.2-11.4 cm); inside diam. 3½-4 in. (8.9-10.2 cm), depth 2½ in. (6.4 cm).
Eggs: 3-6, commonly 4-5; av. 28.02 x 20.44 mm. Uniformly oval. Shell smooth, has slight gloss. 2 distinct ground colors recognized: olive (usual) or buff, rarely a bluish type; marked with dark brown, grayish dots and spots. Many look like miniature American Crow eggs. Incubation by both sexes, probably mostly by female; 17–18 days. 1 brood in North; 2 broods in South; 3 reported occasionally.
Notes: For a typically noisy bird, this species is remarkably quiet around its nest. Behavior varies: some incubating birds flush quickly, others have been lifted from nest and returned without objection. 63 nests in Pennsylvania: 20 in white pine, 18 in hemlock, 2 in red spruce, 2 fir, 12 white oak, 5 alder, 1 each pitch pine, sourgum, viburnum, dogwood. Frequently nests near houses, sometimes in porch vines, on trellises.

SCRUB (FLORIDA) JAY *Aphelocoma coerulescens*

Breeding range: Resident only in Florida peninsula.

Habitat: Scrub oak, a type of vegetation peculiar to Florida, occupying scattered areas of sandy soil in central lake region, strip along eastern coast, smaller tracts of southwestern coast. Characteristically includes sand pine (*Pinus clausa*), shrubby oaks (*Quercus*) of several species, wild olive (*Osmanthus*), common wax myrtle (*Myrica cerifera*), rosemary (*Ceratiola eriocoides*), saw palmetto (*Serenoa repens*), which form dense impenetrable thickets. Scrub Jays so partial to this habitat that it is futile to look elsewhere.

Nest: In scattered colonies (up to 6 nests) in small tracts of scrub; may also be solitary. Oak twigs formed into thick-walled cup, lined with rootlets. Built by both sexes. Similar to Blue Jay nest but at low elevation, 4–12 ft. (1.2–3.7 cm) above ground. Construction requires about 5 days.

Eggs: 2–5; av. 27.5 x 20.3 mm. Usually oval. Shell smooth, little gloss. Greenish, blotched and spotted with irregular brown markings, typically wreathed at larger end. Incubation by female; 16–19 days.

Notes: Fearless around human beings at nest; incubating bird often may be handled without protest. For taking photograph (see illus.) author had to ask companion to hold incubating bird that refused to stay off nest.

136

COMMON RAVEN *Corvus corax*

Breeding range: Resident n. Wisconsin, n. Michigan, New York, (mountains), New Hampshire, Vermont, Maine, cen. Pennsylvania •south in mountains to nw. Georgia.

Habitat: Remote forest wilderness, mountains, seacoasts, wooded marine islands.

Nest: Typically solitary; nests far apart, often several miles. Large structures, mostly in coniferous trees or on cliff ledges. Built of tree branches, sticks, twigs, grapevine; deeply hollowed, thickly lined with animal hair, mosses, grasses, bark shreds. Often built on top of nest from previous year. Outside diam. 2–4 ft. (61–121.9 cm); inside diam. 1 ft. (30.5 cm), depth 6 in. (15.2 cm).

Eggs: 3–6, commonly 4–5; av. 50.2 x 34.3 mm. Oval to long-oval. Shell slightly rough, little or no gloss. Greenish with brown or olive markings, variously patterned (large versions of American Crow eggs). Incubation by female (male may sit for short intervals occasionally); about 3 wks.

Notes: Raven has retreated with encroachment of civilization. 17 Pennsylvania nests: 13 on cliffs; 3 in hemlocks, 45–80 ft. (13.7–24.4 m) above ground; 1 in white pine, 85 ft. (25.9 m) up. Nest found frozen to icy cliff March 13, 1965, had 4 incubated eggs in deep inner cup lined with deer hair 4 in. (10.2 cm) thick (see illus.).

137

AMERICAN (COMMON) CROW *Corvus brachyrhynchos*

Breeding range: Throughout e. U.S.

Habitat: Forests, farm woodlots, parks, wooded islands.

Nest: Solitary nest in deciduous or coniferous tree. Generally placed in crotch or near trunk on supporting limbs, 10–70 ft. (3.0–21.3 m) above ground, av. over 25 ft. (7.6 m). Large substantial basket of sticks, twigs, bark, vines, lined with shredded bark fibers, moss, grass, feathers, fur, hair, roots, leaves, etc. Building by both sexes; takes about 12 days. Outside diam. 22 x 26 in. (55.9 x 65.9 cm), height 9 in. (22.9 cm); inside diam. 6 x 7 in. (15.2 x 17.8 cm), depth 4½ in. (11.4 cm).

Eggs: 3–8, commonly 4–6; av. 41.40 x 29.13 mm. Typically oval. Shell slightly rough, has some gloss. Bluish or grayish green, irregularly blotched and spotted with browns and grays. Incubation by both sexes; 18 days. 1 brood in North; often 2 broods in South. Eggs vary considerably in shape, size, color, markings.

Notes: 217 nests in Pennsylvania, Delaware, New Jersey: 112 in oak; 62 in other hardwoods, including 13 in maple, 11 in beech; 24 in pine, 17 in cedar, 2 in hemlock. 22 nests in Maine, all in conifers except 1 in oak. Several records of American Crows building on chimney tops. Rarely lays abnormal red eggs (erythrism). 2 sets of eggs found in 1 nest hatched different dates. 2 Crows reported sitting on nest with 5 well-incubated eggs (mated pair?).

138

FISH CROW *Corvus ossifragus*

Breeding range: S. New England along coast, and inland along rivers affected by tides, to Florida (throughout most of state except keys), and along Gulf Coast to Louisiana. Resident from New Jersey south.

Habitat: Wooded marine shorelines; edges of brackish seashores, bays, tidal rivers. In Florida, both salt and freshwater environment (lakes, marshes, rivers).

Nest: Often in loose colonies, 2–4 pairs in same area; also solitary nests. In tops of tall trees, deciduous and coniferous, 20–80 ft. (6.1–24.4 m) above ground. Sticks, twigs, bark fibers; lined with bark strips, grasses, roots, hair, feathers, etc. Both sexes build. Outside diam. 14–18 in. (35.6–45.7 cm), height 10–14 in. (25.4–35.6 cm); inside diam. 6½–7½ in. (16.5–19.1 cm), depth 5–6 in. (12.7–15.2 cm).

Eggs: 4–5, rarely more; av. 37.17 x 26.97 mm. Oval. Shell slightly rough, with some gloss. Bluish or grayish green, irregularly blotched and spotted with browns, grays. *Indistinguishable from eggs of American Crow except for smaller size.* Incubation by both sexes: 17–18 days. 1 brood.

Notes: 138 nests in New Jersey: 80 in holly 12–30 ft. (3.7–9.1 m); 34 in cedar 5½–25 ft. (1.7–7.6 m); 9 in oak 18–50 ft. (5.5–15.2 m); 9 in pine 17–90 ft. (5.2–27.4 m); 2 in maple; 1 each in beech, gum, sassafras, wild cherry.

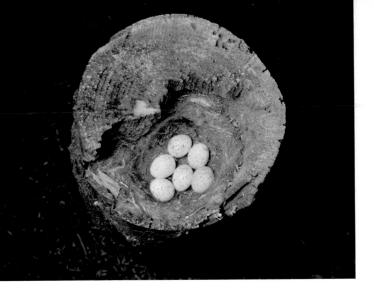

BLACK-CAPPED CHICKADEE *Parus atricapillus*

Breeding range: Resident from Wisconsin to Maine, south to Illinois, Ohio, Pennsylvania, W. Virginia, n. New Jersey, and in mountains of N. Carolina, Tennessee.

Habitat: Deciduous and coniferous forests, rural woodlands.

Nest: In holes made by birds themselves in soft, rotting wood of dead stub, typically 4–10 ft. (1.2–3.0 m) above ground; also natural cavities, abandoned woodpecker holes, birdhouses. Both sexes excavate, scattering chips away from immediate area. Bottom of 5–8 in. (12.7–20.3 cm) cavity lined by female with wool, hair, fur (rabbit), moss, feathers, insect cocoons, cottony fibers. Excavation requires 7–10 days, building 3–4 days. Entrance hole diam. 1⅜ in. (3.5 cm); diam. of cavity at rim of nest cup 2⅜ in. (6 cm); depth of cavity about 5 in. (12.7 cm); depth of cup 1 in. (2.5 cm).

Eggs: 5–10, commonly 6–8; av. 15.2 x 12.2 mm. Oval to short-oval. Shell smooth, very thin, has little or no gloss. White; rather evenly spotted and dotted with reddish brown, concentrated at larger end. *Indistinguishable from eggs of Carolina Chickadee.* Incubation by female alone; 12–13 days. Male feeds mate on nest. Before clutch complete, eggs kept covered with soft nest lining.

Notes: Species rarely parasitized by Brown-headed Cowbird; cavity entrance too small.

CAROLINA CHICKADEE *Parus carolinensis*

Breeding range: E. Illinois, cen. Indiana, cen. and ne. Ohio, cen. and e. W. Virginia, nw. Maryland, se. Pennsylvania, cen. New Jersey south to Gulf Coast and Florida.

Habitat: Deciduous and coniferous forests, rural woodlands.

Nest: Both sexes excavate, 5–6 in. (12.7–15.2 cm) deep, in soft wood of rotting tree stub, 5–6 ft. (1.5–1.8 m) above ground. Excavation requires up to 2 wks. Loosened chips discarded 5–20 ft. (1.5–6.1 m) away from cavity. May also nest in natural cavity, abandoned woodpecker hole, birdhouse. Bottom of cavity thickly lined by female with moss, animal hair, rabbit fur, feathers, and down of milkweed, thistle, cinnamon fern. Entrance diam. 1½ in. (3.8 cm); diam. of cavity at rim of nest cup 2¼ in. (5.7 cm).

Eggs: 5–8, commonly 6; av. 14.8 x 11.5 mm. Oval to short-oval. Shell smooth, very thin, little or no gloss. White; rather evenly spotted and dotted with reddish brown, concentrated at larger end. *Indistinguishable from eggs of Black-capped Chickadee.* Incubation by female, 13 days. Male feeds mate on nest. Before clutch complete, female covers eggs with soft nest lining.

Notes: Throughout much of their ranges there seems to be a gap of up to several miles (or km) between northern range limits of Carolina and southern range limits of Black-capped Chickadee.

BOREAL (BROWN-CAPPED) CHICKADEE
Parus hudsonicus

Breeding range: Ne. Wisconsin, n. Michigan, ne. New York, n. Vermont, n. New Hampshire, Maine.

Habitat: Coniferous forests, muskegs, peat bogs.

Nest: Cavity, dug by both birds, in rotting stub, commonly birch, cedar, spruce, 1–12 ft. (0.3–3.7 m) above ground. Also natural tree cavities, abandoned woodpecker holes. Entrance hole commonly on side, occasionally at open top of stub. Bottom lined with fur, hair, cottony plant down, bark strips, moss, feathers. Depth of cavity 6 in. (15.2 cm).

Eggs: 4–9, commonly 5–7; av. 16.0 x 12.2 mm. Oval to short-oval, some rather pointed. Shell smooth, little or no gloss. White; sparingly, unevenly sprinkled with reddish-brown dots and small spots, often concentrated at larger end. Incubation probably by female; 12–13 days. 1 brood.

Notes: Nests difficult to find. Female sits tight while incubating; generally will not flush when stub is tapped. Author found nest in Maine, May 26, by watching male carry food to incubating female in rotted spruce stub, 3 ft. (.9 m) above ground. Once, while female incubated 7 eggs, male brought beakful of cattail down to add to nest lining. Both birds very tame; entered nest cavity while author stood beside it.

142

TUFTED TITMOUSE *Parus bicolor*

Breeding range: S. Wisconsin, s. Michigan, cen. New York, s. New England south to Gulf of Mexico and cen. Florida.

Habitat: Deciduous, coniferous forests; swamps, orchards, suburban shade trees.

Nest: Inside natural tree cavity, abandoned woodpecker hole, 2–87 ft. (0.6–26.5 m) above ground; occasionally in birdhouse. Is not believed to excavate own nest hole. Bottom of cavity lined with bark strips, dead deciduous leaves, moss, grass; nest cupped, padded with hair, fur, bits of string, cloth.

Eggs: 4–8, commonly 5–6; av. 18.4 x 14.1 mm. Oval to long-oval. Shell smooth, little or no gloss. White or creamy; evenly speckled with small spots, dots, often concentrated at larger end. Eggs covered with nest material when unattended. Incubation by female only; 13–14 days. Male feeds incubating female after calling her from nest. Pair bonds appear generally to be permanent.

Notes: Female observed pulling hair for nest from a live squirrel's tail, a woodchuck's back, and also from a man's head and beard. Like Great-crested Flycatcher, this species commonly uses shed snakeskins as nest material. Female sits tight while incubating; generally cannot be dislodged by tapping on outside of nest.

143

WHITE-BREASTED NUTHATCH *Sitta carolinensis*

Breeding range: Resident throughout e. U.S. except s. Florida.
Habitat: Mixed woodlands, village trees, orchards.
Nest: In natural cavity in tree, 15–50 ft. (4.6–15.2 m) above ground; in old woodpecker hole, birdhouse. Cavity lined by female with bark shreds, twigs, grasses, rootlets, fur, hair. Reported sometimes to excavate own cavity, but this considered rare or doubtful.
Eggs: 5–10, commonly 8; av. 18.8 x 14.3 mm. Oval to short-oval. Shell smooth, very little gloss. White; usually heavily marked with light brown and lavender spots, often densest at larger end. Incubation by female; reported to be 12 days. 1 brood. Pair bond may extend beyond 1 nesting season, or may even be permanent.
Notes: Nesting in large cavities in tall trees puts species in competition with squirrels for nesting sites. Strange behavior called "bill sweeping," seen only during breeding season, may be territorial defense mechanism. Both birds engage in prolonged (several minutes) sweeping of bill in wide arc in or outside cavity, generally with insect held in bill. Unproven theory is that crushed insect may repel squirrels searching for available cavity. It is considered unlikely that this is courtship behavior.

RED-BREASTED NUTHATCH *Sitta canadensis*

Breeding range: Ne. Wisconsin, n. Michigan, n. New York, n. New England, and in mountains to e. Tennessee, w. N. Carolina.
Habitat: Coniferous forests.
Nest: Generally in excavated cavity in rotted stub or branch of dead tree, 5–40 ft. (1.5–12.2 m) above ground, av. 15 ft. (4.6 m); old woodpecker holes, rarely birdhouses. Cavity lined with bark shreds, grass, moss, feathers. Entrance hole diam. 1½ in. (3.8 cm); hole slants for 3–4 in. (7.6–10.2 cm) then goes straight down for about 4 in. Both birds invariably smear pitch (resin) heavily around entrance to cavity, continuing to do so during nesting period (see illus.).
Eggs: 4–7, commonly 5–6; av. 15.2 x 11.9 mm. Oval to short-oval or long-oval. Shell smooth, little or no gloss. White; heavily or sparingly spotted and dotted with reddish brown. Similar to eggs of White-breasted Nuthatch but smaller. Incubation by female; said to be 12 days. 1 brood.
Notes: All nuthatches perform some sort of nest entrance modification (see White-breasted Nuthatch, Brown-headed Nuthatch). The Red-breasted dabs globules of pitch around hole; this may prevent insects, small mammals, or other birds from entering. To avoid pitch, female entering cavity generally flies straight in. Dead body of nuthatch has been found stuck to entrance hole in birch.

BROWN-HEADED NUTHATCH *Sitta pusilla*

Breeding range: N. Mississippi, n. Alabama, n. Georgia, cen. S. Carolina, se. Virginia, se. Maryland, s. Delaware south to Gulf Coast and s. Florida.

Habitat: Open pine woods.

Nest: In old woodpecker hole in tree stub, fencepost; sometimes both sexes dig cavity in decaying pine stub, fire-blackened stump, dead tree; 2–50 ft. (0.6–15.2 m) above ground, av. less than 10 ft. (3 m). Cavity lined with pine seed husks, inner bark strips, wood chips, grasses, cotton, feathers. Cavity usually 6–9 in. (15.2–22.9 cm) deep.

Eggs: 3–9, commonly 5–6; av. 15.5 x 12.3 mm. Oval or short-oval. Shell smooth, practically no gloss. White; profusely marked (more than any other nuthatch eggs) with evenly distributed fine reddish-brown dots, small spots, blotches. Incubation by female; said to be 14 days. 1 brood.

Notes: Like other New World nuthatches, this species has its individual modification of nest behavior; it calks or "weather-strips" with pieces of cottony plant down any cracks, holes, crevices in cavity that might expose interior to outside of stub or tree. Not done by all pairs. Leaves or husks of pine seeds are typically used nest material; occasionally make up entire nest.

146

BROWN CREEPER *Certhia familiaris*

Breeding range: Northern border of U.S. to s. Wisconsin and Illinois, cen. Michigan, n. Ohio, ne. Pennsylvania, s. New England, New York, n. New Jersey, and in mountains to e. Tennessee, w. N. Carolina.

Habitat: Coniferous, deciduous, or mixed forests; timbered swamps.

Nest: Behind loose slab of bark still attached to living or dead tree, av. 5–15 ft. (1.5–4.6 m) above ground. Foundation of twigs, leaves, bark shreddings; lined with finer bark shreds, grasses, feathers (occasionally), mosses. Shape of structure conforms with space in which placed; center neatly cupped; sides of nest continue upward, ending in points (crescent-shaped like hammock, half-moon). Female builds, male may carry material. Building prolonged; birds work intermittently up to 1 month.

Eggs: 4–8, commonly 5–6; av. 15.1 x 11.8 mm. Oval to short-oval. Shell smooth, little or no gloss. White or creamy white; peppered, spotted with reddish brown, sometimes wreathed. Similar to eggs of Black-capped and Carolina Chickadees. Both sexes incubate; 14–15 days.

Notes: May occasionally nest in holes in trees if loose bark not available. Author found nest in nw. Pennsylvania behind permanent shutter of summer cottage near lake.

NORTHERN HOUSE-WREN *Troglodytes aedon*

Breeding range: Wisconsin to Maine, south to Kentucky, Virginia, Tennessee, n. Georgia.

Habitat: Farmland, open forests, suburban gardens, parks.

Nest: In natural cavity in tree, stub, fencepost; old woodpecker hole; often birdhouse. Male arrives first, establishes territory, builds dummy nests of twigs in all or most of available nest sites. Female may or may not accept prechosen site; may or may not accept male's incomplete twig nest. On base of twigs, female builds cup of grasses, plant fibers, rootlets, feathers, hair, rubbish.

Eggs: 5–8, commonly 6–7; av. 16.4 x 12.7 mm. Oval to short-oval. Shell smooth, has slight gloss. White; thickly speckled with minute reddish or cinnamon-brown dots; color deepest at larger end. Incubation by female alone; 12–15 days, typically 13. 2 broods. Not permanently mated; may form new pair bonds between broods.

Notes: Species has nested in radiator of unused auto, top of pump, empty cow skull, leg of work pants on clothesline, flowerpot, pocket of scarecrow, boots, shoes, in or on nests of other birds. May destroy nests, eggs, young of same or different species within their territory. Author watched Northern House-Wren puncture 4 eggs of Rufous-sided Towhee while female absent from nest.

148

WINTER WREN *Troglodytes troglodytes*

Breeding range: N. and e. Wisconsin, n. Michigan, New York, w. Massachusetts, Vermont, New Hampshire, Maine; in mountains to n. Georgia.

Habitat: Forests, mainly coniferous; heavily wooded swamps, boreal bogs, rocky outcrops.

Nest: Most often a well-hidden cavity in upturned roots of fallen tree; also in or under stumps, live tree roots; in old woodpecker holes, mossy hummocks, rocky crevices. Cavity filled with moss, grasses, weed stems, fine twigs, rootlets; lined with hair, feathers. Occasionally a round mass of twigs and moss with small round entrance on side, attached to open branch of coniferous tree. Size of nest varies with space available in cavity; large for small bird. Unlined dummy nests built by male.

Eggs: 4–7, commonly 5–6; av. 16.7 x 12.5 mm. Oval, less rounded than eggs of Black-capped Chickadee, which they resemble. Shell smooth, little or no gloss. Clear white; spotted, dotted, with reddish brown, often wreathed. Sex of incubating bird unknown; period unrecorded, probably about 2 wks.

Notes: Author has flushed bird from upturned roots without finding nest until bird returned to hidden opening.

BEWICK'S WREN
Thryomanes bewickii   p. 160

CAROLINA WREN *Thryothorus ludovicianus*

Breeding range: Se. Wisconsin, se. Michigan, Ohio, Pennsylvania, se. New York, s. New England south to Gulf Coast and Florida.
Habitat: Brushy forests, shrubby thickets, farmlands, parks, suburban gardens.
Nest: Built in natural cavity, woodpecker hole, birdhouse, upturned roots, stone walls, under bridges; nook or cranny around human dwelling or outbuilding. To 10 ft (3 m) above ground, rarely higher. Bulky mass of leaves, twigs, mosses, rootlets, weed stalks, strips of inner bark, debris; generally domed, with side entrance; lined with feathers, hair, moss, wool, fine grasses. Both sexes build in about 5 days; female does most of the lining. Some building after egg-laying starts.
Eggs: 4–8, commonly 5–6; av. 19.1 x 14.9 mm. Oval to short-oval. Shell smooth, little or no gloss. White, pale pink; typically marked with heavy brown spots, often concentrated at larger end. Incubation by female alone; 14 days. Male feeds mate on nest. Time spent on nest during incubation unusually long for passerine. 2 broods; sometimes 3 in South.

Notes: Incubating Northern House-Wren leaves nest 27–43 times daily; Carolina Wren 6–7 times. Lays largest of eastern wren eggs. Like Great-crested Flycatcher, this species often uses cast-off snakeskin as nest material.

150

LONG-BILLED MARSH WREN *Telmatodytes palustris*

Breeding range: Wisconsin to n. Vermont, Maine, south to Gulf Coast and Florida.

Habitat: Freshwater or brackish marshes, banks of tidal rivers, shores of inland ponds.

Nest: Lashed to standing cattails, reeds, rushes, sedges, small bushes, trees; commonly 1–3 ft. (.3–.9 m) above water. Oblong structure with side opening (not so globular as nest of Short-billed Marsh Wren); woven of wet cattails, reeds, grasses; lined with cattail down, feathers, rootlets, fine plant material. Male builds 1–10 incomplete unlined dummy nests in territory, mostly during 10 or more days before the female arrives. Brood nest is built by female in 5–8 days; has sill or short tunnel at entrance projecting farther into nest than any other part of lining. Nest cavity small compared to entire structure. Outside height of entire nest 7 in. (17.8 cm); outside width 3 in. (7.6 cm); diam. of opening about 1¼ in. (3.2 cm).

Eggs: 3–6, commonly 5; av. 16.5 x 12.4 mm. Oval. Shell smooth, not glossy until well incubated. Dull brown, cinnamon; evenly sprinkled with dark brown dots and spots, often partly or totally obscuring ground color; usually capped. Rarely may be all white. Incubation by female alone; 13 days. Males monogamous or polygamous. 2 broods.

151

SHORT-BILLED MARSH WREN *Cistothorus platensis*

Breeding range: Wisconsin to Maine, south to Ohio R. valley, W. Virginia, Virginia.

Habitat: Wet meadows, grass and sedge marshes, hayfields. Prefers drier areas than Long-billed Marsh Wren, generally avoids cattail marshes.

Nest: Sometimes single, sometimes in colonies where conditions at best. Globular structure (not oval like Long-billed Marsh Wren's) of dried or green sedges with entrance, diam. 1 in. (2.5 cm), barely discernible on side. Well hidden and woven into growing vegetation, 2–3 ft. (.6–.9 m) above ground or water. Lined with feathers, fur, soft plant down. Male builds numerous unlined dummy nests, generally easier to find than brood nest built by female. Av. outside height of entire nest 4 in. (10.2 cm); outside width 3½ in. (8.9 cm); front to back 3½ in.

Eggs: 4–8, commonly 7; av. 16 x 12 mm. Oval, and sometimes pyriform. Shell smooth, thin, fragile, with slight gloss. Pure white. Incubation by female alone; 12–14 days. Typically 2 broods; sometimes 1, rarely 3.

Notes: 35–40 singing males counted in 10 acre (4 ha) marsh. In dry hayfield in nw. Pennsylvania, author found 9 dummy nests in 1 territory; unable to find brood nest. Near Oconto, Wisconsin, Short and Long-bills had adjacent territories; latter used wetter sites.

152

NORTHERN (COMMON) MOCKINGBIRD
Mimus polyglottos

Breeding range: S. Wisconsin, Illinois, Indiana, Michigan, Ohio, Pennsylvania, s. New York, Connecticut, Massachusetts, se. Maine south to Gulf Coast and Florida. Species steadily extending range northward.

Habitat: Farmlands, open woods, parks, gardens, cities, villages.

Nest: In tree, shrub, vine, 3–10 ft. (0.9–3.0 m) above ground. Bulky, loosely laid outer layer of thorny twigs; inner layer dry leaves, plant stems, moss, hair; lining, brown rootlets. Male places material in possible nest sites as courtship behavior; female decides on location; both sexes build. Usually new nest built for each brood. Outside diam. 7 in (17.8 cm), height 4½ in. (11.4 cm); inside depth 1¾ in. (4.4 cm).

Eggs: 3–5, commonly 4; av. 24.3 x 18.3 mm. Typically oval, occasionally short- or long-oval. Shell smooth, has slight gloss. Shades of blue and green; heavily marked with brown spots, blotches. Incubation by female alone; 12–13 days. Commonly 2 broods. Male may occasionally be bigamous.

Notes: Strongly partial to sites near houses; porch vines, foundation and garden plantings favored. In South majority of population nests in towns and cities. In 182 nests in Tennessee, 114 had 4 eggs, 42 had 3 eggs, 26 had 5 eggs.

GRAY CATBIRD *Dumetella carolinensis*

Breeding range: Wisconsin to Maine, south to cen. Mississippi, cen. Alabama, cen. Georgia, cen. Florida.

Habitat: Woodland undergrowth, shrubby marsh borders, hedgerows, gardens.

Nest: Built in dense thickets, briars, vine tangles, shrubs, low trees, typically well concealed by foliage, 3–10 ft. (0.9–3.0 m) above ground. Substantial, bulky foundation of twigs, grapevine, leaves, grasses, paper, weed stems; deeply cupped; neatly lined with rootlets. Built by both sexes, mostly female, in 5–6 days.

Eggs: 3–5, commonly 4; av. 23.3 x 17.5 mm. Oval to short-oval. Shell smooth, glossy. Deep greenish blue, unmarked (much darker than eggs of any eastern thrushes). Incubation by female alone; 12–13 days.

Notes: Unusual nests have been found on ground and at 50–60 ft. (15.2–18.3 m) above ground. Of 190 nests found in Pennsylvania, only 5 had 5 eggs. Rarely parasitized by Brown-headed Cowbird; female ejects parasitic egg. Experiments show Gray Catbird can detect color and size of Cowbird egg; yet leaf placed over eggs in nest not removed before female resumed incubation. Author found nest in Pennsylvania containing white shoestring, 8 in. (20.3 cm) strip of white bandage, piece of paper napkin, 3 cellophane cigar wrappers, in addition to usual material.

154

BROWN THRASHER *Toxostoma rufum*

Breeding range: Throughout e. U.S. Permanent resident in South.

Habitat: Thickets, brushy fields, hedgerows, woodland borders.

Nest: Placed on ground under small bush or as high as 14 ft. (4.3 m), av. 2–7 ft. (0.6–2.1 m), in tree, shrub, vine. Loosely constructed foundation of thorny twigs as long as 12 in. (30.5 cm) is base for large cup of dry leaves, small twigs, grass stems, grapevine, inner bark; lined with rootlets. Both sexes build in 5–7 days. Outside diam. about 12 in. (30.5 cm), height 3¾ in. (9.5 cm); inside diam. 3¾ in., depth, 1 in. (2.5 cm).

Eggs: 2–5, commonly 4; av. 26.5 x 19.4 mm. Oval to short- or long-oval. Shell smooth, has slight gloss. Pale bluish white (sometimes has greenish tinge); evenly and rather thickly covered with small reddish-brown spots or fine dots. Incubation by both sexes; typically 12–13 days. 2nd brood soon after young are fledged; may find new mates for 2nd nesting.

Notes: In 52 Tennessee nests, 31 had 4 eggs, 13 had 3, 7 had 5, 1 had 2. In 17 Tennessee nests, 9 hatched in 13 days, 6 in 12 days, 1 in 11 days, 1 in 14 days. Of 109 Tennessee nests, only 1 on ground (frequent site in New England). Author found nest on ground under leaning tombstone in Pennsylvania. The largest passerine known to be parasitized by Brown-headed Cowbird.

155

AMERICAN ROBIN *Turdus migratorius*

Breeding range: Wisconsin to Maine, south to Gulf Coast, s. Georgia, n. Florida (rarely).

Habitat: Cities, villages, farmlands, gardens, open woods.

Nest: Built in shrub, tree fork, horizontal branch; or on almost any substantial ledge, principally on house or outbuilding; rarely on ground. Deep cup, molded by contours of female's body; made of grasses, weed stalks, strips of cloth, string, worked into wet or soft mud; lined with fine grasses. Female carries mud in bill. Outside diam. 6½ in. (16.5 cm), height 3 in. (7.6 cm); inside diam. 4 in. (10.2 cm), depth 2½ in. (6.4 cm).

Eggs: 4, occasionally 3, rarely 5; av. 28.1 x 20.0 mm. Oval, short-oval, or long-oval. Shell smooth, has slight luster when laid, becomes glossy with incubation. "Robin's-egg blue," unmarked. Incubation by female; 12–14 days. 2, possibly 3 broods.

Notes: Lack of orientation may cause female to build many nests side by side on long beam, girder, fire escape steps. Author found

13 nests side by side in various stages of construction on cottage porch beam. Eggs were laid and incubated in 1 nest. Winter nestings reported in Ellwood City, Pennsylvania, Jan. 1965; Columbus, Ohio, Dec. 1965; eggs in former, young in latter; both unsuccessful. Brown-headed Cowbird eggs invariably removed by American Robin when laid in its nest.

156

WOOD THRUSH *Hylocichla mustelina*

Breeding range: Wisconsin to Maine (mostly southern), south to Gulf Coast, n. Florida. Species gradually extending range northward.

Habitat: Cool, humid forests, mainly deciduous; parks, gardens.

Nest: Anchored 6–50 ft. (1.8–15.2 m) above ground, av. about 10 ft. (3 m) in fork or horizontal limb of tree. Firm, compact cup of grasses, bark, moss, paper, mixed with leafmold, mud; molded by contours of female's body; lined with rootlets. Similar to nest of American Robin but smaller, invariably with leaves in foundation and rootlets instead of grass in lining. Site selection and building by female alone; complete in about 5 days. No evidence birds ever use nest 2nd time. Outside diam. 4–5½ in. (10.2–14.0 cm), height 2–5¾ in. (5.1–14.6 cm); inside diam. 2¾ x 3¼ in. (7.0 x 8.3 cm), depth 1¼–2 in. (3.2–5.1 cm).

Eggs: 3–4, occasionally 2, rarely 5; av. 25.4 x 18.6 mm; smaller, generally more pointed at one end than American Robin eggs. Typically oval. Shell smooth, has slight gloss. Pale blue or bluish green; unmarked (slightly paler than eggs of American Robin). Incubation by female alone; 13 days. Male usually guards nest when female absent. Typically 2 broods. Pair remains together for 2nd nesting.

Notes: Becoming more tolerant of people, often choosing site close to house when wooded area nearby.

157

HERMIT THRUSH *Catharus guttatus*

Breeding range: Northern border of U.S. south to cen. Wisconsin, n. Michigan, New York, Massachusetts, Connecticut, New Jersey, and in mountains to Virginia.

Habitat: Coniferous or mixed forests.

Nest: Typically on ground, usually well hidden under small tree, bush, fern; compact, bulky structure of twigs, bark fibers, grasses, ferns, mosses; lined with conifer needles, plant fibers, rootlets; built by female alone. Occasionally nest is in tree, 2–4 ft. (0.6–1.2 m) above ground. Inside diam. 2¾ in. (7 cm), depth 2 in. (5.1 cm).

Eggs: 3–4; av. 22.1 x 16.8 mm. Oval or long-oval. Shell smooth, has slight gloss. Very pale blue; typically unmarked (rarely spotted). Similar to eggs of Veery but paler blue. Incubation by female alone; 12 days. Male feeds incubating mate.

Notes: Competition between Hermit Thrush and Veery for ground nesting sites lessened by habitat preferences. Hermit very wary; will usually leave nest at 1st sign of intrusion. Author found nests

in open sphagnum bog in Maine, where surroundings were constantly wet; built of fresh green moss, spruce twigs, *Usnea,* lined with red stems of Turk's-cap moss, skeletonized leaves. Author found exposed nest 8 ft. (2.4 m) from ground on dead arched limb of hemlock in Cook Forest State Park, Pennsylvania.

158

SWAINSON'S THRUSH *Catharus ustulatus*

Breeding range: Northern border of U.S. south to n. Wisconsin, n. Michigan, New York, Vermont, New Hampshire, Maine; in mountains to W. Virginia.

Habitat: Spruce, fir, birch forests.

Nest: In small tree, commonly on horizontal branch near trunk, 2–20 ft. (0.6–6.1 m) above ground, av. 4–8 ft. (1.2–2.4 m). Bulky well-made cup of twigs, mosses, cedar and birch bark, grasses, rootlets, wet leaves; lined with lichens, skeletonized leaves, fine strips of bark, animal hair. Female builds in about 4 days. Outside diam. 4–4½ in. (10.2–11.4 cm), height 3–3½ in. (7.6–8.9 cm); inside diam. 2¼–2½ in. (5.7–6.4 cm), depth 1½–1¾ in. (3.8–4.4 cm).

Eggs: 3–4, rarely 5; av. 22.4 x 16.5 mm. Oval. Shell smooth, has very little gloss. Pale blue; evenly spotted, blotched with brown, generally heaviest about larger end. Same size and color as Gray-cheeked Thrush eggs (which are more faintly and sparsely marked). Incubation by female alone; 12–13 days.

Notes: Of 21 nests found in New England, 11 were in spruce, 10 in balsam. In mountainous regions of New England, typically breeds at lower altitude than similar Gray-cheeked Thrush. Author watched female start nest in spruce in Maine on June 14; on June 21 she was incubating 3 eggs.

GRAY-CHEEKED THRUSH *Catharus minimus*
(including Bicknell's Thrush)

Breeding range: Northern border of U.S. south to se. New York (Catskills), nw. Massachusetts (Berkshires); n. New Hampshire, n. Vermont, n. Maine.

Habitat: Spruce, fir forests at high elevations, 3000 ft. (914.4 m) to timberline.

Nest: In relatively inaccessible nesting sites in wild, isolated regions of high mountains, often placed in evergreens, occasionally birches, 3–12 ft. (0.9–3.7 m) above ground. Foundation of twigs and mosses, placed on divergent branches close to trunk. Walls built of moss, supporting twigs; female forms cup by rotating body inside structure. Lined with fine black rootlets. Outside often ornamented with gray-green lichens. Mossy appearance lacking in nest of similar Swainson's Thrush. Outside diam. 4½–5 in. (11.4–12.7 cm), height 3¾ in. (9.5 cm); inside diam. 2½–2¾ in. (6.4–7.0 cm), depth 1¾ in. (4.4 cm).

Eggs: 3–4; av. 21.9 x 16.6 mm. Oval to short-oval. Shell smooth, has slight gloss. Pale blue or bluish green, very sparingly marked with pale brown dots and splotches (fewer, paler markings than eggs of Swainson's Thrush). Incubation by female alone; 13–14 days. 1 brood.

BEWICK'S WREN *Thryomanes bewickii*
(proper order after Winter Wren, p. 149)

Breeding range: Mississippi Valley and s. Appalachian Plateau from s. Wisconsin, s. Michigan to cen. and sw. Pennsylvania, south to n. Mississippi, cen. Alabama, cen. Georgia, cen. S. Carolina.

Habitat: Open woodlands, farmlands, gardens, brushy areas.

Nest: Some still in primitive sites: knotholes in fallen trees, natural cavities, old woodpecker holes, brush heaps. Mainly in man-made sites: birdhouses, fenceposts, cans, empty barrels, discarded clothing, abandoned automobiles, crevices in walls, mailboxes, etc. Nest bulky; size governed by cavity it fills. Mass of sticks, chips, leaves, debris is foundation for deep cup of feathers, hair, moss, dead leaves.

Eggs: 4–11, commonly 5–7; av. 16.4 x 12.7 mm. Oval to short-oval. Shell smooth, little or no gloss. White; irregular brown, purple, gray spots, dots, often concentrated in wreath at larger end. Incubation probably by female alone; said to average 14 days. Normally monogamous, but polygyny may occur occasionally. Probably 2 broods.

Notes: There is evidence that although Northern House-Wrens and Carolina Wrens may live in same area without friction, Bewick's Wren conflicts with both (exceptions have been noted, however).

VEERY *Catharus fuscescens*

Breeding range: Wisconsin to Maine, south to n. Illinois, n. Indiana, Ohio, Pennsylvania, New Jersey; in mountains to n. Georgia.

Habitat: Moist deciduous woods, bottomland forests, damp ravines.

Nest: Built on or close to ground, in low shrub, often in brush pile. Twigs, weed stalks, grapevine, on pile of dead leaves; lined with soft bark strips, rootlets, grasses. Large nest for size of bird, usually well concealed by surrounding living plants. Building requires 6–10 days. Outside diam. to 10 in. (25.4 cm), height 5 in. (12.7 cm); inside diam. 2½ in. (6.4 cm), depth 2 in. (5.1 cm).

Eggs: 3–5, commonly 4; av. 22.4 x 16.7 mm. Oval. Shell smooth, has slight gloss. Pale blue; unmarked, rarely spotted. Resemble eggs of Hermit Thrush, Wood Thrush. Incubation by female alone; 11–12 days.

Notes: Frequent victim of Brown-headed Cowbird. Makes no attempt to remove eggs; usually incubates and raises young interlopers. Author found 3 nests in tussocks of grass on floor of woods near Oconto, Wisconsin, containing 3 Cowbird eggs, 1 Veery egg; 5 Cowbird eggs, 1 Veery egg; 3 Cowbird eggs, 3 Veery eggs. All females were incubating. 4 of 7 nests in Michigan held 2 Cowbird eggs each: 60 percent of Veeries, 75 percent of Cowbirds fledged.

161

EASTERN BLUEBIRD *Sialia sialis*

Breeding range: Throughout e. U.S. Resident in South.

Habitat: Farmlands, roadside fence lines, open woods, swamps, gardens.

Nest: Carelessly arranged in natural cavity in tree, old woodpecker hole, or one of thousands of birdhouses in suitable locations throughout bird's range. Loosely built cup of fine grasses, weed stalks. Female normally builds nest in 4–5 days, rarely 2–12 days. Male rarely may carry some material. Outside diam. varies with cavity; inside diam. 2½ x 3 in. (6.4 x 7.6 cm), depth about 2 in. (5.1 cm).

Eggs: 3–6, commonly 4–5; av. 20.7 x 16.3 mm. Oval to short-oval. Shell smooth, glossy. Pale blue, bluish white, occasionally pure white; unmarked. Palest of all eastern thrush eggs. Incubation by female alone; 13–15 days, normally 14. 2 broods, sometimes 3. 2nd clutch tends to average 1 egg fewer than 1st.

Notes: In a record of 730 eggs, 40 (or 5.48 percent) were albinistic. In Nashville, Tennessee, 1942, record of 774 eggs, 71 (or 9.1 percent) were white. "Bluebird trails" established in many states phenomenally successful; thousands of birdhouses put up, especially along country roads. In 1970, the Laboratory of Ornithology, Cornell University, published data on 8108 nests of Eastern Bluebirds from its Nest Record Card Program.

162

BLUE-GRAY GNATCATCHER *Polioptila caerulea*

Breeding range: S. Wisconsin, s. Michigan to w. New York; n. New Jersey, se. New York (Long I.), Connecticut, e. Massachusetts; south to Gulf Coast and cen. Florida.

Habitat: Oak woods, mixed forests, pinelands, wooded swamps.

Nest: Saddled to small horizontal tree limb or fork, 4–70 ft. (1.2–21.3 m), av. less than 25 ft. (7.6 m) above ground. Cup-shaped, compactly built of plant down, fiber, oak catkins; bound together with insect silk, spider web; covered externally with bits of lichen, plant down; lined with fine pieces of inner bark, tendrils, plant down, feathers (sometimes). Compares with nest of Ruby-throated Hummingbird in beauty of construction. Both sexes build in 1–2 weeks, preceding egg-laying by 10–14 days. Outside diam. 2–2½ in. (5.1–6.4 cm), height 2¼–2½ in. (5.7–6.4 cm); inside diam. 1¼ in. (3.2 cm), depth 1¼–1⅜ in. (3.2–3.5 cm).

Eggs: 4–5; av. 14.5 x 11.2 mm. Oval to short-oval. Shell smooth, has little or no gloss. Pale bluish, bluish white; generally covered evenly with a few small reddish-brown spots, fine dots; often wreathed. Incubation by both sexes; 13 days.

Notes: Unusual characteristic of this bird: it tears up a completed or partly completed nest and reuses the material to build another nest nearby. Author has seen this several times; believes that awareness of possible discovery during building may be cause.

163

GOLDEN-CROWNED KINGLET *Regulus satrapa*

Breeding range: N. Wisconsin, n. Michigan, n. New York, n. New England south in higher mountains to Tennessee, N. Carolina. Resident in much of range.

Habitat: Coniferous forests, preferably spruces.

Nest: Firmly fastened to twigs of horizontal limb into which nest is woven; 6–60 ft. (1.8–18.2 m) above ground in conifer, usually spruce. A hanging mass of mosses, lichens, open at top; lined with delicate strips of inner bark, fine black rootlets, grouse feathers (with quills pointing downward, tips arching over eggs). Rim of open top contracted or arched on all sides over deep hollow beneath. Female alone builds in 9 days or longer. Outside diam. 2¾ in. (7 cm), height 3¾ in. (9.5 cm), oblong, not spherical. Diam. of opening 1½ in. (3.8 cm).

Eggs: 5–10, commonly 8-9, deposited in 2 layers; av. 13.3 x 10.4 mm. Oval to long-oval. Shell smooth, no gloss. White to cream; spotted, blotched with browns, grays. *Indistinguishable from eggs of Ruby-crowned Kinglet.* Incubation by female; period unknown; begins before entire clutch laid. 2 broods.

Notes: Positive identification of nest and eggs not possible without seeing bird. General color of nest (variety of green mosses, gray lichens) blends well with surrounding spruce foliage, making structure very difficult to see from ground. Author found nest in Maine with 1 Brown-headed Cowbird and 8 Golden-crowned Kinglet eggs.

164

RUBY-CROWNED KINGLET *Regulus calendula*

Breeding range: N. Wisconsin, n. Michigan, n. and cen. New York, n. Vermont, n. New Hampshire, Maine; possibly Massachusetts.
Habitat: Coniferous forests.
Nest: Attached to pendent twigs beneath horizontal branch of conifer, typically spruce, 2–100 ft. (0.6–30.5 m) above ground; well concealed, usually at end of branch where foliage is thickest; in color nest looks like surrounding foliage. Deep pensile cup of mosses, lichens, small twigs, plants; lined with fur, feathers. Outside diam. at center 2½ in. (6.4 cm), height 4–4½ in. (10.2–11.4 cm); narrows at top to form circular opening 1¼ in. (3.2 cm) in diam.
Eggs: 5–11, commonly 7–9; av. 13.7 x 10.8 mm. Oval. Shell smooth, no gloss. Pale buffy white, dirty white, clear white; evenly covered with fine reddish-brown dots, spots, often concentrated around larger end. *Indistinguishable from eggs of Golden-crowned Kinglet.* Female alone incubates; is completely concealed inside nest.
Notes: Identification of nest and eggs not positive without seeing bird. Male characteristically highly agitated when intruder approaches nest, thus disclosing area. Author found 7 Ruby-crowned Kinglet eggs, 1 Brown-headed Cowbird egg in nest; 8 Kinglet eggs, 1 Cowbird egg in another, Mt. Desert I., Maine. Ruby-crowned nests generally found nearer to ground than nests of Golden-crowned.

165

CEDAR WAXWING *Bombycilla cedrorum*

Breeding range: Wisconsin to Maine, south to s. Illinois, s. Indiana, cen. Kentucky, e. Tennessee, n. Alabama, n. Georgia. Irregular in breeding areas; common some years, absent other years.
Habitat: Open woods, orchards, shade trees (avoids dense woods).
Nest: Placed on horizontal limb of tree, 4–50 ft. (1.2–15.2 m) above ground, av. 6–20 ft. (1.8–6.1 m). Loosely woven of grasses, twigs, weed stems, string, cottony fibers, yarn; lined with rootlets, fine grasses, plant down. Both sexes build in 5–7 days. Outside diam. 4½–6 in. (11.4–15.2 cm), height 3½–4½ in. (8.9–11.4 cm); inside diam. 2½–3 in. (6.4–7.6 cm), depth 2 in. (5.1 cm).
Eggs: 4–5, occasionally 3, rarely 2 or 6; av. 21.8 x 15.6 mm. Oval. Shell smooth, has little or no gloss. Pale gray, pale bluish gray; lightly, irregularly spotted with dark brown, blotched with pale brownish gray. Incubation by female; 12–13 days, starting before clutch complete. Male feeds incubating mate. Commonly 2 broods. Pair remains mated for both broods.

Notes: Small amount of space demanded for nesting territory results in occasional colonial nestings. In Connecticut, 17 nests found within radius of 150 yds. (137.2 m); in Ontario 11 nests in radius of 25 ft. (7.6 m). In 65 complete egg sets in Ohio, 41.6 percent had 5 eggs, 40 percent had 4, 18.4 percent had 3 or 2.

LOGGERHEAD SHRIKE *Lanius ludovicianus*

Breeding range: S. Wisconsin, s. Michigan, w. New York, locally in s. New England, south to Gulf Coast and Florida. Resident in South.

Habitat: Open country with scattered trees, shrubs; hedgerows, orchards.

Nest: Built 5–30 ft. (1.5–9.1 m) above ground, av. 8–15 ft. (2.4–4.6 m) in dense foliage in trees, shrubs. Bulky, well-made structure of woven sticks, twigs, weed stems, grasses, bark fibers, in Florida Spanish moss; lined with rootlets, bark fibers, feathers, cotton, cottony materials. Both birds carry nest material; female does most building. Nests early in South (Feb.–March), where it prefers live oaks, thorny trees.

Eggs: 4–6, commonly 4–5; av. 24.2 x 18.7 mm. Oval to long-oval. Shell smooth, no gloss. Dull white, grayish or buffy; spotted, blotched with browns, grays, often concentrated at larger end. Incubation by female alone; 16 days (may be less in some geographic races of species). Male feeds incubating mate. 2 broods, possibly 3 in South.

Notes: Author found several Florida nests buried deep in clumps of mistletoe as high as 30 ft. (9.1 m) above ground (see illus.). Usually solitary nester, but 14 nests found in hedgerow of 13 dwarf thorn trees (*Crataegus*) along levee in Mississippi; 8 contained eggs, others under construction.

167

COMMON STARLING *Sturnus vulgaris*

Breeding range: Resident throughout e. U.S.

Habitat: Cities, suburbs, wooded farmlands, orchards, parks, gardens, cliffs.

Nest: Solitary or in colonies (5 nests found in dead limb of 1 willow tree). Any cavity or hole almost anywhere; prefers natural cavities in trees, old or new woodpecker holes, birdhouses, 2–60 ft. (0.6–18.3 m) above ground, av. 10–25 ft. (3.0–7.6 m). Cavity filled with mass of material: grasses, weed stems, twigs, corn husks, dried leaves, cloth, feathers. Size of nest depends on size of cavity to be filled. Cup formed in trash; lined with fine grass, feathers. Nest slovenly built, carelessly kept (fouled by excrement). Inside diam. 3 in. (7.6 cm).

Eggs: 4–5, often 6, rarely 7; av. 29.2 x 21.1 mm. Shape varies greatly, short-oval to long-oval. Shell smooth, has slight gloss. Pale bluish or greenish white, unmarked. Incubation by both sexes; 11–13 days, commonly 12. Typically 2 broods.

Notes: Dominant species well fitted to survive in competition with other hole-nesting birds. Cannot enter birdhouses with openings less than 1½ in. (3.8 cm) diam. Highways cutting through hills provide nesting cavities among exposed rocks. Author found nesting colony on rocky shore of uninhabited sea island 7 miles (11.3 km) off Maine Coast.

WHITE-EYED VIREO *Vireo griseus*

Breeding range: S. Illinois, s. Indiana, Ohio to New York, Massachusetts, south to Gulf Coast and Florida.

Habitat: Dense shrubby regions, deciduous forest undergrowth, briar thickets, old fields, often along streambanks.

Nest: Cone-shaped structure suspended from forked twigs of low shrub, tree, 1–8 ft. (0.3–2.4 m) above ground, av. 2–6 ft. (0.6–1.8 m). Woven of small pieces of soft wood, bark shreds, held together with cobwebs; lined with fine plant stems, pieces of fine dry grass. Distinguished from round, cup-shaped nest of Red-eyed Vireo by exterior conelike pointed bottom. Outside diam. 3 in. (7.6 cm), height 3½ in. (8.9 cm); inside diam 2 in. (5.1 cm), depth 2 in.

Eggs: 3–5, commonly 4; av. 18.7 x 14.0 mm. Oval. Shell smooth, has no gloss. White; marked with a few widely scattered fine brown or black spots, dots. Incubation by both sexes; 14–15 days.

Notes: Habitat in Florida differs from most of breeding range: often in dry scrub composed of palmetto or oak. All nests found by author on Sanibel I., Florida, have been within 3 ft. (91.4 cm) of ground suspended from outer branches of common wax myrtle (*Myrica cerifera*).

BELL'S VIREO p. 173
Vireo bellii

YELLOW-THROATED VIREO *Vireo flavifrons*

Breeding range: Cen. Wisconsin, s. Michigan, s. New York, n. Vermont, n. New Hampshire, sw. Maine south to Gulf Coast and cen. Florida.

Habitat: Open woods of oak, maple, other hardwoods; orchards, groves, roadside trees; seldom in dense forests, rarely in conifers.

Nest: Suspended between forks of slender branch of tree, often near trunk, 3–60 ft. (0.9–18.3 m) above ground, typically over 20 ft. (6.1 m). Well-made, thick-walled, deep cup of grasses, strips of inner bark, woven together with spider silk, plant down; decorated on outside with moss, lichens; lined with fine grasses. Nest rim is incurved. Building mostly by female; requires about 1 week. Outside diam. 3 in. (7.6 cm), height 2½ in. (6.4 cm); inside diam. 2 in. (5.1 cm), depth 1½ in. (3.8 cm).

Eggs: 3–5, commonly 4; av. 20.8 x 14.9 mm. Oval, some slightly pointed. Shell smooth, without gloss. White to cream-white; strongly spotted with shades of brown, mostly at larger end. Incubation by both sexes; 14 days.

Notes: Ordinarily, but not always, builds nest near trunk of tree. In Michigan, 14 nests were recorded within 12–20 in. (30.5–50.8 cm) of trunk. Author photographed Pennsylvania nest 35 ft. (10.7 m) above ground, 11 in. (27.9 cm) from trunk in black cherry (see illus.). Author has never found nest below 30 ft. (9.1 m).

SOLITARY VIREO *Vireo solitarius*

Breeding range: N. Wisconsin to New England, south to n. New Jersey, n. Pennsylvania, in mountains to n. Georgia.
Habitat: Mixed evergreen, deciduous woodlands.
Nest: Suspended by upper rim from twig fork on horizontal branch of hardwood or conifer tree, 3½–20 ft. (1.1–6.1 m) above ground, often less than 10 ft. (3 m). Compactly built basketlike structure of strips of inner bark, soft plant fibers, grasses, weed stems, rootlets, hair; neatly lined with moss stems, conifer needles, fine grasses, vine tendrils; decorated externally with lichens, paper (bits of old hornet nests). Male carries material; female does most or all building. Outside diam. 3 x 3½ in. (7.6 x 8.9 cm), height 3½ in.; inside diam. 2 x 2¼ in. (5.1 x 5.7 cm), depth 1½ in. (3.8 cm).
Eggs: 3–5, commonly 4; av. 19.5 x 14.4 mm. Oval, some quite pointed. Shell smooth, without gloss. White, creamy white; sparingly spotted, dotted, mostly at larger end, with brown, black. Incubation by both sexes; period not definitely known, probably 13–14 days. Possibly 2 broods, especially in South.
Notes: Birds remarkably tame. Observers have lifted incubating bird off nest. Male sometimes sings while incubating. All Pennsylvania nests found by author were in hemlock or white pine.

BLACK-WHISKERED VIREO
Vireo altiloquus p. 173

171

RED-EYED VIREO *Vireo olivaceus*

Breeding range: Throughout e. U.S. except s. Florida.
Habitat: Open deciduous woods with thick undergrowth of saplings; occasionally mixed woods.
Nest: Deep-cupped pensile structure suspended in horizontal fork of slender tree branch (often sapling), 2–60 ft. (0.6–18.3 m) above ground, av. 5–10 ft. (1.5–3.0 m). Built of grasses, paper, bark strips, rootlets, vine tendrils, bound to supporting twigs and covered on outside with spider webbing; decorated externally with lichens. Built by female in about 5 days. Outside diam. 2¾ x 3 in. (7.0 x 7.6 cm), height 2⅛–3³⁄₁₆ in. (5.4–8.1 cm); inside diam. 2⅛ x 2⁵⁄₁₆ in. (5.4–5.9 cm), depth 1³⁄₁₆–2⅛ in. (3.0–5.4 cm); wall thickness ½ in. (1.3 cm). Walls thinner than in nests of most vireos.
Eggs: 2–4, commonly 4; av. 20.3 x 14.5 mm. Oval, rarely somewhat long-oval. Shell smooth, little or no gloss. White; sparingly marked with fine brown, black dots, spots, chiefly toward larger end. Incubation mostly or entirely by female; 12–14 days, and may begin before clutch complete. Eggs laid 3–5 days after nest completed. Occasionally 2 broods.

Notes: Measurements of 45 territories in Cheboygan Co., Michigan, indicate average 1.7 acres (.7 ha) per pair. In same area, 87 of 114 nests parasitized by Brown-headed Cowbird. Author found bird incubating 4 Cowbird, no Vireo eggs, in Pennsylvania.

BLACK-WHISKERED VIREO *Vireo altiloquus*
(proper order after Solitary Vireo, p. 171)

Breeding range: Florida Keys north along west and east coasts to cen. Florida. Does not breed inland.
Habitat: Mostly mangroves along coastlines and islands.
Nest: Commonly in red mangroves but sometimes in other trees, shrubs, as high as 15 ft. (4.6 m) above ground. Deep cup narrow at top, suspended between twigs; woven of dried grass, lichens, spider webs; lined with palm threads, fine grass.
Eggs: 3, sometimes 2; av. 21.0 x 15.1 mm. Long-oval. Shell smooth, has little or no gloss. White; sparingly marked with few scattered brown dots, spots.
Notes: In 3 nestings observed by author on Sanibel I., Florida, birds ignored red mangroves to build in sea hibiscus trees (*Hibiscus tiliaceus*).

PHILADELPHIA VIREO *Vireo philadelphicus*

Breeding range: N. New Hampshire, n. and cen. Maine.
Habitat: Second-growth forests, roadside trees, deserted farms, occasionally in village shade trees (Jackman, Maine).
Nest: Deep, neat cup attached by spider web and *Usnea* to horizontal forked twig of tree branch, 10–40 ft. (3.0–12.2 m) above ground. Made of birch bark, grasses, lichens, plant down; lined with fine grasses, decorated with paper-birch bark. Both sexes build. Outside diam. 2¾ x 3³⁄₁₆ in. (7.0 x 8.1 cm), height 2⅝ in. (6.7 cm); inside diam. 1½ x 2 in. (3.8 x 5.1 cm), depth 1⁵⁄₁₆ in. (3.3 cm).
Eggs: 3–5, commonly 4; av. 19.2 x 14.0 mm. Long-oval. Shell smooth, has no gloss. White; sparingly spotted with brown, black. Similar to eggs of Red-eyed Vireo but slightly smaller. Incubation by both sexes; 14 days. Male sings on nest.

BELL'S VIREO *Vireo bellii*
(proper order after White-eyed Vireo, p. 169)

Breeding range: Locally in sw. Wisconsin, Illinois, Indiana, Ohio.
Habitat: Lowland thickets, forest edges, brushy bottomlands, briar patches.
Nest: Suspended 2–3 ft. (.6–.9 m) above ground in slender fork of shrub, small tree. Plant fibers, bark, leaves, bits of paper, cocoons, spider webs; lined with fine grasses, few hairs. Building takes 4–6 days; male may or may not help. Outside diam. 2⅜ x 3 in. (6.0 x 7.6 cm), height 3–3⅜ in. (7.6–8.6 cm); inside diam. 1½ x 1¾ in. (3.8 x 4.4 cm), depth 1¼–1¾ in. (3.2–4.4 cm).
Eggs: 3–5, commonly 4; av. 17.4 x 12.6 mm. Oval, sometimes pointed. Shell smooth, has no gloss. White; fine brown or black dots scattered mainly about larger end. Incubation by both sexes; 14 days, and may start before clutch complete.

WARBLING VIREO *Vireo gilvus*

Breeding range: Wisconsin to Maine, south to e. Kentucky, n. Mississippi, n. Alabama, n. and cen. N. Carolina, se. Virginia.
Habitat: Open, mixed, or deciduous woods, orchards, roadside and village shade trees.
Nest: Higher above ground than most vireo nests, 20–90 ft. (6.1–27.4 m), in horizontal fork of slender branch, usually well away from trunk, often in poplar. Neat and closely built cup of bark strips, leaves, grasses, feathers, plant down; fastened and woven with spider webs; lined with fine plant stems, horsehair. Rim overhangs deep cup; typically protected by canopy of overhead leaves. Building by both sexes; about 1 wk. Greatest outside diam. about 3½ in. (8.9 cm), narrowing to 2 in. (5.1 cm) at top opening.
Eggs: 3–5, commonly 4; av. 19.1 x 14.2 mm. Oval. Shell smooth, has little or no gloss. White; sparsely dotted with browns, black. Incubation by both sexes, 12 days.

Notes: Several species of vireos sing while incubating — none more vociferously than this one. Author has found most nests by listening for Purple Finchlike song of male. Trees and height above ground of Pennsylvania nests found by author: red maple, 45 ft. (13.7 m); black oak, 20 ft. (6.1 m); elm, 40 ft. (12.2 m); wild cherry, 50 ft. (15.2 m); poplar, 30 ft. (9.1 m); aspen, 30 ft.

BLACK-AND-WHITE WARBLER *Mniotilta varia*

Breeding range: Wisconsin to Maine, south to n. Mississippi, cen. Alabama, cen. Georgia, s. S. Carolina, se. N. Carolina.

Habitat: Deciduous woodlands, especially hillsides, ravines.

Nest: On the ground, typically at the base of tree, stump, rock; under log, fallen tree branch; usually hidden from above, concealed in drift of leaves. Built of dry skeletonized leaves; inlaid with grasses, weed fibers, inner bark strips (grapevine), rootlets, sometimes hair. Rarely built at top of stump 15 in. (38.1 cm) or less above ground. Female builds; male accompanies her. Outside diam. 3¾–4½ in. (9.5–11.4 cm), height 2¼ in. (5.7 cm); inside diam. 1¾–2 in. (4.4–5.1 cm), depth 1½ in. (3.8 cm); wall of nest 1 in. (2.5 cm) thick; bottom of nest ½ in. (1.3 cm) thick.

Eggs: 4–5; av. 17.2 x 13.3 mm. Oval to short-oval. Shell smooth, slight gloss. White, creamy white; finely sprinkled over entire surface with spots, dots, small blotches of various shades of brown; principally at larger end. Incubation by female; 11–12 days. 1 brood.

Notes: Common victim of Brown-headed Cowbird. Record number of 8 Cowbird eggs, 2 warbler eggs found in Michigan nest with female incubating all 10. Nest with 5 Cowbird eggs, 2 warbler eggs also reported. Except for Louisiana Waterthrush, this is earliest warbler to arrive on northern breeding grounds in spring.

PROTHONOTARY WARBLER *Protonotaria citrea*

Breeding range: Cen. and s. Wisconsin, s. Michigan, n. Ohio, nw. Pennsylvania, w. New York, s. New Jersey south to Gulf Coast and cen. Florida.

Habitat: Forested bottomland, flooded river valleys, swamps.

Nest: Only cavity-nesting warbler in e. U.S. In natural cavity, old woodpecker hole (usually Downy Woodpecker), birdhouse, 3–32 ft. (0.9–9.8 m) above water or ground, av. 5–10 ft. (1.5–3.0 m). Male selects territory, nest site, places some material before female's spring arrival. Female does most of building with mosses, rootlets, twigs, leaves. Egg cavity neatly rounded, cup-shaped hollow; smoothly lined with fine grasses, leaf stems, feathers. Nest complete 6–10 days; several days' delay before eggs laid. Inside diam. 2 in. (5.1 cm), depth 1½ in. (3.8 cm).

Eggs: 3–8, commonly 4–6, often 7; av. 18.47 x 14.55 mm. Oval to short-oval. Shell smooth, somewhat glossy. Creamy; boldly, liberally spotted, blotched with brown shades over entire egg. Incubation by female; 12–14 days, usually 13, starting day before last egg laid. Typically 2 broods, sometimes 1, especially in North.

Notes: Of 84 nests in s. Michigan in natural situations 29 were over standing water, 32 over running water, 23 over dry land; of these, 43 were in natural openings, 41 in woodpecker holes.

SWAINSON'S WARBLER *Limnothlypis swainsonii*

Breeding range: S. Illinois, s. Indiana, s. Ohio, w. W. Virginia, s. Virginia, se. Maryland south to Gulf Coast and n. Florida.

Habitat: In se. Atlantic Coastal Plain, typically in wooded canebrake swamps; in mountainous areas, wooded ravines, rhododendron and laurel thickets.

Nest: Difficult to find, often at edge of or even outside singing territory of male. In coastal lowlands, commonly in cane (*Arundinaria*) or palmetto. In highlands, nest built in shrubs, small trees, masses of vines, briars, rhododendron, laurel, 2–10 ft. (0.6–3.0 m) above ground, often far from water. Nest bulky, loosely constructed, well concealed; of leaves, mosses, pine needles; lined with fine grasses. Built by female.

Eggs: 3, sometimes 4, rarely 5; av. 19.5 x 15.0 mm. Elliptical. Shell smooth, has slight gloss. White, rarely spotted. Except for very rare Bachman's Warbler (*Vermivora bachmanii*), Swainson's is only warbler in U.S. that typically lays *white, unmarked eggs*. Incubation by female; 13 days.

Notes: At W. Virginia nest observed from blind by author for 12 consecutive hours, male never sang within 100 yds. (91.4 m) of nest.

WORM-EATING WARBLER
Helmitheros vermivorus p. 195

GOLDEN-WINGED WARBLER *Vermivora chrysoptera*

Breeding range: Wisconsin, s. Michigan, cen. New York, s. Connecticut, e. Massachusetts, s. Vermont south to n. Illinois, n. Indiana, s. Ohio, w. Pennsylvania, n. New Jersey; in mountains to n. Georgia.

Habitat: Brushy fields, overgrown pastures, openings in deciduous forests, woodland edges, hillside thickets.

Nest: On or close to ground, supported by weed stalks (goldenrod), tufts of grass. Coarse bulky structure of grasses, tendrils, bark shreds on foundation of dead leaves; lined with hair, fine grasses. Built by female. Outside diam. 3⅝–5 in. (9.2–12.7 cm), height 3–5 in. (7.6–12.7 cm); inside diam. 1¾–2½ in. (4.4–6.4 cm), depth 1⁵⁄₁₆–2½ in. (3.3–6.4 cm).

Eggs: 3–6, commonly 4–5; av. 16.7 x 13.0 mm. Oval to short-oval. Shell smooth, has slight gloss. White, creamy white; variety of brown markings with underlying speckles, spots; denser toward larger end. Generally more heavily marked than similar Blue-winged Warbler eggs. Incubation by female; 10–11 days.

Notes: Author observed female Golden-winged Warbler place 1st leaves in goldenrod clump on May 18. Nest completed in 5 days. 1st egg laid May 23; incubation started May 27, when 5th egg was laid. This species and Blue-winged Warbler sometimes hybridize where ranges overlap.

BLUE-WINGED WARBLER *Vermivora pinus*

Breeding range: S. Wisconsin, s. Michigan, n. Ohio, nw. Pennsylvania, w. and cen. New York, s. New England south to s. Illinois, cen. Tennessee, Kentucky, n. Alabama, n. Georgia, N. Carolina, n. Virginia, ne. Maryland, Delaware.

Habitat: Swamps, stream edges, overgrown pastures, woodland edges, bottomlands.

Nest: Close to or on ground, built among and attached to upright stems of weeds, grass clumps; often very narrow, deep, supported on sturdy foundation of dead leaves. Made of coarse grasses, dead leaves, bark shreds (often grapevine); lined with fine bark shreds, grass stems, horsehair. Female builds.

Eggs: 4–5, rarely 6; av. 15.7 x 12.5 mm. Oval to short-oval. Shell smooth, has slight gloss. White; finely dotted, sparingly spotted with shades of brown, usually heaviest at larger end. Less heavily marked than similar Golden-winged Warbler eggs. Incubation by female; 10–11 days.

Notes: Although female is generally reported as building nest alone, author watched male bringing material equally often as female during 1st day of construction, Butler Co., Pennsylvania. Where ranges overlap, this species hybridizes with closely related Golden-winged Warbler. Habitats also overlap somewhat, but Blue-winged Warbler tends to choose moister situations than the Golden-winged.

TENNESSEE WARBLER *Vermivora peregrina*

Breeding range: Northern border of U.S. south to n. Wisconsin, n. Michigan, ne. New York, s. Vermont, cen. New Hampshire, s. Maine.

Habitat: Open deciduous, coniferous forests, swales, forest clearings in second-growth timber.

Nest: Sometimes single, sometimes in small colonies, several occupying same forest clearing. Built on ground, often in damp situation (sphagnum bog), edge of alder swale; almost entirely of lightly arranged dry grasses; lined with finer grasses, sometimes hair; usually completely concealed by surroundings. Outside diam. 3–4 in. (7.6-10.2 cm), height 2–3¼ in. (5.1-8.3 cm); inside diam. 1⅛–2 in. (2.9-5.1 cm), depth 1⅛–1½ in. (2.9-3.8 cm).

Eggs: 4–7, commonly 6 (larger clutch than most boreal warblers except Cape May, which nests in tree); av. 16.1 x 12.4 mm. Oval to short-oval. Shell smooth, slight luster. White, creamy white; marked with reddish-brown dots, small spots, scattered over entire egg or concentrated mostly at larger end. Incubation by female; probably 11–12 days.

Notes: Eggs similar to but slightly larger than eggs of Nashville Warbler; nest grassier. Nashville rarely if ever lays clutch of 6 eggs (commonly 4–5). Nest in photograph was at edge of alder swale 50 ft. (15.2 m) from nest of Nashville.

NASHVILLE WARBLER *Vermivora ruficapilla*

Breeding range: Northern border of U.S. south to n. Illinois, s. Michigan, n. Ohio, W. Virginia, Pennsylvania, w. Maryland, n. New Jersey, Connecticut.

Habitat: Slashings, swales, edges of bogs, mixed forest undergrowth, forest edges.

Nest: Invariably on ground, set in well-concealed depression in moss, often with overhead cover of blueberry, clubmoss, bunchberry. Small, compact shallow cup of rootlets, bark fibers, grasses; lined with fine grasses, moss stems, hair. Female builds; 7–9 days. Outside diam. 3¼ in. (8.3 cm), height 1¾ in. (4.4 cm); depth, 1 in. (2.5 cm).

Eggs: 4–5; av. 15.7 x 12.1 mm. Oval to short-oval. Shell smooth, has slight gloss. White, creamy white; dotted with shades of brown; markings may be scattered over entire egg or concentrated in wreath at larger end. Incubation by female; 11–12 days.

Notes: Nest neat, not grassy like similarly located Tennessee Warbler nest. Nashville Warbler rarely if ever lays 6 eggs (common for clutch of Tennessee). Author's records include 8 nests in Pennsylvania and Maine — 5 with 5 eggs, 3 with 4 eggs; none parasitized by Brown-headed Cowbird. Finding nest without following or flushing incubating bird virtually impossible.

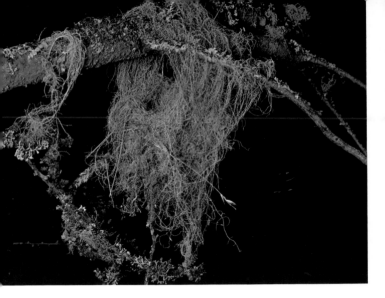

NORTHERN PARULA *Parula americana*

Breeding range: Throughout e. U.S. to cen. Florida.

Habitat: Coniferous, deciduous forests where mosslike lichens or bromeliads hang from tree branches. Also in conifers, hardwoods without lichens and airplants.

Nest: In northern range, completely hidden in festoons of *Usnea* hanging from tree branches, 6–100 ft. (1.8–30.5 m) above ground; in southern range, in Spanish moss; elsewhere, in conifers (hemlocks), mixed hardwoods. Within mosslike "beards," pendent nest built of fine grasses, tendrils, hair, plant down; opening at side or top. From ground nest looks size and shape of tennis ball held in bottom of beard. Elsewhere, open nests are built in accumulated trash, piles of leaves, hanging clusters of twigs, on horizontal tree branches, 10–40 ft. (3.0–12.2 m) above ground. Sometimes oriolelike in shape.

Eggs: 3–7, commonly 4–5; av. 16.5 x 12.1 mm. Oval to short-oval. Shell smooth, has slight gloss. White, creamy white; dotted, spotted with browns. Incubation by female; at least 12 days.

Notes: Where *Usnea* and Spanish moss are not available, nests are extremely varied. Author found nest in W. Virginia built within piece of burlap caught in outer branches of tree. Other nests: composed almost entirely of heavy brown wrapping cord and small quantity of wool; composed entirely of leaf skeletons; built chiefly of fine grasses.

182

YELLOW WARBLER *Dendroica petechia*

Breeding range: Wisconsin to Maine, south to n. Alabama, n. Georgia. Also a subspecies in Florida Keys.

Habitat: Along waterways, edges of swamps, marshes, brushy bottomlands, small trees, orchards, hedgerows, roadside thickets.

Nest: Often in colonies in ideal habitat; individual territories as small as ⅖ acres (.16 ha); also single. Placed in upright fork or crotch of shrub, tree, briars 2–12 ft. (0.6–3.7 m) above ground, av. 3–8 ft. (0.9–2.4 m). Strong, compact cup of firmly interwoven milkweed fibers, hemp, grasses, plant down; lined with felted plant down, hair, fine grasses. Walls thicker, less neatly built than in American Redstart's nest. Female builds in about 4 days. Outside diam. 2¼–3 in. (5.7–7.6 cm), height, 2–5 in. (5.1–12.7 cm); inside diam. 1¾–2 in. (4.4–5.1 cm), depth 1¼–1½ in. (3.2–3.8 cm).

Eggs: 3–6, commonly 4–5; av. 16.6 x 12.6 mm. Oval to short-oval. Shell smooth, has slight gloss. Grayish white, bluish or greenish white; splashed with brown, gray markings; often wreathed at larger end. Incubation by female; 11–2 days.

Notes: Common victim of Brown-headed Cowbird. Has devised ingenious way of combating parasite: builds 2nd story on top of Cowbird eggs, burying them. Nest may also contain warbler eggs when superstructure is added. As many as 6 stories have been found with Cowbird eggs buried in each layer.

MAGNOLIA WARBLER *Dendroica magnolia*

Breeding range: Northern border of U.S. south to cen. Wisconsin, cen. Michigan, nw. Pennsylvania, New York, nw. New Jersey, n. Massachusetts; in mountains to sw. N. Carolina.

Habitat: Coniferous forests.

Nest: Well hidden in bushy top or horizontal branch of small conifer (Christmas tree), 1–15 ft. (0.3–4.6 m) above ground, av. 2–6 ft. (0.6–1.8 m). Loosely made of fine grass stems, fine twigs, weed stalks; lined with black rootlets, moss stems. *Coal-black* rootlets invariably in lining. Built mostly or entirely by female in 4–6 days. Outside diam. 2¾–4 in. (7.0–10.2 cm); inside diam. 1¾–2 in. (4.4–5.1 cm).

Eggs: 3–5, commonly 4; av. 16.3 x 12.3 mm. Oval to short-oval. Shell smooth, has slight gloss. White, creamy white; spotted, splashed with reddish brown, hazel, purple, lavender; usually wreathed at larger end. Incubation by female; 11–13 days.

Notes: Of 16 nests found in Maine by author, 10 contained 4 eggs, 2 had 3 eggs, 2 had 1 Brown-headed Cowbird each, 1 had 2 warbler eggs, 1 had 3. Of 2 nests found in Pennsylvania by author, each had 2 Cowbird eggs and 2 warbler eggs. All were lined with characteristic black rootlets. Thick stands of small evergreens preferred, but occasionally nest placed in large tree beside clearing.

CAPE MAY WARBLER p. 193
Dendroica tigrina

184

BLACK-THROATED BLUE WARBLER
Dendroica caerulescens

Breeding range: N. Wisconsin, n. Michigan, New York, Maine south to n. Ohio, nw. and cen. Pennsylvania, n. Maryland, n. Connecticut; in mountains to ne. Georgia.

Habitat: Mixed conifers, hardwood forests, with heavy undergrowth; cut-over areas.

Nest: Built close to ground, 1–4 ft. (0.3–1.2 m) in low tree, shrub; partial to rhododendron, laurel, hemlock, small spruce, fir, maple. Well concealed, bulky, of shreds of dead wood, papery bark, twigs, bud scales, leaves; anchored and woven together with spider, insect webbing; lined with fine black rootlets, hair. Built mostly by female in 4 days; male may bring material, occasionally shape nest. Outside diam 3½ in. (8.9 cm), height 2¼–5 in. (5.7–12.7 cm); inside diam. 2 in. (5.1 cm), depth 1½ in. (3.8 cm).

Eggs: 3–5, commonly 4 (in record of over 200 nests, only 4 sets of 5); av. 16.9 x 12.8 mm. Oval to short-oval. Shell smooth, has no gloss. White, creamy white; 2 types of markings: spots of 2–3 brown shades with gray undertones; only 1 brown shade with drab undertones. Incubation by female; 11–13 days, typically 12.

Notes: Preferred site varies: In New Hampshire, 15 nests built in mountain laurel, 9–15 in. (22.9–38.1 cm) above ground; in Pennsylvania in rhododendron; on Mt. Desert I., Maine, small spruces.

YELLOW-RUMPED (MYRTLE) WARBLER
Dendroica coronata

Breeding range: Northern border of U.S. south to n. Wisconsin, n. Michigan, n. New York (mountains), w. Massachusetts, ne. Pennsylvania (Poconos).

Habitat: Mixed and coniferous forests.

Nest: Typically on horizontal branch of spruce, cedar, hemlock, often near trunk, 4–50 ft. (1.2–15.2 m) above ground, av. 20 ft. (6.1 m). Occasionally nests in hardwoods: maple, apple, birch. Neat, deep cup of small twigs, bark strips, plant down, fibers; lined with hair, fine grasses, *many feathers.* Outside diam. 3–3½ in. (7.6–8.9 cm), height 2¼ in. (5.7 cm); inside diam. 2 in. (5.1 cm), depth 1½ in. (3.8 cm).

Eggs: 4–5, sometimes 3; av. 17.5 x 13.3 mm. Oval to short-oval. Shell smooth, has slight gloss. White, creamy white; peppered, spotted, blotched with brown, often wreathed at larger end. Incubation by female; 12–13 days. 2 broods occasionally suspected.

Notes: Characteristic nest arrangement of lining of feathers is identification factor. Shafts of feathers are woven or imbedded into lining of nests so that tops bend inward over cup, forming screen for eggs when female is not incubating (see illus.). Of 7 nests found by author in Maine, all had this feather arrangement; eggs almost invisible from above. Ruffed Grouse feathers commonly used.

186

BLACK-THROATED GREEN WARBLER *Dendroica virens*

Breeding range: N. Wisconsin, cen. Michigan to Maine, south to n. Ohio, n. Pennsylvania, w. Massachusetts; in mountains to n. Alabama, n. Georgia. Also subspecies in coastal S. Carolina.

Habitat: Coniferous, mixed forests.

Nest: Compact, well-built, deep cup saddled to branch or fork of conifer in thick foliage, 3–80 ft. (0.9–24.4 m) above ground; sometimes in hardwoods: birch, maple, others. Of fine bark, twigs, mosses, grasses, lichens, spider webs; lined with thick felting of hair, fur, fine stems, rootlets, feathers. Built in about 4 days mostly or entirely by female. Outside diam. 3–4 in. (7.6–10.2 cm), height 2 in. (5.1 cm); inside diam. 2 in., depth 1½ in. (3.8 cm).

Eggs: 4–5; av. 17.0 x 12.7 mm. Oval to short-oval. Shell smooth, has slight gloss. Creamy white or grayish white; spotted, dotted, scrawled, with reddish brown, purple, lavender; commonly wreathed at larger end. Incubation mostly or entirely by female; 12 days. Possibly 2 broods occasionally.

Notes: Curled, papery strips of white birch bark built into outside walls of nest make it easier to find in dark coniferous forests (see illus.). In nest building, it is believed male assists female only on 1st day, if at all. Said to be seldom victimized by Brown-headed Cowbird.

CERULEAN WARBLER *Dendroica cerulea*

Breeding range: S. Wisconsin, s. Michigan, se. and sw. Pennsylvania, n. New Jersey, New York, Connecticut (Hartford) south to cen. Alabama, cen. N. Carolina, cen. Virginia, s. Maryland, s. Delaware.

Habitat: Upper stories of tallest trees in deciduous forests with little undergrowth.

Nest: On horizontal branch of tree, 20–60 ft. (6.1–18.3 m) above ground; far from trunk, 10–20 ft. (3.0–6.1 m), typically with an open area below. Dainty, compactly built, gray, knotlike shallow structure of fine grasses, plant fibers, bark strips, weed stems, mosses, lichens, neatly interwoven; lined with fine fibers, mosses, hair; bound on outside with spider silk. From ground resembles nests of Eastern Wood-Pewee, Blue-gray Gnatcatcher, in knotlike appearance. Very shallow, unwarblerlike. Outside diam. 2¾ in. (7.0 cm), height 1¾–2 in. (4.4–5.1 cm); inside diam. 1¾–1⅞ in. (4.4–4.8 cm), depth ⅞–1 in. (2.2–2.5 cm).

Eggs: 3–5, commonly 4; av. 17 x 13 mm. Oval to short-oval. Shell smooth, has slight gloss. Grayish white, creamy white, greenish white; peppered, spotted, blotched with brown; usually wreathed at larger end. Incubation by female; period unknown, probably 12–13 days.

Notes: Ten nests found in Pennsylvania, all in oaks except 1 (shagbark hickory), 24–60 ft. (7.3–18.3 m) above ground, 6–20 ft. (1.8–6.1 m) from bole.

188

BLACKBURNIAN WARBLER *Dendroica fusca*

Breeding range: Northern border of U.S. south to cen. Wisconsin, cen. Michigan, se. New York, s. New England, cen. Pennsylvania; south in mountains to n. Georgia.

Habitat: Mostly coniferous also deciduous forests.

Nest: Typically high, as far as 84 ft. (25.6 m) above ground in big trees; in conifers throughout range, also in hardwoods in South. Saddled to horizontal limb, usually far from trunk, or in small fork near top of tree. Of twigs, plant down, invariably *Usnea* where available, spider silk; lined with hair, black rootlets, fine grasses. Built by female alone. Outside diam. 3 in. (7.6 cm), height 1½ in. (3.8 cm); inside diam. 1¾ in. (4.4 cm), depth 1⅛ in. (2.9 cm).

Eggs: 4–5; av. 17.2 x 12.8 mm. Oval to short-oval. Shell smooth, has slight gloss. White, greenish white; spotted, splashed with brown shades, undertones of gray; in wreath around larger end or spotted over entire egg. Incubation by female alone; period unknown, probably 11–12 days.

Notes: In suitable habitat, species tends to congregate in loosely scattered colonies; elsewhere nests singly. One of most difficult of warbler nests to discover; commonly found by following female. Nest illustrated, 49 ft. 8 in. (15.1 m) above ground in top of spruce, on Mt. Desert I., Maine.

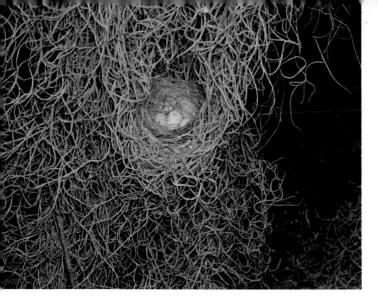

YELLOW-THROATED WARBLER *Dendroica dominica*

Breeding range: Eastern race (*D. d. dominica*): along Atlantic Coastal Plain, Florida to cen. New Jersey. Western race, Sycamore Warbler (*D. d. albilora*): Gulf states north to s. Michigan, s. Wisconsin, s. Ohio, sw. W. Virginia.

Habitat: Cypress swamps, pinewoods festooned with Spanish moss (*Tillandsia*) in South; in West and North, partial to sycamores.

Nest: In coastal areas invariably in clumps of Spanish moss hanging from horizontal limbs of live oaks (mostly), pines, cypresses; 10–120 ft. (3.0–36.6 m) above ground, av. 30–60 ft. (9.1–18.3 m); far out from trunk. Inland, open nests, typically saddled to horizontal branch of sycamore, pine. In *Tillandsia,* female lines cup-shaped pocket with grasses, weeds, feathers, strands of moss (woven into nest). Open nests of bark strips, grasses, weed stems, plant down; lined with plant down, feathers. Outside diam. 2½ in. (6.4 cm), height 2 in. (5.1 cm); inside diam. 1⅝ in. (4.1 cm), depth 1¾ in. (4.4 cm).

Eggs: 4, sometimes 5; av. 17.1 x 13.0 mm. Oval to short-oval. Shell smooth, somewhat glossy. Pale green, grayish white; dotted, blotched with dull shades of lavender and gray overlaid with brown, grays; usually wreathed. Incubation by female; period unknown, probably 12–13 days. 2 broods likely in South.

Notes: Nest illustrated, 45 ft. (13.7 m) above ground, 8 ft. (2.4 m) from trunk on limb of slash pine in Leon Co., Florida.

CHESTNUT-SIDED WARBLER *Dendroica pensylvanica*

Breeding range: Wisconsin to Maine, south to Illinois, n. Ohio, Pennsylvania, cen. New Jersey, cen. Maryland; in mountains to nw. S. Carolina, n.-cen. Georgia, se. Tennessee.

Habitat: Shrubby rural areas (neglected pastures); roadside shrubs, briar tangles, hedgerows; undergrowth in cut-over timber.

Nest: Placed at low elevation, 1–4 ft. (0.3–1.2 m) above ground, well concealed in briars, vines, shrubs. Loosely woven, thin-walled cup made of coarse or fine strips of inner bark, shredded weed stems, grasses, plant down; lined with fine grasses, sometimes hair. Built entirely by female in about 5 days. Outside diam. 2½ x 3½ in. (6.4 x 8.9 cm), height 2 in. (5.1 cm); inside diam. 1¾ in. (4.4 cm), depth, 1¾ in.

Eggs: 3–5, commonly 4; av. 16.7 x 12.4 mm. Oval to long-oval. Shell smooth, has slight gloss. White, creamy white, greenish white; dotted, spotted, blotched, splashed with gray, brown, lilac. Considerable variation in color and number of markings. Incubation by female; 11–12 days.

Notes: In 14 nests studied in Michigan, av. height above ground was exactly 2 ft. (.6 m). Meadowsweet was nesting site for 6 of 17 nests in same area, 3 in raspberry, 2 in red osier dogwood; 1 each in meadowrue, sensitive fern, sedge, bracken fern, sweet gale, gooseberry.

BAY-BREASTED WARBLER *Dendroica castanea*

Breeding range: Northeastern border of U.S. south to s. Maine, cen. Vermont, cen. New Hampshire, n. New York.

Habitat: Coniferous forests.

Nest: Saddled on horizontal limb of dense conifer 4–40 ft. (1.2–12.2 m) above ground, av. 15–25 ft. (4.6–7.6 m); usually 5–10 ft. (1.5–3.0 m) out from trunk. Loosely woven of conifer twigs that protrude on all sides, coarse dried grasses, spider silk; lined with rootlets, hair, fine grasses. Female, accompanied by male, gathers material and builds. Outside diam. 3½–5 in. (8.9–12.7 cm), height 2–2¾ in. (5.1–7.0 cm); inside diam. 2–2½ in. (5.1–6.4 cm), depth 1¼–1½ in. (3.2–3.8 cm).

Eggs: 4–7, commonly 5; av. 17.7 x 12.9 mm. Oval to long-oval. Shell smooth, has slight gloss. White, pale blue-white, pale green-white; peppered, spotted, blotched with browns, grays. Incubation by female alone. Male feeds mate on nest, stands guard beside nest when she is absent.

Notes: Maine data on 10 clutches: 8 sets of 5, 1 set of 4, 1 set of 6. At 10:30 A.M. June 17, 1970, Mt. Desert I., Maine, author found 4 eggs in nest on horizontal limb of spruce 15 ft. (4.6 m) above ground. At 10:50, returned with camera for photograph, found female incubating. Bird refused to leave nest until pushed off. Nest then contained 5 eggs (see illus.). Many observers report fearlessness of female at nest.

192

BLACKPOLL WARBLER *Dendroica striata*

Breeding range: Northeastern border of U.S. south to cen. Maine and mountains of New York, Vermont, New Hampshire, w. Massachusetts.

Habitat: Low coniferous forests, especially spruces.

Nest: In conifer, commonly 2–7 ft. (0.6–2.1 m) above ground against trunk of tree supported by 1 or 2 horizontal branches, well concealed by overhanging limbs. Somewhat bulky; built of small twigs, bark, grasses, weeds, mosses, *Usnea,* hair; lined with plant fibers, fine rootlets, hair, with liberal lining of feathers (characteristic). Female builds. Outside diam. 4½ in. (11.4 cm), height 3 in. (7.6 cm); inside diam. 2 in. (5.1 cm), depth 1½ in. (3.8 cm).

Eggs: 4–5, sometimes 3; av. 17.9 x 13.4 mm. Oval to long-oval. Shell smooth, has little gloss. White, creamy buff, pale green; evenly speckled with brown spots; blotched with subdued shades of lavender commonly concentrated at large end. Incubation by female; about 11 days, and may begin before clutch complete.

Notes: Male does not incubate but feeds mate on nest. Following male with food is means of finding nest with eggs. All 17 nests observed on Grand Manan I., New Brunswick, were in spruce, mostly within 5 ft. (1.5 m) of ground: 10 contained 5 eggs, 6 had 4, 1 had 3. Yellow-rumped Warbler's nest, also lined with feathers, is more compact, built out from trunk.

CAPE MAY WARBLER *Dendroica tigrina*
(proper order after Magnolia Warbler, p. 184)

Breeding range: N. Maine, n. New Hampshire (rarely), n. Vermont (irregularly), ne. New York (possibly in Adirondacks), n. Michigan.

Habitat: Open stands of coniferous trees; dense forests shunned.

Nest: Invariably in uppermost clump of needles, as near top as possible, in spirelike crown of spruce, fir; in thick foliage against or near main tree stem, resting on twigs, foliage. Cannot be seen from ground even with field glasses. Height from ground determined by tree height, usually 30–60 ft. (9.1–18.3 m) within 2–4 ft. (0.6–1.2 m) of top. Female builds somewhat bulky structure with exterior of green moss (sphagnum), interwoven with twigs, fine grass stems, bound with plant down; felt-lined with hair, rootlets, feathers, fur. Outside diam. 4 in. (10.2 cm), height 2½ in. (6.4 cm); inside diam. 1¾ in. (4.4 cm); depth 1 in. (2.5 cm).

Eggs: 4–9, commonly 6–7; av. 16.8 x 12.5 mm. Oval to short-oval. Shell smooth, has practically no gloss. Creamy white; richly spotted, blotched with reddish brown concentrated at larger end; occasionally has black scrawls. Incubation by female; period unknown.

Notes: Following female to nest is difficult — she usually lands near base, works up through tree.

PINE WARBLER *Dendroica pinus*

Breeding range: Throughout e. U.S.; local, is rare or absent outside pine woodlands. Resident in South.

Habitat: Open pine woods.

Nest: Saddled to horizontal limb of pine, well out from trunk, 8–80 ft. (2.4–24.4 m) above ground, av. 30–50 ft. (9.1–15.2 m); well concealed, completely hidden from below in cluster of fine needles. Well made; compactly built of weed stems, bark strips, pine needles, pine twigs, spider webs; lined with fern down, hair, pine needles, feathers.

Eggs: 3–5, commonly 4; av. 18.1 x 13.5 mm. Oval to short-oval. Shell smooth, has no gloss. White, grayish white, greenish white; speckled, spotted, blotched with shades of brown; normally concentrated in wreath at larger end. Incubation by female (male suspected of sharing to some extent); period unknown, probably 12–13 days. 2 broods in South, possibly 3 occasionally.

Notes: Attachment of this species to pine trees as nesting site is so persistent that it is practically useless to look for nests elsewhere. Nest have been found, rarely, in cedar, cypress. 15 species of trees  in *Pinus* genus known to be used; any type of pine within breeding range appears to be suitable. S. Carolina nest 135 ft. (41.1 m) above ground is record height. Throughout its range, the Pine Warbler is one of the 1st warblers to nest each spring.

KIRTLAND'S WARBLER *Dendroica kirtlandii*

Breeding range: Twelve counties in n. Lower Peninsula, Michigan; approximately 85 miles (136 km) north-south, 100 miles (160 km) east-west.

Habitat: Jack pine stands of more than 80 acres (32.4 ha), the trees 6–18 ft. (1.8–5.5 m) high, 8–20 yrs. old, with heavy ground cover.

Nest: On or in ground in thick cover under or near jack pines; cup of grasses, dead sedge leaves, pine needles; lined with hair, mosses, grasses, rootlets. Built by female in 2–4 days.

Eggs: 3–6, commonly 5; av. 18.5 x 14.0 mm (largest eggs of any species in genus *Dendroica*). Oval to short-oval. Shell smooth, has slight gloss. Creamy white; dotted, blotched with shades of brown. Incubation by female; 13–16 days, av. 14 (longest period of any N. American warbler). 1 brood.

Notes: Living pine-branch thickets near ground crucial nesting requirement, not height or age of tree.

WORM-EATING WARBLER *Helmitheros vermivorus*
(proper order after Swainson's Warbler, p. 177)

Breeding range: N. Illinois, s. Indiana, s. and cen. Ohio, sw. Pennsylvania, cen. and se. New York, e. and sw. Massachusetts, s. Connecticut south to w. Tennessee, n. Alabama, n. Georgia, nw. S. Carolina, e. N. Carolina.

Habitat: Deciduous forests, especially brushy hillsides.

Nest: On the ground, concealed under drift of leaves, usually protected overhead by shrubs, briars, saplings. Built of skeletonized leaves; lined with hair moss (*Polytrichium*), fine grass, hair. Typically on hillside or bank of ravine.

Eggs: 3–6, commonly 4–5; av. 17.4 x 13.6 mm. Oval to short-oval. Shell smooth, slight gloss. White, dotted sparingly or profusely with shades of brown, often concentrated at large end. Incubation by female; 13 days.

CONNECTICUT WARBLER *Oporornis agilis*
(proper order after Kentucky Warbler, p. 201)

Breeding range: N. Wisconsin, n. Michigan.

Habitat: Muskegs, tamarack, spruce bogs.

Nest: On or near ground, well hidden by surrounding vegetation, in wet moss (sphagnum) or dry ground. Deep rounded cup on foundation of leaves or sunk in moss; lined with grasses.

Eggs: 4–5; av. 19.5 x 14.3 mm. Oval. Shell smooth, has slight gloss. Creamy white; dotted, spotted, blotched with browns. Incubation by female; period unknown.

Notes: Approaching nest, female lands 30–40 ft. (9.1–12.2 m) away, walks quietly through underbrush. Male usually sings far from nest.

PRAIRIE WARBLER *Dendroica discolor*

Breeding range: S. Wisconsin (rarely), Michigan, Illinois, Ohio, Pennsylvania, New York, s. New Hampshire, Massachusetts, s. Maine south to Gulf Coast and s. Florida.

Habitat: Dry, brushy clearings, sproutlands, pine barrens, burned-over areas, roadside vegetation, Christmas tree plantings.

Nest: Sometimes in loose colonies with territories well defined; also singly. Attached to bushes, briars, tree limbs or crotches, typically at low elevations — 1–10 ft. (0.3–3.0 m) above ground, occasionally higher. Compact cup of plant down, bark shreds, woven with fine grasses, bound with spider silk; interwoven with supporting vegetation; lined with hair, grasses, feathers. Built by female alone. Outside diam. 2¾ x 3 in. (7.0 x 7.6 cm), height 3¼ in. (8.3 cm); inside diam. 2 in. (5.1 cm), depth 2 in.

Eggs: 3–5, commonly 4; av. 15.9 x 12.3 mm. Oval to short-oval. Shell smooth, has slight gloss. White, creamy white, greenish white; spotted, dotted with browns, grays; typically wreathed at larger end. Incubation by female; 12–13 days.

Notes: Range is expanding northward, influenced to a great extent by availability of Christmas tree plantings. Author has followed range extension from sw. Pennsylvania northward almost by movement from one pine planting to another.

PALM WARBLER *Dendroica palmarum*

Breeding range: Locally in n. Wisconsin, n. and cen. Michigan; Maine.

Habitat: Two types: wet muskeg and sphagnum bogs; open barrens, dry forests of spruce (east) and jack pine (west).

Nest: In loose colonies in favorable habitat; also singly. Buried in sphagnum moss, lichen-covered hummocks, often under small trees, shrubs, in heathlike bogs. Also above ground in dry areas in lower branches of young conifers. Almost entirely of dry grasses, weed stalks; lined with fine grasses, feathers worked in. Built by female. Outside diam. 3½ in. (8.9 cm), height 2½ in. (6.4 cm); inside diam. 2 in. (5.1 cm), depth 2 in.

Eggs: 4–5; av. 17.4 x 12.9 mm (east); 16.7 x 13.1 mm (west). Oval to short-oval or long-oval. Shell smooth, has slight gloss. White, creamy white; spotted, dotted, blotched with shades of brown; commonly wreathed at larger end. Incubation probably by female alone; period unknown, probably 12–13 days. Male feeds incubating mate. Possibly 2 broods.

Notes: Author found 2 distinct colonies of this species on Mt. Desert I., Maine. Of 9 nests found: 6 were on ground buried in sphagnum moss (all had 4 or 5 eggs); 3 were in young spruce trees on hillside. Of the latter, 2 were 18 in. (45.7 cm) above ground; 1 was 24 in. (61 cm) above ground and of these, 2 contained young, 1 had 4 eggs.

OVENBIRD *Seiurus aurocapillus*

Breeding range: Wisconsin to Maine, south to n. Alabama, n. Georgia.

Habitat: Deciduous forest floors, especially with low undergrowth.

Nest: Built on ground in depression in dead leaves; top arched with dead leaves and surrounding vegetation, shaped like an old-fashioned oven with opening at ground level to 1 in. (2.5 cm) above ground. Invisible from above. Made of grasses, plant fibers, weed stems, leaves, rootlets, mosses, bark; lined with fine rootlets, fibers, and hair. Female alone builds in about 5 days. Outside diam. 6½ in. (16.5 cm), height of nest and roof, 4½–5 in. (11.4–12.7 cm); inside diam. 3 in. (7.6 cm), opening 1½ in. (3.8 cm) high, 2¼ in. (5.7 cm) wide — smaller than inner cavity.

Eggs: 3–6, commonly 4–5; av. 20.2 x 15.5 mm. Oval to short-oval. Shell smooth, has very slight gloss. White; dotted, spotted with reddish brown, lilac; usually wreathed at large end. Incubation by female alone; 11½–14 days, av. 12¼ days (information based on observations of 76 eggs in 21 nests). 1 brood.

Notes: Female sits tight on nest; usually will not flush until nearly stepped on. Commonly victimized by Brown-headed Cowbird. No record ever found of nests above ground. Of 27 nests, 2 had 3 eggs, 6 had 4, 18 had 5, 1 had 6.

NORTHERN WATERTHRUSH *Seiurus noveboracensis*

Breeding range: Wisconsin to Maine, south to ne. Ohio, n. Pennsylvania, W. Virginia (mountains), Massachusetts.

Habitat: Wooded swamps, swampy borders of streams, lakes.

Nest: On ground in upturned roots of fallen trees or roots of living trees; in hollows in decaying stumps; sides of overhanging banks. Built by female of mosses, small twigs, bark strips, skeletonized leaves; lined with mosses, hair, fine grasses. Outside diam. varies with location; inside diam. about 2 in. (5.1 cm), depth 1½ in. (3.8 cm).

Eggs: 4–5, occasionally 3, rarely 6; av. 19.1 x 14.6 mm. Very similar to eggs of Louisiana Waterthrush and Ovenbird; slightly smaller. Oval to short-oval. Shell smooth, has no gloss. White; dotted, spotted, blotched, sometimes scrawled with browns, grays. Incubation by female; period unknown.

Notes: Incubating female sits tight; will not flush until intruder is very close. Author searched for nest with eggs for 20 yrs. before finding 2 in 1970, in Maine and Pennsylvania. Both in upturned roots of fallen trees, both above pools formed in holes previously occupied by roots, both in deepest parts of thick, tangled swamps. Maine nest shown above. 10 nests found by James Bond in Pocono Swamp, Pennsylvania, all in upturned roots of fallen trees, each contained 4 or 5 eggs.

199

LOUISIANA WATERTHRUSH *Seiurus motacilla*

Breeding range: Sw. Wisconsin, s. Michigan, w. and cen. New York, s. Vermont, Connecticut, Rhode Island south to s. Mississippi, s. Alabama (absent from coastal plain), cen. and sw. Georgia, cen. S. Carolina, cen. and ne. N. Carolina.

Habitat: Ravines, small streams, mountain brooks, occasionally wooded swamps with flowing water.

Nest: Built in hole in steep bank of stream or in overturned roots close to running water, hidden by overhanging roots, weeds, or grass. Bulky, well-insulated mass of dead wet leaves, packed close together, reinforced by twigs; cup in top; lined with dry grasses, small rootlets, plant stems, hair. Leaves in front create pathway to nest. Both sexes build in 4–6 days; female more active. Outside diam. 3½ in. (8.9 cm), height varies — 8 in. (20.3 cm) or more; inside diam. 2½ in. (6.4 cm), depth 2½ in.

Eggs: 4–6; av. 19.9 x 15.5 mm. Oval to short-oval. Shell smooth, has slight gloss. White, creamy white; dotted, spotted, blotched, with browns, grays; commonly wreathed at large end. Eggs similar to those of Ovenbird and Northern Waterthrush. Incubation by female alone; 12–14 days. 1 brood.

Notes: Habitats of this species and Northern Waterthrush seldom overlap even when ranges do. Of 14 Pennsylvania nests, 13 were close to water along banks of streams.

KENTUCKY WARBLER *Oporornis formosus*

Breeding range: Sw. Wisconsin (locally), Illinois, s. Indiana, cen. and e. Ohio, s. and w. Pennsylvania, New York (lower Hudson Valley), sw. Connecticut (rarely) south to s. Mississippi, s. Alabama, nw. Florida, cen. Georgia, S. Carolina.

Habitat: Deciduous woodland thickets; moist, shady ravines.

Nest: On or near ground, sometimes in base of shrub, concealed by surrounding vegetation. Cup of grasses, plant fibers, rootlets built on a bulky foundation of dead leaves 4–6 in. (10.2–15.2 cm) deep; lined with rootlets, weed stalks, grasses. Like Golden-winged Warbler, but unlike many ground-nesting birds, this species builds nest slightly above ground level.

Eggs: 4–5, rarely 6; av. 18.6 x 14.3 mm. Short-oval to long-oval. Shell smooth, has slight gloss. White, creamy white; blotched, dotted, spotted with grays, browns, usually concentrated at large end. Incubation by female; 12–13 days. 1 brood.

Notes: Foundation of a Maryland nest contained 200 leaves. In a series of 25 egg sets: 13 of 4, 10 of 5, 2 of 6. Common victim of Brown-headed Cowbird. Record of 47 Pennsylvania nests: 39 with 1 Cowbird each, 7 with 2, 1 with 3. During nest building, birds may desert if disturbed often. When incubating, female generally permits close approach before flushing.

CONNECTICUT WARBLER
Oporornis agilis p. 195

MOURNING WARBLER *Oporornis philadelphia*

Breeding range: N. Wisconsin, n. Michigan, n. Ohio, n. Pennsylvania, w. New York; in mountains in Maryland and W. Virginia; w. Massachusetts, n. New Hampshire, w. and n. Maine.

Habitat: Slashings, dry brushy clearings, roadside tangles, swampy thickets.

Nest: Built on or near ground — 1 ft. (30.5 cm) or less, in tangle of briars or herbaceous plants (jewelweed, ferns, goldenrod, grass tussock). Bulky exterior of dry leaves, vine stalks, coarse grasses, weed stalks, bark pieces; lined with fine grasses, fine rootlets, hair. Outside diam. 5 in. (12.7 cm), height 3½ in. (8.9 cm); inside diam. 2 in. (5.1 cm), depth, 2 in.

Eggs: 3–5, commonly 4; av. 18.2 x 13.8 mm. Oval to short-oval. Shell smooth, has slight gloss. White, creamy white; dotted, spotted, blotched with brown; occasionally black scrawls. Incubation by female; 12 days, and may start day before last egg laid. Male feeds mate at or away from nest during incubation.

Notes: Measurement of 10 nesting territories: 1.6–2.4 acres (.65–.97 ha), av. 1.9 acres (.77 ha) each. In approaching nest female never flies directly to site; lands 30–50 ft. (9.1–15.2 m) away and silently creeps through vegetation. Author has found 4 nests: 1 in tussock of grass (see illus.), 1 in blackberry tangle, 2 in jewelweed; each contained 4 eggs.

COMMON YELLOWTHROAT *Geothlypis trichas*

Breeding range: Throughout e. U.S. Most widespread of American wood-warblers.

Habitat: Wet or dry areas with dense, low cover; fresh and salt-water marshes, swamps, wet bottomlands; brushy thickets, hedgerows.

Nest: Securely lodged in surrounding vegetation on or near ground in weed stalks, grass tussocks, low bushes. Bulky (large for small bird), of coarse grasses, reed shreds, leaves, mosses; lined with fine grasses, bark fibers, hair. Built by female alone in as few as 2 days. Outside diam. 3¼ in. (8.3 cm), height 3½ in. (8.9 cm); inside diam. 1¾ in. (4.4 cm), depth 1½ in. (3.8 cm).

Eggs: 3–5, commonly 4, rarely 6; av. 17.5 x 13.3 mm. Oval to long-oval. Shell smooth, has slight gloss. White, creamy white; dotted with browns, gray, black; commonly wreathed at large end. Incubation by female; 11–13 days, av. 12. 2 broods normally attempted.

Notes: Where desirable habitat was limited, 17 nests found in ½ acre (.2 ha) marsh in Illinois. In Michigan, 11 territorial males counted in 16 acre (6.5 ha) marsh. Of 22 nests near Ann Arbor, Michigan, 10 were parasitized by Brown-headed Cowbird; only 1 Yellowthroat fledged in these nests. In 12 Michigan nests 6 contained 4 eggs, 5 contained 5 eggs, 1 had 6.

YELLOW-BREASTED CHAT *Icteria virens*

Breeding range: S. Wisconsin, s. Michigan, cen. New York, Massachusetts, south to Gulf Coast and n. Florida.

Habitat: Woodland edges, neglected pastures, thick shrubbery, briar thickets.

Nest: 2–6 ft. (0.6–1.8 m) above ground in bush, briar tangle, vines, low tree. Bulky, of leaves, vines, weed stems, grasses; lined with fine grasses, plant stems. Outside diam. 5 in. (12.7 cm), height 3 in. (7.6 cm); inside diam. 3 in., depth 2 in. (5.1 cm).

Eggs: 3–6; commonly 5; av. 21.9 x 16.9 mm. Oval. Shell smooth; rather glossy. White, creamy white; speckled, spotted with browns, lilac, usually over entire egg, sometimes heaviest at large end. Similar to eggs of Ovenbird. Incubation by female; 11 days.

Notes: Author's experience indicates chat, while quite shy, does not desert eggs or young when continuously disturbed, despite repeated claims to contrary. 34 nests found in Pennsylvania and New Jersey were 1½–5 ft. (0.5–1.5 m) above ground; 21 were in

blackberry bushes. Author found Yellow-breasted Chats abundant in low crabapple, hawthorn trees in overgrown Pennsylvania fields. Of 10 nests found there in 1964, none was parasitized by Brown-headed Cowbird. In same area, 11 of 12 nests of Wood Thrush were parasitized.

HOODED WARBLER *Wilsonia citrina*

Breeding range: S. Michigan (locally), s. and cen. Illinois, Ohio, w. Pennsylvania, cen. and s. New York, s. Connecticut, Rhode Island south to Gulf Coast and n. Florida.

Habitat: Undergrowth of deciduous woodlands, thickets, wooded swamps (especially southern areas).

Nest: At low elevations, 1–6 ft. (0.3–1.8 m), av. 2–3 ft. (.6–.9 m), above ground in small bushes, herbaceous plants, vines, saplings; cane (*Arundinaria*) and palmetto in South. Neat, compact; built of dead leaves, grasses, bark strips, plant down, weeds; lined with black rootlets, soft grasses, plant fibers, hair; Spanish moss in South; often fastened with spider silk to very slight support. Measurements of 84 nests averaged: outside diam. 3 in. (7.6 cm), height 3 in.; inside diam. 1½ in. (3.8 cm), depth 2 in. (5.1 cm).

Eggs: 3–4, rarely 5; av. 17.6 x 13.6 mm. Oval to short-oval or long-oval. Shell smooth, has slight gloss. Creamy white; blotched, spotted, dotted with browns, lilac; sometimes with underlay of lavender. Incubation by female; 12 days. Occasionally 2 broods in southern part of range.

Notes: Measurements of heights above ground of 99 nests in Ohio: highest 63 in. (160 cm), lowest 7 in. (17.8 cm), av. 25 in. (63.5 cm). Incubating female with unusual amount of black on head may be mistaken for male.

WILSON'S WARBLER *Wilsonia pusilla*

Breeding range: Maine, n. New Hampshire, n. Vermont.

Habitat: Brushy northern bogs, wooded swamp borders, in or adjacent to alder swales.

Nest: In favorable habitat, species may nest in loose colonies. Nest on ground, often at base of sapling, bush; well concealed in moss or grass hummock in swale, bog, or in dry bordering areas. Bulky structure (large for small bird) almost entirely of dried grasses; some leaves, hair added. Female alone builds in 4–5 days. Outside diam. 3½ in. (8.9 cm), height 3½ in.; inside diam. 1¾ in. (4.4 cm), depth 1½ in. (3.8 cm).

Eggs: 4–6, commonly 5; av. 15.9 x 12.4 mm. Oval to short-oval. Shell smooth, has slight gloss. White, creamy white; dotted, spotted, with reddish brown, usually concentrated at large end. Incubation by female; 11–12 days. 1 brood.

Notes: Author followed progress of nest built in well-concealed dry spot at the base of a blackberry bush near an alder swale in Hancock Co., Maine (see illus.), from day female carried 1st material until young left nest 27 days later. Incubation, which required 11–12 days for 4 eggs, ap-parently began the evening before last egg was laid. Female very tame; eventually permitting her back to be stroked while she incubated. Several males sang in adjacent territories, indicating a loose colony.

CANADA WARBLER *Wilsonia canadensis*

Breeding range: N. Wisconsin, n. Michigan to Maine, south to n. New Jersey, Pennsylvania, nw. Ohio; and in mountains to e. Tennessee, w. Maryland, W. Virginia, w. N. Carolina, nw. Georgia.

Habitat: Heavy woodland undergrowth, swamps, streambanks, moist brushlands, deep ravines, rhododendron thickets.

Nest: On or near ground in mossy hummock, cavity in bank, upturned tree root, rotted moss-covered stump, log. Bulky structure of grasses, weed stems, bark fibers, skeletonized leaves, built on base of large dead leaves; lined with rootlets, plant down, hair. Outside diam. 4½ x 5 in. (11.4 x 12.7 cm), height 2½ in. (6.4 cm); inside diam. 2¼ x 2½ in. (5.7 x 6.4 cm), depth 1½–1¾ in. (3.8–4.4 cm); entrance 2 in. (5.1 cm) wide.

Eggs: 3–5, commonly 4; av. 17.2 x 13.1 mm. Oval to short-oval. Shell smooth, has slight gloss. White, creamy white; dotted, spotted, sometimes blotched with browns, often concentrated at large end. Incubation by female; period unknown, probably 12 days. 1 brood.

Notes: In 1 nest under observation male did not feed female while she incubated but brought food to nest with eggs on several occasions when female was absent, proffering food to eggs. Since male feeds young, this act believed "anticipatory feeding behavior." Of 8 nests found by author, 5 were in cavities in steep banks, 2 in rotted stumps, 1 in mossy hummock (see illus.).

207

AMERICAN REDSTART *Setophaga ruticilla*

Breeding range: Wisconsin to Maine, south to s. Alabama, w. Georgia, N. Carolina.

Habitat: Young or second-growth deciduous (mostly) or coniferous woods, roadside trees, thickets, gardens, parks.

Nest: Placed in pronged fork of tree, shrub, 4–30 ft. (1.2–9.1 m) above ground. Firm, compactly woven cup of plant down, bark fibers, small rootlets, grass stems; lined with fine grasses, weed stems, hair, sometimes feathers; decorated on outside with lichens, birch bark, bud scales, plant down; bound with spider silk. Built entirely by female, typically requiring 1 wk. or more. Similar to Yellow Warbler's nest but has neater construction, thinner walls. American Goldfinch nest wider than high; American Redstart higher than wide. Outside diam. 2¾ in. (7.0 cm), height 3 in. (7.6 cm); inside diam. 1¾ in. (4.4 cm), depth 1½ in. (3.8 cm).

Eggs: 4, sometimes 2–3, rarely 5; av. 16.2 x 12.3 mm. Oval to short-oval. Shell smooth, has slight gloss. White, grayish white, creamy white, greenish white; dotted, spotted, blotched with browns, grays; often concentrated at large end. Incubation by female; 12–13 days. Commonly 1 brood.

Notes: At nest in Ottawa Co., Ohio, female built in 2½–3 days, making 650–700 trips to nest with material. Like Yellow Warbler, sometimes builds nest floor over Brown-headed Cowbird eggs.

208

HOUSE SPARROW *Passer domesticus*

Breeding range: Throughout e. U.S.
Habitat: Cities, villages, farms, parks.
Nest: Commonly in any cavity: birdhouses, porch rafters, holes in walls, billboard braces, tree holes; awnings, behind shutters, etc. Ancestral Weaver Finch type of nest often constructed, especially in rural areas: huge ball of grasses, weeds, trash; opening on side; securely lodged in fork of a tree branch. Built by both sexes; mostly of grasses, weeds; lined with many feathers (chicken), some hair, string. Size varies with size of area to be filled.
Eggs: 3–7, commonly 5; av. 22.8 x 15.4 mm. Oval to long-oval. Shell smooth, slight gloss. White, greenish white; dotted, spotted with grays, browns. Incubation by female; 12–13 days. Normally 2 broods; perhaps 3 occasionally.
Notes: Birds often carry nest material weeks before eggs are laid, causing unfounded speculation that species breeds most of year. Very aggressive in appropriating nest cavities of native birds, often ejecting occupants. Gourdlike nests of Cliff Swallows sometimes usurped; in New York report, pair of Cliff Swallows successfully raised House Sparrow from egg laid in their nest. Have been observed using holes of Bank Swallows as nesting sites. In one season same nest site used by 2 females to raise 4 broods of young.

BOBOLINK *Dolichonyx oryzivorus*

Breeding range: Wisconsin to Maine, south to cen. Illinois, Indiana, Ohio, n. W. Virginia, w. Maryland, Pennsylvania, cen. New Jersey, locally and irregularly farther south.

Habitat: Open fields, especially hayfields, moist meadows.

Nest: Commonly in dense stands of vegetation: hay, clover, alfalfa, weeds. Rarely built off ground in low vegetation. Slight hollow in ground, natural or scraped by female, loosely filled with coarse grasses, weed stalks; lined with fine grasses. Diam. about 2¼-2½ in. (5.7-6.4 cm); depth 1½ in. (3.8 cm).

Eggs: 4-7, commonly 5-6; av. 21.08 x 15.71 mm. Oval to short-oval. Shell smooth, somewhat glossy. Pale gray, buff, cinnamon; heavily, irregularly spotted, blotched with browns. Some so heavily marked ground color almost hidden. Incubation by female; 13 days. 1 brood.

Notes: Nest very difficult to find. Female cannot be followed to it or flushed from it — runs through grass before flying. In approaching nest, birds land some distance away and walk through concealing vegetation. Population decreasing in East as a result of fewer hayfields, earlier mowing, and use of modern cutting and raking equipment. Bobolinks are being replaced in much of habitat by eastward movement of Brewer's Blackbird and by meadow-nesting Red-winged Blackbirds.

EASTERN MEADOWLARK *Sturnella magna*

Breeding range: E. U.S., except s. Florida. Resident south of Ohio R. Valley, and on coast from s. New England south.

Habitat: Open farm fields, meadows, pastures, prairies.

Nest: Natural or scraped depression in ground lined first with coarse dried grasses, with inner lining of finer grasses, sometimes horsehair. Dome-shaped roof or canopy constructed of grasses loosely interwoven with and attached to surrounding vegetation. Opening on side. Female alone builds in 3–8 days, often continues after egg-laying starts. Female may start 1 or more nests before final site determination made. Most nests have obvious trails leading to nest through surrounding vegetation. *Indistinguishable from nest of Western* Meadowlark (see p. 212). Outside diam. 6½ in. (16.5 cm), height 7 in. (17.8 cm), usually higher in rear; opening 3½ in. (8.9 cm) wide, 4 in. (10.2 cm) high.

Eggs: 3–5, rarely 2 or 6; av. 27.75 x 20.35 mm. Oval to short- or long-oval. Shell smooth, has moderate gloss. White; profusely spotted, blotched, dotted over entire surface with browns, lavender, especially at large end. Incubation by female; 13–15 days, av. 14; may begin with laying of 3rd, 4th, 5th egg in 5-egg clutch. Male often polygamous. 2 broods. *Eggs indistinguishable from Western Meadowlark's.*

Notes: See discussion of Western Meadowlark, p. 212.

211

WESTERN MEADOWLARK *Sturnella neglecta*

Breeding range: Wisconsin, n. and cen. Illinois, Michigan. Extending range; song has been reported from as far east as Maine.
Habitat: Same as for Eastern Meadowlark, see p. 211.
Nest: *Indistinguishable from Eastern Meadowlark's.*
Eggs: *Indistinguishable from Eastern Meadowlark's.*
Notes: Eastern and Western Meadowlarks are almost identical in appearance. Nests and eggs are so similar that positive identification of either species, where ranges overlap, depends upon hearing male's song, which is decidedly different for each species and thus diagnostic. Before 1910 Western Meadowlark was considered by American Ornithologists' Union as subspecies of Eastern Meadowlark and was named *Sturnella magna neglecta*. Hybridization may exist, but where ranges overlap typical birds with typical songs are found breeding in same region, even in same fields, a condition not supposed to occur with subspecies. Observer must be careful to see and *hear* male in whose territory nest and eggs are found. Sight of female at nest is insufficient. Since male does not visit

nest during incubation, singing bird must be related to nest by territory. Identification will become a greater problem as species moves eastward. In past 60 yrs., Western Meadowlark has become a common breeder in n. and cen. Illinois, where it was previously considered rare.

212

YELLOW-HEADED BLACKBIRD
Xanthocephalus xanthocephalus

Breeding range: Wisconsin, n. and w. Michigan, n. Illinois (locally). Extending eastward; sight records regularly in Indiana, Ohio.

Habitat: Freshwater sloughs, marshy borders of lakes.

Nest: In large thickly populated colonies, as many as 25–30 nests in an area 225 sq. ft. (21 sq. m), in aquatic vegetation (cattails, reeds) invariably over water 2–4 ft. (0.6–1.2 m) or more deep, 6–36 in. (15.2–91.4 cm) above water level. Bulky structure of water-soaked aquatic vegetation woven to upright growing plants; lined with pieces of broad dry aquatic vegetation. Nest shrinks while drying, drawing stems tight around supports. Built entirely by female in 2–4 days. Female often abandons unfinished nests; may build 3–4 before laying eggs. Outside diam. 5 x 6 in. (12.7 x 15.2 cm), height 4 in. (10.2 cm); inside diam. 3 in. (7.6 cm), depth 2½ in. (6.4 cm).

Eggs: 3–5, commonly 4; av. 25.83 x 17.92 mm. Oval to long-oval. Shell smooth, rather glossy. Pale grayish white, pale greenish white; profusely dotted, blotched over entire egg with browns, grays. Incubation by female alone; 12–13 days, often starting with laying of 2nd egg. Males polygamous, may have 2–3 mates.

Notes: Females land in vegetation 5–6 ft. (1.5–1.8 m) away to approach nest.

RED-WINGED BLACKBIRD *Agelaius phoeniceus*

Breeding range: Throughout e. U.S.

Habitat: Fresh and saltwater marshes, swamps, wet meadows, streamside bushes, dry fields, pastures.

Nest: In loose colonies in cattails, rushes, sedges, reeds, bushes (alder, willow), preferably near or over water; also in weeds, grass tussocks, bushes, low trees in dry areas. Sedge leaves, rushes, grasses, rootlets, mosses bound to surrounding vegetation with milkweed fibers; lined with fine grasses; placed 3 in. to 14 ft. (7.6 cm to 4.3 m) above ground or water. Built entirely by female in 3–6 days.

Eggs: 3–4, rarely more or less; av. 24.80 x 17.55 mm. Oval. Shell smooth, moderately glossy. Pale bluish green; spotted, blotched, marbled, scrawled, with browns, purples, black; mostly concentrated at large end. Incubation entirely by female; 10–12 days, av. 11. Often 2 broods. Males monogamous or polygamous, some mated to 2–3 females. Males probably breed when 2 yrs. old; females 1 yr.

Notes: Road count at Ithaca, New York, revealed densities of breeding males to be 16 per 100 acres (40.5 ha) of marsh, 11 per 100 acres of upland habitat. In 840 nests, 38 percent had 3 eggs, 53 percent had 4. In 926 nests, clutch size av. 3.5 per nest. 25 males in Wisconsin marsh: 5 had 1 mate each, 16 had 2, 4 had 3.

ORCHARD ORIOLE *Icterus spurius*

Breeding range: Cen. Wisconsin, s. Michigan (locally), Ohio, cen. New York, s. New England (sparingly) south to Gulf Coast and n. Florida.

Habitat: Farms, suburbs, country roadsides, orchards, open woodlands. Shuns heavy forests.

Nest: Hung between horizontally forked branches of tree, shrub; well concealed among leaves, 4–70 ft. (1.2–21.3 m) above ground, commonly 10–20 ft. (3.0–6.1 m); in South, often within festoons of Spanish moss. Deeply hollowed, thin-walled, basketlike structure with contracted rim, securely woven of grasses; lined with finer grasses, some plant down. Depth usually less than outside diam.; not as pendulous as nest of Northern Oriole. Invariable use of grasses, often for entire structure, diagnostic. Built by female in 3–6 days. Outside diam. 3½–4 in. (8.9–10.2 cm), height 2½–4 in. (6.4–10.2 cm); inside diam. 2½–3 in. (6.4–7.6 cm), depth 2¼–3 in. (5.7–7.6 cm).

Eggs: 3–7, commonly 4–5; av. 20.47 x 14.54 mm. Oval. Shell smooth, has no gloss. Pale bluish white; spotted, blotched, scrawled with browns, purples, grays, over entire egg; sometimes concentrated at large end. Incubation by female; 12–14 days; female fed by male while on nest. Normally 1 brood.

Notes: Propensity of species to nest in same tree with Eastern Kingbird observed often.

215

NORTHERN (BALTIMORE) ORIOLE *Icterus galbula*

Breeding range: Wisconsin to Maine, south to cen. Mississippi, cen. Alabama, n. Georgia, w. S. Carolina, w. N. Carolina, cen. Virginia, n. Maryland.

Habitat: Suburban shade trees, groves, orchards, parks, roadsides.

Nest: In elms, maples, willows, apples by preference; also many other trees; 6–60 ft. (1.8–18.3 m) above ground, av. 25–30 ft. (7.6–9.1 m). Attached by rim to drooping branch; intricately woven deep pouch of plant fibers (milkweed, Indian hemp), hair, yarn, string, grapevine bark; Spanish moss in South; lined with hair, wool, fine grasses, cottony materials; opening at top, rarely at side. Female normally builds new nest every year in 4½–8 days. Outside height 3½–8 in. (8.9–20.3 cm), av. 5 in. (12.7 cm); oval entrance 2 x 3¼ in. (5.1 x 8.3 cm); inside width, 2½ in. (6.4 cm), depth av. 4½ in. (11.4 cm).

Eggs: Typically 4, often 5, rarely 6; av. 23.03 x 15.45 mm. Oval

to long-oval. Shell smooth, has slight gloss. Pale grayish white, pale bluish white; streaked, scrawled, blotched with browns, black; generally concentrated at large end. Incubation by female; 12–14 days. 1 brood.

Notes: June 8, 1972, Northern Orioles were found nesting in Key West cemetery — 1st record for Florida.

216

RUSTY BLACKBIRD *Euphagus carolinus*

Breeding range: Northern border of U.S. south to n. Vermont, n. New Hampshire, cen. Maine, ne. New York (Adirondacks).

Habitat: Tree-bordered marshes, swampy woodlands, muskegs.

Nest: Single, not in colonies. Commonly placed in thick growth of evergreens (spruce, balsam), also in deciduous bushes in marshes, along stream borders, 2–20 ft. (0.6–6.1 m) above ground or water, usually less than 10 ft. (3 m). Bulky but well built of twigs, lichens, leaves, grasses, with inner cup of wet rotting vegetation ¼–½ in. (0.6–1.3 cm) thick; lined with green grasses, fine twigs. Outside diam. 7 in. (17.8 cm), height 5½ in. (14 cm); inside diam. 3½ in. (8.9 cm), depth 2½ in. (6.4 cm).

Eggs: 4–5; av. 25.8 x 18.6 mm. Oval. Shell smooth; has slight gloss. Pale bluish green; spotted, blotched with browns, grays; usually heaviest at large end. Aid to identification: absence of scrawls typically present on eggs of other blackbird species. Incubation by female alone; about 14 days. Male feeds incubating mate.

Notes: Birds attached to nesting site, returning from year to year. Nests so well constructed they last several years; nevertheless female builds new nest annually. Each pair demands large breeding territory; nests ½ mi. (.8 km) or more apart.

PAINTED BUNTING *Passerina ciris*
(proper order after Indigo Bunting, p. 227)

Breeding range: N. Mississippi, sw. Tennessee, se. N. Carolina south to the Gulf Coast and cen. Florida.

Habitat: Towns, thickets, bushy fields, roadsides.

Nest: Firmly attached to twigs or other supporting vegetation at low elevations, commonly 3–6 ft. (0.9–1.8 m), in bushes, vine tangles, low trees. Sometimes placed as high as 14 ft. (4.3 m) above ground in festoons of Spanish moss. Shallow cup, well made, woven of grasses, weed stems, leaves; lined with fine grasses, rootlets, hair. Built by female in as little as 2 days (may complete lining after 1st egg laid).

Eggs: 3–4, rarely 5; av. 18.9 x 14.5 mm. Oval to short-oval. Shell smooth, has slight gloss. White, bluish white, grayish white; spotted with reddish brown; markings often concentrated at large end. Incubation by female alone; 11–12 days, often beginning with laying of next to last egg. Normally 2 broods; in South 3 reported occasionally.

Notes: While female tends fledged young unassisted, she carries fresh nesting material to new site for 2nd brood. Just before egg-laying male suddenly, dramatically, takes charge of 1st brood, which female then abandons. Not all females have 2 broods. Some mate with polygamous males, which may at the same time be mated to double-brooded females.

BREWER'S BLACKBIRD *Euphagus cyanocephalus*

Breeding range: Wisconsin, Michigan, n. Illinois, n. Indiana.
Habitat: Open farmlands, roadsides, towns, gardens, groves, marsh edges.
Nest: In loose colonies or single; on ground in thick weedy cover, in shrubs or in trees as high as 150 ft. (45.7 m) above ground. Sturdy structure of interlaced twigs, grasses, often strengthened by mud, cow dung; lined with rootlets, grasses, horsehair. Ground nests most common in eastern part of range. Built by female. Outside diam. 5–6 in. (12.7–15.2 cm), height 3¼ in. (8.3 cm); inside diam. 3 in. (7.6 cm), depth 1½ in. (3.8 cm).
Eggs: Commonly 5, often 4, 6, occasionally 3, 7; av. 25.49 x 18.60 mm. Oval to long-oval. Shell smooth, has slight gloss. Light gray, greenish gray; spotted, blotched with grayish brown, sepia; sometimes ground color completely obscured by overlay of dark brown dots, blotches. Incubation by female; 12–14 days. Females probably breed 1st year; males 2nd. Males monogamous or polygamous (normally 2 mates, occasionally 3, rarely 4).

Notes: In early 1900s, limit of eastern range was Red River Valley, Minnesota. Eastern expansion triggered by production of suitable habitat plus population buildup in Minnesota. Within 60 yrs. species has expanded range 700 miles (1126 km) in Great Lakes region. Since 1926 eastern extension very rapid.

218

BOAT-TAILED GRACKLE *Cassidix major*

Breeding range: Atlantic Coast, s. New Jersey to Florida Keys; Gulf Coast to Louisiana; inland throughout Florida. Resident in southern part of range.

Habitat: Open coastal areas, islands, fresh and saltwater marshes. In Florida, dooryard bird in cities, suburbs, farms, roadsides.

Nest: In colonies, generally near or over water in willows, cattails, saw grass, bulrushes; 1–4 ft. (0.3–1.2 m) above ground or water; also in trees up to 40–50 ft. (12.2–15.2 m) above ground, av. 10–12 ft. (3.0–3.7 m). Bulky, loosely constructed, open cup on foundation of grasses, rushes, vines; woven around tree twigs or stems of surrounding vegetation; lined with mud, then with fine grasses, weed stems. Female builds in 4–5 days. Nests vary greatly in size, depending on location; inside diam. av. 4–5 in. (10.2–12.7 cm), depth 2¾–4 in. (7.0–10.2 cm).

Eggs: Normally 3, occasionally 4, rarely 2, 5; av. 31.60 x 22.49 mm. Long-oval to oval. Shell smooth, has slight gloss. Light blue, pale bluish gray; boldly spotted, scrawled with browns, grays, purples, black. Incubation by female alone; 13 days; starts before clutch complete. Males monogamous or polygamous. Probably 2 broods.

Notes: Some observers contend males promiscuous, not polygamous; and that females leave males when sexual mating accomplished.

219

COMMON GRACKLE *Quiscalus quiscula*

Breeding range: Throughout e. U.S. Resident in much of range.
Habitat: Cities, suburbs, farms, marshes, swampy thickets, coniferous groves.
Nest: Usually in small colonies of 20–30 pairs in deciduous, coniferous trees up to 60 ft. (18.3 m) above ground; also in shrubs, roadside plantings; natural cavities, ledges; cattail marshes, 1–3 ft. (30.5–91.4 cm) above water. Loose, bulky structure of weed stalks, grasses, debris; sometimes reinforced with mud on inside; lined with grasses, feathers, fine debris. Female builds in about 11 days. Nests sometimes deserted in early stages of construction. Outside diam. 7–9 in. (17.8–22.9 cm), height 5–8 in. (12.7–20.3 cm); inside diam. 4–4½ in. (10.2–11.4 cm), depth 3–3¾ in. (7.6–9.5 cm).
Eggs: 3–6, commonly 5; av. 28.53 x 20.89 mm. Oval. Shell smooth, has slight gloss. Pale greenish white, pale yellow-brown; blotched, scrawled, spotted with dark browns, purples. Incubation by female alone; 11–12 days. Probably 1 brood.
Notes: Unusual nesting sites include a cavity in the lower part of an Osprey's nest in New Jersey; Wood Duck nesting boxes in

pond at Somesville, Mt. Desert I., Maine. American Robin found incubating 4 Grackle eggs in Robin's nest; female Grackle tried to dislodge Robin; broken Robin egg on ground under nest. Robin incubated 6 days before nest destroyed.

220

BROWN-HEADED COWBIRD *Molothrus ater*

Breeding range: Wisconsin to Maine, south to Gulf Coast and n. Florida.

Habitat: Farmlands; open deciduous, coniferous woods; forest edges, suburban gardens, shade trees.

Nest: Parasitic species; builds no nest. Lays eggs in nests of other birds, depending on host to hatch eggs, raise young.

Eggs: 1 egg laid per day until clutch of 6 or more laid, often in different nests. After interval of several days, 2nd clutch laid. Possibly 3–4 clutches per season. Total of eggs laid probably 11–20. Av. size 21.45 x 16.42 mm. Typically oval; shape varies greatly. Shell granulated, moderately glossy. White, grayish white; evenly dotted with browns; often heavier markings at large end. Incubation by host; 11–12 days.

Notes: Of 214 species known to have been parasitized, 121 have raised young Cowbirds successfully. Yellow Warbler and Song Sparrow are most heavily victimized. Record numbers Cowbird eggs in 1 nest of: Wood Thrush, 9; 4 species each, 8; 3 species each, 7. Author found Red-eyed Vireo in Pennsylvania incubating 4 Cowbird eggs, no Vireo eggs. Cowbird lays egg at dawn; removes egg of host day before or day after parasitic egg laid. Host may desert nest, build floor over Cowbird egg, throw it out, or accept it. Gray Catbird and American Robin known to throw eggs out.

221

SCARLET TANAGER *Piranga olivacea*

Breeding range: Wisconsin to Maine, south to n. Mississippi, cen. Alabama, cen. Georgia, nw. S. Carolina, W. Virginia, Maryland.
Habitat: Deciduous, coniferous woodlands; groves, parks, orchards, roadsides.
Nest: 8–75 ft. (2.4–22.9 m) above ground, well out on limb of tree, commonly oak. Small, flimsy, flat cup built by female of twigs, rootlets; lined with weed stems, grasses. Eggs sometimes seen from ground through shallow bottom of nest.
Eggs: 3–5, commonly 4; av. 23.3 x 16.5 mm. Oval, sometimes short-oval. Shell smooth, moderately glossy. Pale blue, pale green; irregularly dotted, spotted, blotched with browns; markings often concentrated at large end, sometimes capped; generally not so bold as on eggs of Summer Tanager. Smaller than eggs of Rose-breasted Grosbeak. Incubation by female alone; 13–14 days.
Notes: Of 29 nests studied in Pennsylvania only 1, containing full clutch of 4 eggs and no Brown-headed Cowbird eggs, was accessible for photography (see illus.; note string used to attach nest to branch). 19 nests were in oaks, 4 in maples, 2 each in hemlock, apple, 1 each in elm, tulip. 8 were 60 ft. (18.3 m) or more from ground, highest 75 ft. (22.9 m); 11 were between 35–50 ft. (10.7–15.2 m), lowest was 9 ft. (2.7 m) in oak.

222

SUMMER TANAGER *Piranga rubra*

Breeding range: Illinois, Ohio, W. Virginia, Maryland, Delaware south to Gulf Coast and Florida.

Habitat: Open, dry, deciduous (mostly), coniferous woods, groves, orchards, roadsides.

Nest: Placed on horizontal limb (often oak) 10–35 ft. (3.0–10.7 m) above ground, well out from trunk. Flimsy, flat, well-concealed cup of weed stems, bark, leaves, grasses, Spanish moss, spider silk; lined with fine grasses. Only female carries material and builds, accompanied by male. Outside diam. 3¼ x 4⅝ in. (8.3 x 11.0 cm), height 2³⁄₁₆ in. (5.6 cm); inside diam. 2⁷⁄₁₆ x 3 in. (6.2 x 7.6 cm), depth 1⅜ in. (3.5 cm).

Eggs: 3–4, rarely 5; av. 23.1 x 17.1 mm. Commonly oval, varying to short- or long-oval. Shell smooth, moderately glossy. Pale blue, pale green; speckled, spotted, blotched with browns, faint undertones of gray; markings well distributed over entire egg, sometimes concentrated or capped at large end. Markings bolder than on similar eggs of Scarlet Tanager. Incubation by female; 11–12 days. Male usually feeds incubating mate. 1 brood.

Notes: Where ranges of 2 species of tanagers overlap, positive identification of similar nest and eggs should not be made until bird is seen. Georgia nest (illus. above) in post oak only 11 ft. (3.4 m) from ground.

223

CARDINAL *Cardinalis cardinalis*

Breeding range: Throughout e. U.S.; local, rare, or absent in northern border regions. Still extending range northward.

Habitat: Thickets, forest edges, groves, suburban gardens, parks; deep forests typically shunned.

Nest: Placed in dense shrubbery, small deciduous, coniferous tree, thicket, vine, briar tangle, 3-20 ft. (0.9-6.1 m) above ground, generally below 10 ft. (3 m). Loosely built of twigs, vines, some leaves, bark strips, grasses, weed stalks, rootlets; lined with fine grasses, hair. Female builds in 3-9 days, occasionally assisted by male. Period as long as 6 days may elapse between nest completion and laying of 1st egg.

Eggs: 2-5, commonly 3-4; av. 25.3 x 18.2 mm. Typically oval, sometimes long- or short-oval. Shell smooth, somewhat glossy. Grayish, bluish, greenish white; dotted, spotted, blotched with browns, grays, purples. Some so thickly marked, ground color almost obliterated; others sparingly spotted. Incubation by female; 12-13 days (male has been observed on nest occasionally). Normally 2-3 broods, rarely 4.

Notes: Similar nest of Gray Catbird invariably contains many leaves in foundation (absent or sparse in Cardinal nest), is generally smaller, lined with rootlets (lining of fine grasses in Cardinal nest). Cases of 2 females sharing same nest simultaneously reported several times. 1 nest shared with Song Sparrow.

ROSE-BREASTED GROSBEAK *Pheucticus ludovicianus*

Breeding range: Wisconsin to Maine, south to cen. Illinois, cen. Indiana, cen. Ohio, w. Pennsylvania, s. New Jersey, e. Maryland (locally); in mountains to cen. Tennessee, n. Georgia.

Habitat: Moist, deciduous, second-growth woods, swamp borders, thickets, old orchards, suburban trees, shrubs.

Nest: Generally in fork of deciduous tree, shrub (occasionally conifer), 6–26 ft. (1.8–7.9 m) above ground, av. 10–15 ft. (3.0–4.6 m). Nest often so flimsy that eggs may be seen through lining from ground.

Eggs: 3–6, commonly 4; av. 24.6 x 17.7 mm. Typically oval. Shell smooth, has slight gloss. Pale gray, green, blue, bluish green; dotted, spotted, blotched with browns, purples; generally wreathed or capped at large end. Similar to eggs of Scarlet Tanager but larger and usually more heavily marked. Incubation by both sexes; 12–14 days. Both birds sing while incubating, especially male. Typically 1 brood, occasionally 2.

Notes: In Cook Forest State Park, Pennsylvania, author found nest in fork formed by 4 branches of rhododendron; nest contained 757 twigs 1–5 in. (2.5–12.7 cm) long. Lining was ¾ in. (1.9 cm) thick, made entirely of hemlock twigs. Nests have been found in wide variety of shrubs and trees. Apparently any small tree or shrub will do so long as it provides sufficient shelter.

225

BLUE GROSBEAK *Guiraca caerulea*

Breeding range: S. Illinois, cen. Kentucky, se. Pennsylvania, Maryland, s. New Jersey south to Gulf Coast and cen. Florida.

Habitat: Old fields overgrown to brambles; brushy edges, scrubby thickets, open groves, hedgerows.

Nest: Placed in low tree or bush, tangle of vegetation (vines, briars), 3–8 ft. (0.9–2.4 m) above ground, typically at edge of an open area. Compact, rather deep structure of grasses, bark strips, leaves, weed stems, snakeskins, cotton; lined with rootlets, hair (sometimes), grasses. Inside diam. 2⅜ in. (6 cm), depth 2 in. (5.1 cm).

Eggs: 3–5, commonly 4; av. 22.0 x 16.8 mm. Typically oval. Shell smooth, has slight gloss. Unlike all other grosbeak eggs, white or pale blue, unmarked (rarely spotted with browns). Pale blue color often fades before hatching. Incubation probably by female; period unknown. Typically 2 broods.

Notes: Although not so well known as the Great-crested Flycatcher for its characteristic use of cast-off snakeskins in nest construction, the Blue Grosbeak probably uses this material as often as the

Great-crested Flycatcher. In 23 nests reported in New Mexico, 21 had snakeskins as a foundation. A Georgia nest was reported almost entirely covered with cast-off snakeskins. In southern part of range nest often placed near ground in sweet gum (see illus.).

INDIGO BUNTING *Passerina cyanea*

Breeding range: Wisconsin to Maine, south to s. Mississippi and cen. Florida.

Habitat: Open brushy fields, clearings, hedgerows, roadside thickets, edges of woods, overgrown fence rows; avoids mature forests.

Nest: Placed in crotch of bush, shrub, low tree, tangle of black-berries, cane thicket (*Arundinaria*); firmly attached by rim and sides to supporting plants 2–12 ft. (0.6–3.7 m) above ground in dense cover. Well-woven cup of dried grasses, bark strips, twigs, weeds on base of leaves; lined with fine grasses, cotton, rootlets, sometimes hair, feathers. Sometimes uses snakeskins in foundation. Spanish moss often used in outer structure. Shape may be oval or round. Female builds alone. Outside diam. 3¼–4½ in. (8.3–11.4 cm), height 2½–3 in. (6.4–7.6 cm); inside diam. 1¾–2¾ in. (4.4–7.0 cm), depth 1½–2½ in. (3.8–6.4 cm).

Eggs: 2–6, commonly 3–4; av. 18.7 x 13.7 mm. Oval to short-oval. Shell smooth, has slight gloss. White, pale bluish white; unmarked. Resemble eggs of Blue Grosbeak but smaller. Incubation by female alone; 12–13 days. 1 or 2 broods.

Notes: Heavily parasitized by Brown-headed Cowbird.

PAINTED BUNTING
Passerina ciris p. 217

DICKCISSEL *Spiza americana*

Breeding range: N. Wisconsin, s. Michigan; sporadically in w. Ohio, w.-cen. New York, s. Pennsylvania, Maryland; south to W. Virginia (locally), Georgia, Alabama, Mississippi. Extending range north and south.

Habitat: Meadows, hayfields, prairies.

Nest: Placed on or near ground, typically well hidden in rank growth of clover, alfalfa, grass, weeds. Bulky but substantial shallow cup of weeds, grass stems, leaves; lined with finer grasses, rootlets, hair; loosely interwoven with surrounding vegetation. Female alone builds in about 4 days. Av. size 10 nests: outside diam. 4¹³⁄₁₆ (12.2 cm), height 2½ in. (6.4 cm); inside diam. 2⅜ x 2¹¹⁄₁₆ in. (6.0 x 6.8 cm), depth 1¹³⁄₁₆ in. (4.6 cm).

Eggs: 3–5, commonly 4; av. 20.8 x 15.7 mm. Oval to long-oval. Shell smooth, glossy. Pale blue, unmarked. Incubation by female alone; 11–12 days. Typically 2 broods. Incubation may start with laying of next to last egg. Male may occasionally be polygamous.

Notes: Of 78 Illinois nests, 68 were in meadows. Nests very difficult to find. Female approaches from distance walking on ground; after eggs hatch shyness diminishes. Species erratic in distribution; may fluctuate from year to year in entire region.

EVENING GROSBEAK *Hesperiphona vespertina*

Breeding range: N. Wisconsin, n. Michigan, n. New York, Vermont, New Hampshire, Maine, Massachusetts (locally). Has bred in Connecticut.

Habitat: Coniferous forests.

Nest: Placed in conifer 20–60 ft. (6.1–18.3 m) above ground; occasionally in deciduous tree. Female builds frail, loosely constructed elliptical cup almost entirely of twigs interwoven with mosses or lichens; lined with rootlets. Outside diam. $4\frac{5}{16}$ x $5\frac{7}{8}$ in. (11.0 x 14.9 cm), height $5\frac{1}{8}$ in. (13 cm); inside diam. $3\frac{3}{16}$ x $3\frac{11}{16}$ in. (8.1 x 9.4 cm), depth $2\frac{13}{16}$ in. (7.1 cm).

Eggs: 2–5, commonly 3–4; av. 24.5 x 17.5 mm. Oval, rarely slightly pyriform. Shell smooth, has little gloss. Clear blue or blue-green; blotched, spotted with browns, grays, purples, with occasional fine black-pencil markings. Somewhat resemble eggs of Red-winged Blackbird. Incubation by female alone; period unknown.

Notes: With southern winter incursions to feeding stations increasing annually, breeding-range extension anticipated.

PINE SISKIN *Spinus pinus*
(proper order after Pine Grosbeak, p. 231)

Breeding range: N. Wisconsin, cen. Michigan, New York, n. Pennsylvania, Maine, Vermont, New Hampshire; casually in s. New England and mountains to Tennessee, N. Carolina. Erratic and irregular nesters; breeding place may vary from year to year within this range.

Habitat: Coniferous forests.

Nest: May be single, but typically in loose colonies. Concealed on horizontal conifer branch, generally well out from trunk, 6–35 ft. (1.8–10.7 m) above ground, av. 20 ft. (6.1 m), in natural stand or evergreen planting. Female chooses site, builds large shallow cup of twigs, grasses, mosses, lichens, bark strips, rootlets; lines it with mosses, rootlets, hair, fur, feathers. Outside diam. 4 in. (10.2 cm), height $1\frac{1}{2}$ in. (3.8 cm); inside diam. 2 in. (5.1 cm), depth $\frac{3}{4}$–$1\frac{1}{4}$ in. (1.9–3.2 cm).

Eggs: 2–6, commonly 3–4; av. 16.6 x 12.4 mm. Oval to short-oval. Shell smooth, has very little gloss. Pale greenish blue; spotted, dotted with browns, black, generally wreathed at large end. Incubation by female alone; 13 days, and said to start with 1st egg, which reduces chance of frozen eggs in early nestings. Male feeds female throughout incubation period.

Notes: Pine Siskins vary from year to year in choice of breeding place. From mid-March to May, the urge to nest breaks wandering winter flocks into pairs wherever they may be throughout their range. Small territory established and defended around nest — 3–6 ft. (0.9–1.8 m) — but birds continue to feed in flocks.

PURPLE FINCH *Carpodacus purpureus*

Breeding range: Cen. Wisconsin to Maine, south to n. Illinois, n. and e. Ohio, w. and ne. Pennsylvania, n. New Jersey; in mountains to Maryland, W. Virginia.

Habitat: Coniferous forests, roadside conifers, Christmas tree plantings.

Nest: Almost always placed on horizontal branch of conifer (fork of small tree), 5–60 ft. (1.5–18.3 m) above ground. Female builds well-concealed, neat, shallow cup of twigs, grasses, weed stems, bark strips, rootlets; lined with fine grasses, hair.

Eggs: 3–5, commonly 4; av. 20.2 x 14.6 mm. Oval to short-oval. Shell smooth, has slight gloss. Pale greenish blue; dotted, spotted, scrawled in short lines with browns and black; markings scattered over entire egg, generally heaviest at large end. Incubation by female; 13 days.

Notes: Commercial evergreen plantings (Christmas trees) have influenced range extension of species. Author has seen and heard of numerous nests in spruces, pines, at edges of busy parking lots  and city parks. Species noted for ability to conceal nest in clusters of needles. Often nest cannot be seen from ground. In courtship, male occasionally picks up nesting material (conifer twig or needle) as he approaches mate. This gesture does not indicate male's participation in nest construction.

HOUSE FINCH *Carpodacus mexicanus*

Breeding range: Se. New York, Connecticut, Rhode Island, e. Massachusetts, New Jersey, e. Pennsylvania, Delaware. Extending range.

Habitat: Cities, suburbs, parks, farms, open woods; adapts easily to civilized environment.

Nest: Site quite varied. Twigs, grasses, debris placed in tree cavities, birdboxes, building ledges.

Eggs: 2-6, commonly 4-5; av. 18.8 x 13.8 mm. Typically oval. Shell smooth, has slight gloss. Pale bluish green; sparingly spotted, dotted with black. Incubation by female; 12-14 days. 2 or more broods.

Notes: Shipped illegally from California to New York as "Hollywood Finches" in 1940; released by dealers to avoid prosecution. Quickly established as breeding bird on Long I. and has been increasing range ever since.

PINE GROSBEAK *Pinicola enucleator*

Breeding range: N. New England mountains (infrequent resident). Has nested in n. Wisconsin.

Habitat: Cold spruce forests, typically at high elevations.

Nest: Low in conifer or underbrush of coniferous forest. Bulky structure of mosses, twigs, grasses, lichens; lined with hair. Resembles nest of Blue Jay.

Eggs: 2-5, commonly 4; av. 26.0 x 18.3 mm. Oval to long-oval. Shell smooth, has slight gloss. Pale grayish green; spotted, blotched with browns, purples, black. Incubation by female; 13-14 days. Male feeds incubating mate. 1 brood.

PINE SISKIN *Spinus pinus* p. 229

LE CONTE'S SPARROW *Ammospiza leconteii*
(proper order after Henslow's Sparrow, p. 237)

Breeding range: N. and cen. Wisconsin, n. Michigan; casually farther south.

Habitat: Grassy meadows, prairies, marsh borders.

Nest: Typically placed slightly above ground beneath tangle of dead rushes, grasses, sedges, where dead and fallen vegetation is thickest. Female alone builds well-concealed, shallow, well-rounded cup of dry grasses interwoven with surrounding standing stems. Nest similar to nest of Henslow's Sparrow. Outside diam. 3½ x 4½ in. (8.9 x 11.4 cm); inside diam. 2¼ in. (5.7 cm), depth 1¼ in. (3.2 cm).

Eggs: 3-5, commonly 4; av. 18.0 x 13.7 mm. Oval. Shell smooth, has slight gloss. Grayish white; dotted, spotted, blotched with browns, black, generally over entire egg. Incubation by female; period unknown, probably 12-13 days.

Notes: Species is more numerous than generally realized. Its very secretive habits and insectlike song, not easily recognized as that of a bird, may cause many bird watchers to pass it by.

AMERICAN GOLDFINCH *Spinus tristis*

Breeding range: Wisconsin to Maine, south to n. Mississippi, cen. Alabama, cen. Georgia.

Habitat: Open country, overgrown fields with scattered trees; villages, groves, farms.

Nest: Generally placed in 4 (more or less) upright branches or in fork of horizontal limb of tree, 1–33 ft. (0.3–10.1 m) above ground, av. 4–14 ft. (1.2–4.3 m). Durable neat cup of fine vegetable fibers woven and lined with thistle and cattail down. Female builds in 4–5 days. Some nests tend to be deeper than wide. Av. of 79 nests: outside diam. 2⅞ in. (7.3 cm), height 2¹³⁄₁₆ in. (7.1 cm); inside diam. 2 in. (5.1 cm), depth 1⅝ in. (4.1 cm).

Eggs: 4–6, commonly 5; av. 16.2 x 12.2 mm. Oval to short-oval. Shell smooth, has very little gloss. Pale bluish white, unmarked. Incubation by female alone; 12–14 days. Male feeds incubating mate.

Notes: Nesting time appears correlated with maturing thistles; seeds used as food, down for nest building. Nests generally close to adequate food supply. Earliest nests with eggs recorded (1933–49) in 264 Michigan nests July 6; latest, Sept. 25. Nests found after young have left identified by thick rim of excrement left by fledglings.

RED CROSSBILL *Loxia curvirostra*

Breeding range: N. Wisconsin, n. Michigan, New York, n. New England, e. Massachusetts south in mountains to Tennessee, N. Carolina. Locally erratic and irregular.

Habitat: Coniferous forests.

Nest: Placed well out from trunk on branch of conifer, often saddled in thick tuft of needles, 5–80 ft. (1.5-24.4 m) above ground, av. 10–40 ft. (3.0-12.2 m). Loosely arranged, bulky structure of twigs, rootlets, decayed wood, bark strips, *Usnea;* well lined with mosses, fine grasses, feathers, fur. Abundance of food probably governs choice of nesting area. Outside diam. 4½–5½ in. (11.4-14.0 cm), height 3–3½ in. (7.6-8.9 cm); inside diam. 2–2½ in. (5.1-6.4 cm), depth 1¼–1¾ in. (3.2-4.4 cm).

Eggs: 3–5, commonly 4; av. 20.4 x 14.8 mm. Oval to long-oval. Shell smooth, has slight gloss. Pale bluish white or greenish white; spotted, dotted with browns, purples; mostly wreathed or capped at large end. Incubation by female alone; 12–14 days; attentive for long periods of time. 1 brood.

Notes: Date of nesting very irregular; usually in late winter and early spring; less often in Sept., Oct., rarely in May, June, July. Many observers report nests found by following male, which feeds incubating female every 2 or 3 hours during day. Female seldom leaves nest; close sitter. Her olive-green coloring blends with evergreen needles around nest, making detection difficult or impossible. *Nest indistinguishable from White-winged Crossbill's.*

WHITE-WINGED CROSSBILL *Loxia leucoptera*

Breeding range: N. Wisconsin, n. Michigan, casually and irregularly to New York, Vermont, Maine.

Habitat: Spruce forests.

Nest: Placed on horizontal spruce limb 5–70 ft. (1.5-21.3 m) above ground, av. 8–15 ft. (2.4-4.6 m). Deep cup of twigs, rootlets, weed stalks, mosses, lichens, bark strips; lined with fine grasses, feathers, hair, bark shreds. Outside diam. 4 in. (10.2 cm), height 2–2½ in. (5.1-6.4 cm); inside diam. 2¼–2½ in. (5.7-6.4 cm), depth 1¼–1½ in. (3.2-3.8 cm).

Eggs: 2–5, commonly 3–4; av. 20.9 x 15.0 mm. Oval to long-oval. Shell smooth, has very little gloss. Pale bluish or greenish white; spotted, blotched, sometimes scrawled with browns, purples. Incubation by female alone; period unknown. Male feeds incubating mate on nest.

Notes: Erratic nesting species; many breed Jan. to May. Nesting biology very similar to that of closely related Red Crossbill. *Nest indistinguishable from Red Crossbill's.*

RUFOUS-SIDED TOWHEE *Pipilo erythrophthalmus*

Breeding range: Wisconsin to s. Maine, south to Florida and Gulf Coast.

Habitat: Open brushy fields, barrens, thickets, hedgerows, slashings, woodland and roadside edges, suburbs, parks.

Nest: Typically placed on or near ground under or in small bush; sometimes 2–5 ft. (0.6–1.5 m) above ground in low bush or tree (especially late nestings). Bulky, firmly built of leaves, bark strips, weed stalks, twigs, grasses; lined with fine grasses, hair (sometimes), bark shreds, pine needles. Built by female in about 5 days.

Eggs: 3–5, sometimes 6; av. 23.1 x 17.0 mm. Oval to short-oval. Shell smooth, has slight gloss. Grayish or creamy white; dotted, spotted with reddish brown; may be wreathed or capped at large end. Incubation by female alone; 12–13 days. Typically 2 broods, sometimes 3 (South).

Notes: Pair remains mated for 2nd or 3rd broods. All nestings generally within original territory. Ranks 6th among species most frequently parasitized by Brown-headed Cowbird. Larger number of parasitic eggs reported from single nests of Rufous-sided Towhee than from any other species. Iowa record, 8 Cowbird eggs, 5 Towhee eggs in 1 nest; Illinois, 8 Cowbird eggs, 1 Towhee egg in single nest. Nest material gathered within a radius of about 60 ft. (18.3 m) from nest site.

234

SAVANNAH SPARROW *Passerculus sandwichensis*

Breeding range: Wisconsin to Maine, south to Indiana, Ohio, Pennsylvania, n. W. Virginia, New Jersey, Delaware, Maryland.
Habitat: Meadows, prairies, hayfields; bay shores, saltmarshes, barrier beaches.
Nest: Colonial nesting believed infrequent except where favorable habitat is limited. Very well concealed in scratched or natural hollow in ground; typically hidden from view by canopy of surrounding vegetation. Hollow filled with coarse grasses; lined with finer grasses, sometimes rootlets, hair. Outside diam. usually about 3 in. (7.6 cm); depth about 1⅜ in. (3.5 cm).
Eggs: 3–6, commonly 4–5; av. 19.5 x 14.7 mm. Typically oval. Shell smooth, has slight gloss. Pale greenish blue, dirty white; commonly heavily spotted, blotched with browns, often wreathed at large end; sometimes dotted over entire egg or in wreath; wide variation in markings even within same clutch. Incubation entirely or mostly by female; 12 days. 2 broods.
Notes: Habitat varies greatly. Author has found nests in saltmarshes in Maine, high dry pastures in Pennsylvania, wet meadows in Wisconsin, but discovered uniformity in nest location and construction.

GRASSHOPPER SPARROW *Ammodramus savannarum*

Breeding range: Wisconsin to Maine, south to cen. Gulf states, Florida. Absent from Atlantic Coastal Plain.

Habitat: Grasslands (especially cultivated), meadows, prairies, hayfields. Shrubby fields avoided.

Nest: In depression in ground, rim typically level with or slightly above ground, well concealed by canopy of grasses, weeds, commonly domed at back. Orchard grass, clover, alfalfa are favored surrounding plants. Built by female of dried grasses; lined with fine grasses, rootlets, occasionally hair. Outside diam. 4½–5½ in. (11.4–14.0 cm), height 2–2¼ in. (5.1–5.7 cm); inside diam. 2½–3¼ in. (6.4–8.3 cm), depth 1¼ in. (3.2 cm).

Eggs: 3–6, commonly 4–5; av. 18.6 x 14.4 mm. Typically oval. Shell smooth, has slight gloss. Creamy white; sparingly spotted, blotched with reddish browns, undermarked with shades of gray, purple; markings scattered over entire egg or concentrated at large end. Incubation by female alone; 12–13 days. 2 broods.

Notes: Nests difficult to find. Female sits close; when flushed, slips off, runs a short distance through grass, then flies. Approaching nest, never flies directly to it. Actions of neither sex attracts attention to nest location.

HENSLOW'S SPARROW *Ammodramus henslowii*

Breeding range: Wisconsin, cen. Michigan, New York, s. Vermont, s. New Hampshire south to W. Virginia, N. Carolina, n. Kentucky, s. Illinois.

Habitat: Neglected weedy fields, wet meadows, thick grasslands, saltmarsh borders.

Nest: Commonly in loose colonies with each territory at least 1 acre (.4 ha). Single nestings not unusual. Well hidden on or in ground, on or near base of grass clump with vegetation often arching over nest to form partial roof. Occasionally 6–20 in. (15.2–50.8 cm) above ground in clump of vegetation, usually lacking canopy. Of grasses; lined with finer grasses, some hair, forming deep cup. Built in 4–5 days by female. Outside diam. 3 in. (7.6 cm), height 1–2 in. (2.5–5.1 cm); inside diam. 2 in.

Eggs: 3–5; av. 18.3 x 14.1 mm. Oval. Shell smooth, has slight gloss. Creamy white, pale greenish white; thickly, evenly dotted, spotted with reddish brown, often wreathed at large end. Incubation by female; 11 days; starts with laying of last or next to last egg. Typically 2 broods.

Notes: In location, typical nest comparable to that of Savannah Sparrow. Shy, unobtrusive, secretive birds with unbirdlike song; easily overlooked. When disturbed at nest, female runs through grass.

LE CONTE'S SPARROW   p. 231
Ammospiza leconteii

SHARP-TAILED SPARROW *Ammospiza caudacuta*

Breeding range: Atlantic Coast Maine to N. Carolina.
Habitat: Salt and brackish marshes.
Nest: In large, loose colonies under favorable conditions — meadowlike saltmarshes, generally in higher portions not flooded except in unusually high tides. On ground in dense, matted beds of dried rushes, grasses, among driftwood, dried seaweed, or raised few inches (or cm) above ground in upright stems of coarse sedges. Female alone builds; of coarse dry grass, seaweed, loosely woven together; lined with finer, similar material. Typically more bulky than nest of Seaside Sparrow. Outside diam. 3½–4½ in. (8.9–11.4 cm), height 3½–4 in. (8.9–10.2 cm); inside diam. 2–2½ in. (5.1–6.4 cm), depth 1½–2 in. (3.8–5.1 cm).
Eggs: 3–5, rarely 6; av. 19.4 x 14.6 mm. Oval. Shell smooth, has slight gloss. Pale greenish white; dotted, spotted with browns with

underlying markings of pale grayish purples; usually well scattered, but may be wreathed. Typically smaller than eggs of Seaside Sparrow, markings finer. Incubation by female alone; 11 days. Commonly 2 broods.
Notes: Nest very difficult to locate. Birds shy, wary, very mouselike in movements. When flushed, quickly drop into cover. Territories often overlap; very little defense evident. Suspected of occasionally hybridizing with related Seaside Sparrow.

SEASIDE SPARROW *Ammospiza maritima*
(includes Dusky Seaside, Cape Sable Seaside Sparrows)

Breeding range: Atlantic and Gulf Coasts, Massachusetts to Louisiana.

Habitat: Saltmarshes (species is strictly maritime).

Nest: In wetter portions of saltmarsh washed by daily tides, often in *Spartina* or *Juncus;* on ground among marsh grasses above high-tide line or 8–12 in. (20.3–30.5 cm) above ground in bushes, especially marsh-elder (*Iva frutescens*). Well-concealed open cup of grass stems, lined with finer grasses; built by female. Typically not so bulky as nest of Sharp-tailed Sparrow. Outside diam. 3–4½ in. (7.6–11.4 cm), height 2–3½ in. (5.1–8.9 cm); inside diam. 2–2½ in. (5.1–6.4 cm), depth 1½ in. (3.8 cm).

Eggs: 3–6, commonly 4–5; av. 20.9 x 15.5 mm. Oval. Shell smooth, has slight gloss. White, pale greenish white; dotted, spotted, blotched with reddish brown; often wreathed at large end. Tend to be larger and have bolder markings than Sharp-tailed Sparrow eggs. Incubation by female alone; period unknown. 1 brood.

Notes: Unlike Sharp-tailed Sparrow, establishes definite territory in saltmarsh, advertises (by song) and defends it against encroachment by other males. Nests often close together, 50–100 yds. (45.7–91.4 m), where environmental conditions are at optimum.

239

VESPER SPARROW *Pooecetes gramineus*

Breeding range: Wisconsin to Maine, south to n. N. Carolina, Tennessee.

Habitat: Open, dry uplands, wild or cultivated — shortgrass pastures, meadows, prairies, corn-stubble fields.

Nest: Ordinarily in a depression in ground under cover of surrounding plants, or in grass tussock. Built of dry grasses, weed stalks, rootlets; lined with finer grasses, rootlets, occasionally hair.

Eggs: Commonly 4, often 5, sometimes 3 or 6; av. 20.7 x 15.2 mm. Oval. Shell smooth, has slight gloss. Creamy white, pale greenish white; dotted, spotted, blotched, scrawled with 1 or more shades brown, gray; considerable variation. Incubation by female (male may assist occasionally); 12–13 days. 2 broods.

Notes: Territories typically larger than for some other grassland sparrows. Conspicuous singing perches (trees, bushes, fences) probably prerequisite to territory selection. Although Vesper Sparrow considered frequent victim of Brown-headed Cowbird (Friedmann), author has found no young or eggs of Cowbird in 18 nests in Pennsylvania, Wisconsin, Michigan. Author found species nesting frequently in Kirtland's Warbler range in Michigan (on ground in jack pine woods). Mating of same pair 2 successive yrs. verified in Michigan.

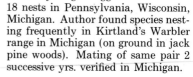

240

LARK SPARROW *Chondestes grammacus*

Breeding range: Wisconsin, Michigan south to cen. Alabama, east to e. Ohio, cen. Pennsylvania, W. Virginia.

Habitat: Prairies, weedy fields, poor pastures, open knolls, cultivated lawns.

Nest: Commonly a depression in the ground, often in a bare or eroded place, filled with grasses and lined with rootlets, fine grasses; usually shaded by a clump of grass or weeds. Sometimes a more bulky structure on a foundation of small twigs placed in low tree or shrub. Both male and female share in selecting nest site, but female alone does building in 3–4 days.

Eggs: 4–5, sometimes 3, rarely 6; av. 20.1 x 15.9 mm. Oval. Shell smooth, has slight gloss. Creamy or grayish white; spotted, blotched, scrawled with dark browns, black, purple; often capped at large end. Markings resemble those on eggs of Vesper Sparrow but are darker, bolder, more likely to be wreathed or capped. Incubation by female; 11–12 days. Probably 1 brood.

Notes: Male's territorial defense wanes after incubation is underway. Birds often feed in flocks during nesting season. In early part of 20th century, species dramatically invaded some eastern states as breeding bird. In recent years, marked reduction in number of nests reported in eastern limits of range.

241

BACHMAN'S (PINE WOODS) SPARROW
Aimophila aestivalis

Breeding range: Ne. Illinois, cen. Indiana, Ohio, sw. Pennsylvania, e. W. Virginia, nw. Virginia, cen. Maryland south to Gulf Coast and cen. Florida.

Habitat: Open pine woods with understory of shrubs, grassy ground cover; weedy, abandoned fields, grassy orchards.

Nest: On ground in open or beneath brush, tree, shrub; in Florida, commonly hidden under saw palmetto (*Serenoa repens*). Built by female of coarse grasses, weed stems; lined with fine grasses. May be domed during construction by bird itself, arched above by surrounding vegetation, or may lack canopy. May be round — inside diam. 2½ in. (6.4 cm), depth 2 in. (5.1 cm) — or cylindrical — outside diam. 4½ in. (11.4 cm), height including dome 7–8 in. (17.8–20.3 cm); inside diam. ¾ x 2 in. (1.9 x 5.1 cm), depth 1¾ in. (4.4 cm).

Eggs: 3–5; av. 19.3 x 15.3 mm. Oval. Shell smooth, has slight gloss. White, unmarked. Incubation by female; only known record 13–14 days. Typically 2 broods, sometimes 3 (South).

Notes: Birds elusive, shy; only male's song, which he often renders 50–100 yds. (45.7–90.4 m) from nest, is attention-compelling. Nest very difficult to find; neither John J. Audubon nor John Bachman ever succeeded in finding one.

242

DARK-EYED (SLATE-COLORED) JUNCO
Junco hyemalis

Breeding range: Northern border of U.S. to n. Wisconsin, cen. Michigan, New York (mountains), w. and cen. Massachusetts, in mountains to Georgia.

Habitat: Coniferous, mixed forests and forest edges.

Nest: Commonly on ground under concealing weeds and grasses; often on slope, roadside bank, rock ledge; in tree roots, under fallen tree or log; sometimes in tree as much as 8 ft. (2.4 m) above ground. Female builds compact structure of grasses, rootlets, bark shreds, mosses, and twigs lined with finer grasses, rootlets, hair. Male sometimes carries nest material.

Eggs: 4–5, occasionally 3, rarely 6; av. 19.4 x 14.4 mm. Oval to short- or long-oval. Shell smooth, has slight gloss. Pale bluish white, grayish; thickly dotted, spotted, occasionally blotched with browns, purple, gray, mostly concentrated at large end; considerable variation in markings. Incubation by female; 12–13 days, may begin with laying of next to last egg. 2 broods.

Notes: Author has found upturned tree roots favorite nesting site. In Pennsylvania, 7 of 11 nests were so placed; 6 in Maine. Similar to site chosen by Yellow-bellied Flycatcher. Nests in slopes and roadside banks are completely hidden by overhanging moss or surrounding grass.

CHIPPING SPARROW *Spizella passerina*

Breeding range: Northern border U.S. south to cen. Mississippi, cen. Alabama, cen. Georgia, n. Florida (rarely).

Habitat: Towns, farms, orchards, garden shrubbery, open woodlands, conifer plantings.

Nest: In tree (often conifer), shrub, vine 1–25 ft. (0.3–7.6 m) above ground, av. 3–10 ft. (0.9–3.0 m); rarely on ground. Made of fine dead grasses, weed stalks, rootlets; lined with hair, fine grasses. Built by female, accompanied by male, in 3–4 days. Av. outside diam. 4⅜ in. (11.2 cm), height 2¼ in. (5.7 cm); inside diam. 1⅞ in. (4.8 cm), depth 1⁷⁄₁₆ in. (3.7 cm).

Eggs: Commonly 4, often 3, rarely 2, 5; av. 17.6 x 12.9 mm. Oval to short-oval. Shell smooth, has slight gloss. Pale bluish green; dotted, spotted, blotched, scrawled, with dark brown, black, purple, mainly at large end. *Indistinguishable from eggs of Clay-colored Sparrow,* although average size slightly larger. Incubation by female; 11–14 days, beginning day before last egg laid. Male feeds incubating mate. 2 broods.

Notes: Horsehair may solely line entire nest; if this unavailable, human or other animal hair used. Although regarded by Friedmann as "extremely common" host of Brown-headed Cowbird, only 3 of 66 nests in Michigan were parasitized, only 1 of 38 nests in another Michigan study, 2 cases in 29 Pennsylvania nests (author). 4 nests in 137 had 5 eggs.

CLAY-COLORED SPARROW *Spizella pallida*

Breeding range: Northern border of U.S. south to sw. Wisconsin, nw. Illinois, cen. and se. Michigan, w. New York (recent).

Habitat: Prairies, pine barrens, conifer plantings, woodland openings, brushy fields, pasturelands.

Nest: Early nests commonly on or near ground; later nests often in trees and shrubs as high as 5 ft. (1.5 m) above ground, usually lower. Female builds rather bulky, well-hidden cup-shaped structure of woven grasses, weed stems, rootlets; lined with fine grasses, rootlets, hair (sometimes). Resembles nest of Chipping Sparrow but not so compact. Male's defended territory generally small — ½ acre (.2 ha) or less. Nests sometimes 30–50 ft. (9.1–15.2 m) apart. For 34 nests in Michigan: av. outside diam. 4 in. (10.2 cm), height 2⅝ in. (6.7 cm); inside diam. 1⅞ in. (4.8 cm), depth 1½ in. (3.8 cm).

Eggs: 3–5, commonly 4; av. 17.1 x 12.7 mm. Oval to short-oval. Shell smooth, has slight gloss. Pale blue-green; dotted, spotted, blotched with dark brown, black scrawls; sometimes underlaid with gray. *Indistinguishable from eggs of Chipping Sparrow;* average slightly smaller. Incubation by both sexes, mostly by female; 10–11½ days, starting after 3rd egg laid. 1 brood.

Notes: One nest contained 384 pieces of grass, another 450 pieces. Often deserts eggs if parasitized by Brownheaded Cowbird.

FIELD SPARROW *Spizella pusilla*

Breeding range: Cen. Wisconsin to s. Maine, south to Mississippi, Alabama (north of coastal plain), s. Georgia.

Habitat: Brushy pastures, clearings, meadows, woodland edges, abandoned hayfields, briar thickets.

Nest: Early nests typically on or near ground; later nests as high as 4 ft. (1.2 m) above ground in low thick shrubs or trees. (In Michigan, of 173 May nests, 135 on ground; none of 240 July nests on ground.) Cup of grasses, leaves, weed stems; lined with fine grasses, rootlets, hair. Female builds, accompanied by male. Of 90 Michigan nests: av. outside diam. 5 in. (12.7 cm), height 2½ in. (6.4 cm); inside diam. 2 in. (5.1 cm), depth 1½ in. (3.8 cm).

Eggs: 3–4, sometimes 2 (late nests), rarely 5 (early nests); av. 17.9 x 13.5 mm. Oval. Shell smooth, has slight gloss. Creamy, bluish white, pale greenish; dotted, spotted, occasionally blotched with reddish brown, pale purple; markings often concentrated at large end. Incubation by female; about 11 days. 2 broods, sometimes 3.

Notes: Unlike Chipping and Song Sparrows, species rarely nests near houses. Males strongly territorial; 2–3 acres (0.8–1.2 ha) average in favorable habitat. 182 of 664 Michigan nests (27.4 percent) were parasitized by Brown-headed Cowbird.

246

WHITE-THROATED SPARROW *Zonotrichia albicollis*

Breeding range: N. and cen. Wisconsin, n. Michigan; nw. W. Virginia, n. Pennsylvania, New York (mainly in mountains, locally elsewhere); New England as far south as w. Massachusetts, nw. Connecticut.

Habitat: Undergrowth and edges of coniferous and northern deciduous forests; clearings, brushy thickets.

Nest: On or close to ground in grass hummock, brush pile; under prostrate tree branch, mat of dead bracken fern or dead grass; in rare cases as high as 3 ft. (.9 m) above ground. Female alone builds nest of coarse grasses, rootlets, pine needles, twigs, bark fibers, mosses; cup is lined with fine grasses, rootlets, hair. Outside diam. 3½ in. (8.9 cm); inside diam. 2⅜ in. (6 cm), depth 1½ in. (3.8 cm).

Eggs: 3–5, commonly 4, sometimes 6; av. 21.0 x 15.4 mm. Oval to long-oval. Shell smooth, has slight gloss. Creamy, bluish white, greenish white, grayish; heavily dotted, spotted, blotched with browns, occasionally scrawled with black; markings mainly concentrated at large end. Ground color sometimes obscured by heavy markings. Incubation by female alone; 12–14 days. Commonly 1 brood, occasionally 2.

Notes: Remarkable record of species nesting in esplanade of public library in downtown Buffalo, N.Y., in 1969 — 31 miles (50 km) from nearest known nest area. Incubating bird sits close.

LINCOLN'S SPARROW *Melospiza lincolnii*

Breeding range: N. Wisconsin, n. Michigan, n. New York, n. New Hampshire, n. and cen. Maine.

Habitat: Tamarack and sphagnum bogs, swamps, wet alder thickets, brushy openings.

Nest: On ground in tussock of grass or sedge, sunk in mosses or lichens, hidden by surrounding vegetation, often just above water. Female builds neat cup of grasses lined with finer grasses. Outside diam. 3½ in. (8.9 cm), height 1¼ in. (3.2 cm); inside diam. 2½ in. (6.4 cm).

Eggs: 3–6, commonly 4–5; av. 19.4 x 14.4 mm. Oval to long-oval. Shell smooth, has slight gloss. Pale greenish white; dotted, spotted, blotched with reddish brown. Markings sometimes concentrated at large end, sometimes so thick they obscure ground color. Practically indistinguishable from eggs of Song Sparrow, but slightly smaller. Incubation by female; about 13 days.

Notes: Male apparently does little if any singing during incubation period. Author, studying this species several years in sphagnum bog in Maine, found it most shy, wary of all sparrows. Rapid flight very low over ground makes bird extremely hard to follow. Author

and party found only 3 nests, 1 with eggs (see illus.), 2 with young, all buried in sphagnum and lichens about 1 ft. (30.5 cm) above water in a hummock that also included leatherleaf, bog rosemary, Labrador tea, black spruce.

248

Index

PAGE NUMBERS in **boldface** type indicate species that are illustrated. Boldface type is used only with the common English names of those species; it is not used after scientific names. English names followed by lightface type numbers indicate species not illustrated. To minimize confusion only common names in general use have been included. Obsolete or little-used vernacular names are not listed.

598.297 Harrison, Hal H.
HAR

A field guide to
birds' nests of 285
species . . .

WREATHED

CAPPED

OVERLAID

SCRAWLED

STREAKED

MARBLED

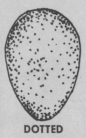

DOTTED

SPOTTED

BLOTCHED

SPLASHED

EGG
MARKINGS